Praise for The Vital Spark

"*The Vital Spark* is the badassery bible whose time has come. It is essential medicine for what ails a woman's soul. Jungian therapist Lisa Marchiano has offered up a treasure trove of insights and practical guidance for women on how to access their inner passion for life   but even more remarkably, on how to embody it with confidence in the world."

SIL REYNOLDS, RN
coauthor of *Mothering and Daughtering*

"With brilliant, fresh readings of fairy tales and other familiar stories, Marchiano guides us through how we lost our inner fire and how to get it back. *The Vital Spark* inspires me to become strong, wild, and whole: the kind of woman I admire. I will be recommending this book to everyone I know. I loved this book; I needed this book; I'll be returning to these pages over and over again. Marchiano's work is essential."

ANNA HOGELAND
psychotherapist and author of *The Long Answer*

"Using myths, fairy tales, and clinical anecdotes, Lisa Marchiano describes how many traits that are essential for women to thrive get banished into the unconscious shadow. As a result, the vital spark that connects us to our aliveness, power, and authenticity is snuffed out. She takes the reader's hand and gently guides us through timeless tales to refind our essential selves."

CONNIE ZWEIG, PHD
author of *The Inner Work of Age*, coauthor of *Romancing the Shadow*

"In *The Vital Spark*, Lisa Marchiano leads us on a quest to uncover the wild woman within so that we might come to live our fullest and most authentic life. She shines a wise and feisty light on the hidden and unowned aspects of being a woman and offers us ways to transcend the smaller stories that the over-culture insists we should inhabit."

SHARON BLACKIE, PHD
author of *Hagitude*

"This book could not have found me at a better time as I move into midlife and find myself outgrowing so many of the roles I once played in my family of origin, my marriage, and within various ideological social networks. The vital spark relates to an inner power and wisdom that one can draw upon when circumstances are no longer tenable. It's about summoning your inner authority in the face of tyranny, without yourself becoming a tyrant. Sometimes life pushes us to the limit, but it's down in that dark underworld where we can potentially draw upon our deepest inner resources. This book is not only a guide through that distressing space, but also a warm companion. I felt like Marchiano was bearing witness to my own specific life journey, and I found comfort that my personal struggles relate to universal coming-of-age themes. Marchiano is a wise teacher and healer, and I look forward to returning to this book many times over!"

MISHA BLAISE
internationally bestselling author and illustrator

"Mixing unique fairy tales, myths, and examples from her psychoanalytic practice and her own experiences, Lisa Marchiano unlocks the ways in which a woman can rediscover her internal 'feminine fire' that for many, independent of culture and geography, has been exiled and buried underground for too long. In this important and meaningful book that amplifies the ways in which a woman can become the heroine of her own life, Marchiano beautifully renders, with nuance and specificity, how to claim what belongs to oneself; how to honor, access, and beneficially express one's anger before it turns into festering resentment; how to set and uphold boundaries; and how to open the door to one's fundamental creativity and intuition, which is easily stifled and silenced by age-old cultural expectations of how a woman should be in the world. All women, at any stage of life, must read this book!"

ALEXIS LANDAU, PHD
author of *The Empire of the Senses* and *Those Who Are Saved*

ALSO BY LISA MARCHIANO

Motherhood: Facing and Finding Yourself

LISA MARCHIANO, LCSW

THE VITAL SPARK

Reclaim Your Outlaw Energies and Find Your Feminine Fire

sounds true
BOULDER, COLORADO

Sounds True
Boulder, CO

Published 2024

Cover design by Jennifer Miles

Book design by Charli Barnes and Linsey Dodaro

"Fire Hazard" by Dorsha Hayes, from The Bell Branch Rings, published by W.L. Bauhan, Inc. (now Bauhan Publishing, Peterborough, New Hampshire) 1972. Used by permission.

"Love After Love" from SEA GRAPES by Derek Walcott. Copyright © 1976 by Derek Walcott. Reprinted by permission of Farrar, Straus and Giroux. All Rights Reserved.

Printed in the United States of America

BK06683
Library of Congress Cataloging-in-Publication Data
Names: Marchiano, Lisa, author.
Title: The vital spark : reclaim your outlaw energies and find your
    feminine fire / Lisa Marchiano.
Description: Boulder, CO : Sounds True, 2024. | Includes bibliographical
    references.
Identifiers: LCCN 2023018401 | ISBN 9781649631008 (trade
paperback) | ISBN
    9781649631015 (ebook)
Subjects: LCSH: Women--Psychology. | Women--Social
conditions. | Vitality.
Classification: LCC HQ1206 .M3428 2024 | DDC 155.3/33--dc23/
eng/20230628
LC record available at https://lccn.loc.gov/2023018401

FSC
www.fsc.org
MIX
Paper | Supporting
responsible forestry
FSC® C103098

In memory of my mother.

DISCLAIMER

All clinical material in this book is either shared with permission or is a composite. All identifying details have been changed.

CONTENTS

BANISHMENT

Before there was Eve, there was Lilith. According to a medieval Jewish text, God decided it wasn't good for Adam to be alone, so he created a woman out of the same clay and named her Lilith. But the two quickly fell to arguing. Lilith refused to lie beneath Adam, and Adam insisted it was his rightful place to be on top. "The two of us are equal," contended Lilith, "since we are both from the earth."[1] But Adam wouldn't listen, so Lilith fled. God sent three angels after her, but she refused to return. After this, God created a second wife for Adam, this time from his rib, so that it was clear that she would be secondary to him.

Unlike Eve, Lilith is one with herself, complete and unique. She is not interested in subordinating herself to someone else. She is, according to Jungian analyst Marie-Louise von Franz, an image of an "unbridled life urge which refuses to be assimilated."[2] For her, autonomy and sovereignty are more important than relationship. Since human society depends on women's willingness to set aside their own needs to tend to others, it is little wonder that we perceive Lilith's fierce independence and assertion of equality as dangerous and demonic. Lilith is said to greedily wait at the bedside of laboring women, eager to snatch and strangle the baby as soon as it is born. She likely provided an explanation for the terrifying reality of stillborn births and early infant mortality in a prescientific world. On a deeper level, we can understand her as the shadowy opposite of a mother's love and concern. She is an image of everything a woman should not be.

The mythic banishment of Lilith speaks to a universal truth. There are qualities such as kindness, empathy, and agreeableness that can help us get and stay connected with each other, and there are fiery qualities such as anger, shrewdness, and forcefulness that can help us get and stay connected to ourselves. Roughly speaking, the first set of attributes fosters relationship, while the second set enables personal empowerment and assertiveness. Both ways of being in the world are important for psychological health and growth. Generally, women in our culture are permitted to access and develop the former qualities, while we are discouraged from expressing or investing in the latter. A woman's fiery nature can be banished because, like Lilith, her male partner expects her to subjugate herself. But this is not the only situation in which women may lose access to their "unbridled life urge." At work or in friendship, or in marriages and partnerships with men or women, we often tend to focus on the other person, sometimes at our own expense.

Most of us, therefore, get cut off from part of our essential nature early in life. As a child, perhaps you sang loudly, told jokes, laughed heartily—but soon got the message that you should be more composed and quieter. Or perhaps you spoke your mind with ease at the dinner table, but later kept your sharp wit and astute insights to yourself, because you were encouraged to be agreeable. Our fiery, independent nature goes underground and is buried under six feet of niceness. Our ability to be selfish and harsh gets exiled to the dark forest of our soul, where it can hardly be recalled. But these traits don't disappear, even when we banish them. They emerge as dark moods—irritability, resentment, or bitterness. They surface in chaotic or passive-aggressive acts that sabotage us or are ineffective—angry outbursts at work, a mysterious compulsion to shoplift. They turn up as symptoms—anxieties, panic attacks, or depression.

THE CENTRAL FIRE

The Swiss psychiatrist Carl Jung once called this life urge that Lilith represents the "central fire."[3] He believed that a spark from this central fire exists in every living creature. But as we meet the demands of adapting to life, we inevitably lose access to some of our spark. We cut ourselves off from potentially valuable qualities in the interest of developing characteristics prized by our teachers, caregivers, or culture. We learn to hide our enthusiasm and feel ashamed of our audacity. We are taught not to be critical, selfish, or angry. The process of sacrificing our original potential wholeness to adapt to the world's demands is universal. We all must betray our essential nature to some extent to get along with others and achieve external goals. However, this process generally affects men and women differently.

As children, girls are praised for being good, well-behaved, quiet, and likable. We are applauded for following the rules, so we learn to cut off our feistiness, loudness, audacity, and aggression. As adults, women may find themselves attuned to the needs and desires of others with whom they are in relationship, often in a way that makes it difficult for them to know their needs and wants. We strain to make ourselves appealing. We accommodate ourselves to our partner's preferences and subordinate our desires in the interest of our children's needs. We learn to be agreeable in social situations and at work. We are the peacemakers, the nurturers, and the facilitators. We make the coffee, do the menial work others don't want to do, or put our creative aspirations on the back burner to midwife someone else's project. By dint of both nature and nurture, we are focused on the needs and desires of others.

Research attests to the fact that, in general, men are more interested in things and women are more interested in people. Though socialization and culture play a role, there is evidence that at least part of this tendency is innate. For example, there are similar sex-based differences in the behavior of male and female chimpanzees. Male neonate humans are more likely to spend a longer time looking at a mobile than a face, while a female infant will be more interested in the face.[4] Women, then, come into the world predisposed to being attuned to other people. In 1982, psychologist Carol Gilligan published her groundbreaking book, *In a Different Voice*. Her work cataloged differences in how men and women navigate their moral worlds and pointed out that women tend to be more compelled by care, responsibility, and relationality.[5]

Personality research consistently finds that women score higher on agreeableness and sensitivity while men score higher on assertiveness. What part of this is due to innate factors or cultural shaping is a fascinating and tangled question that is beyond the scope of this book to put to rest. What concerns us here, however, is that such a discrepancy exists. Because of this, the task of psychological development differs between men and women.

Women are the guardians of feeling values in their environment. This is a sacred charge of the feminine and should not be devalued or refused. The sacrifices a woman makes in the interest of relationships can pay rich dividends and be in the interest of sustaining and nurturing others, organizations, and the culture. Caring for others is often intrinsically deeply meaningful and can be one of the most gratifying things we do. A woman's ability to lovingly attune to and care for the needs of another is fundamental to the continuation of the species. But if we don't have sufficient access to independence and fire, our tendency to focus on others can cause us to lose touch with ourselves and the people we were meant to become. We can become alienated from our souls, which leaves us feeling depleted and inauthentic. Then, we must return to ourselves by reuniting with our Lilith nature, our own "unbridled life urge which refuses to be assimilated."

THE UNLIVED LIFE

For women, finding Lilith will mean reconnecting with the repudiated qualities that she embodies. It will mean permitting ourselves to value autonomy, cunning, and assertiveness in addition to care and relationality. Many of us will have spent our early years investing in our capacity for empathy, attunement, and nurture. This developmental focus will likely have helped us find and sustain a loving relationship, get along with colleagues, and perhaps care for children.

But, on the other hand, we may have forgotten what it means to be fierce and demanding. These banished qualities have been waiting in the shadowy corners of our souls where they have formed a kind of unlived life.

Our unlived life may be very different from the one we are living, and we may meet it first by seeing it in other people. Perhaps when we see someone else being audacious, cunning, or desirous, we feel upset, repelled, or even self-righteous. We can't imagine that we could act that way, and we may judge others—especially women—for doing so. If this is the case, you might want to become curious about your reaction. Strong feelings we have in response to others often indicate that they are displaying a trait we may need to own and develop in ourselves. Be especially wary of feelings that are toned with judgment, such as outrage, indignancy, or moral superiority. When these arise, it is usually a good sign that we are working hard to hold some disowned part of ourselves at bay. If a woman's stubbornness annoys you, ask yourself whether you need to claim your tendency to be unyielding. If she looks selfish as she pursues her heart's desire, consider what has become of yours.

We can't stay cut off from our vital spark without paying a great price. Sooner or later, the unlived life asserts itself. It produces symptoms such as depression, anxiety, or physical ailments. It visits us in dreams filled with troubling imagery. It may even orchestrate accidents or spectacular failures to get our attention. If we continue to ignore it, we will likely become bitter, resentful, and rigid. When the unlived life demands to be known, we may feel frightened as our previous assumptions about our life and identity are challenged. We are asked to admit that we may not be the person we thought we were. It may feel safer to stay small and cling to our former certainty. Being connected with the central fire can be exhilarating, but it can also be terrifying. "Everybody is dealing with how much of their own aliveness they can bear and how much they need to anesthetize themselves," according to the psychoanalyst Adam Phillips.[6] Staying cut off from our vitality is a form of anesthesia.

If we can embrace the challenge presented by the unlived life, we turn our ship around and begin our homeward journey—our return. This part of the voyage may call for a reversal of values from those to which we previously adhered. To fulfill the promise of our original wholeness, we must attend to and develop those traits and attitudes that have become alien and unfamiliar. They may even seem frightening and strange. They have been quietly waiting for us in the wild wasteland of our souls. Finding them will confront us with unlived possibilities and an invitation to reclaim them. Connecting with split-off or undeveloped parts of ourselves can enliven and rejuvenate us. It can allow us to become more of who we were meant to be. And it can help us move toward the potential for wholeness with which we came into the world.

THE POWER OF STORIES

Our tools for this journey back to ourselves are age-old stories and fairy tales. Stories are ancient medicine. They are humankind's earliest method of conveying wisdom. The insights they offer are deep and timeless and have to do with the very bedrock of our nature. Throughout the millennia, the keepers and tellers of these stories have, for the most part, been women. So it is not surprising that fairy tales should mark, with exquisite accuracy and poignancy, the main stations on a woman's psychological journey.

Fairy tales vividly image the retrieval of those split off and unlived parts of ourselves. They can guide us in recovering those values that were disregarded or discarded. They speak of self-betrayals and self-discovery, of aching loss and ultimate triumph. They are the storehouse of the essential psychological experiences that women undergo during our development.

"All fairy tales endeavor to describe one and the same psychic fact," wrote Marie-Louise von Franz, "but a fact so complex and far-reaching and so difficult for us to realize in all its different aspects that hundreds of tales and thousands of repetitions with a musician's variations are needed until this fact is delivered into consciousness; and even then the theme is not exhausted."[7] That fact is the psychological reality of our essential potential for wholeness, a potential that Carl Jung called the Self. If we have known fairy tales mostly through childhood films, we may be surprised by their darkness and brutality. The stories in this book are filled with beauty and magic, but they also contain images of violence and terror. It can be important to remember that they communicate their messages in metaphor. Whether they are enchanting or savage, they reveal universal truths about the soul in the eloquent language of symbol.

"We are participants in a substantial and abiding mystery," writes Jungian Heinz Westman.[8] Fairy tales reveal this mystery by clarifying the universal substrate that joins us all. When one of my clients, Christine, was a child, she listened again and again to a recording of *Beauty and the Beast.* "I think I wore that cassette out," she told me. As a teenager, she devoured *Jane Eyre* and it has since been one of her favorite books. In the course of our work together, we came to realize that these are the same stories. They both tap into the same archetypal bedrock and speak to a yearning for a closer connection with the masculine principle that a girl first encounters through her relationship with her father. As a child, Christine had longed to feel closer to her father, a distant figure often tied up with work who had little interest in his young daughter. The fairy tale reflected a yearning she herself could not consciously understand or find words for.

Jung called the timeless patterns that occur in fairy tales and similar material "archetypes." The archetypal layer of the psyche is like an underground river that runs beneath each of us, connecting us to the inexhaustible storehouse of eternal patterns. We recognize that which is archetypal because of the emotional response it evokes— the shiver of truth, beauty, and awe. Archetypal stories move us and have the potential to heal because they remind us that we are a child of the universe, embedded in and held by the cosmos. The tales in this book come from all over the world. They feature heroines who undertake the difficult quest to find the central fire. All the tales are retellings in my own words of traditional versions.

These universal themes don't only show up in fairy tales. They appear each night in our dreams as well. Dreams and fairy tales spring from the same deep source in the unconscious, and therefore dreams can be full of sorcerers and treasures, talking animals, and strange transformations. Dreams are communications from the Self—the guiding center of the personality. They let us know where we may be out of balance or have the wrong attitude. They speak to us in the mysterious language of image and metaphor. Mining the wisdom of dreams will require us to tune our ear to their symbolic language.

When working with dreams, we assume that, most of the time, everything in the dream is an aspect of our own psyche. Dreams are one of the easiest ways to catch a glimpse of the unlived life. Those parts of ourselves that we have despised and shut away will visit us in our dreams, often in the guise of some element that evokes disgust but at the same time is oddly compelling. Aspects of ourselves that we have split off because they threaten our fragile equilibrium will appear in dreams as frightening monsters who chase or attack us. Dreamwork will be an important resource for learning where we have cut ourselves off from our vital spark—and how we can reconnect with it.

When you are gifted with a dream, ask yourself what the dream maker might be trying to point out to you. What part of yourself have you left behind that is now trying to contact you? Often, the aspect of the dream that is the scariest, the most enraging, or the strangest represents some essential part of your soul that needs to be reclaimed.

GLOWING COALS

When repudiated parts of ourselves fall back into the unconscious, they become wild and feral—untamed and undeveloped yet waiting in the recesses of our soul with all their original energy and potential. The loss of our original wholeness is the price that must be paid if we are to grow up and establish ourselves in the world, but those forgotten parts are not lost forever. "The social goal is attained only at the cost of a diminution of personality," wrote Jung. "Many—far too many—aspects of life which should also have been experienced lie in the lumber room among dusty memories; but sometimes, too, they are glowing coals under gray ashes."[9]

Anna Mary Robertson was born in rural New York in 1860. Her father was a farmer, and she had very little formal education. As a child, she loved to paint what she called "lambscapes" using lemon juice or grape juice as colors.[10] She recalled her delight as a small child when her father would bring home white sheets of paper. At twelve, she left home to work doing chores for other families. One employer noticed how much she admired their Currier and Ives prints and purchased wax and chalk crayons for her.[11]

Anna eventually married and had a farm of her own to care for. She gave birth to ten children, five of whom survived past infancy. Her whole life, she loved to make art. She decorated household objects and embroidered. When she was in her late seventies, arthritis made embroidery too difficult, so she switched to painting. Her exuberant, luminous paintings with their simple themes of country life soon came to the attention of collectors, and she became known to the world as Grandma Moses.

Anna Robertson was born with a burning need to become an artist—a glowing coal banked under gray ash through all the long decades of caring for her children and family and managing the farm. Only late in life did this flame burn brightly enough for the whole world to see. In 2006, her painting "Sugaring Off" sold at Christie's auction house for $1.2 million.

This book is about uncovering these glowing coals and gently fanning them until they burn brightly so we can renew our connection with the central fire—our unbridled life urge. There are numberless possibilities as to what those glowing goals might be, and each of us will have particular aspects of self that we have left on the lumber room floor. We will each have our individual unlived life. However, there are broad themes in women's lives that allow us to examine eight qualities from which we may have alienated ourselves and now need to reclaim. They are shrewdness, disagreeableness, cunning, desire, sexuality, anger, authority, and ruthlessness.

Shrewdness, disagreeableness, and cunning allow us to care for and protect ourselves, respond to danger, and find our unbridled playfulness and humor. Desire and sexuality invigorate us and have to do with our capacity for joy and creative exploration. They help us to feel alive. Anger, authority, and ruthlessness have to do with our ability to take a stand and assert ourselves. Used effectively, they empower us. Together, these outlaw energies help a woman to hew to her own path and become the fullest version of herself possible. In the following pages, we will explore each of these attributes and how developing them can expand the personality and bring a greater sense of wholeness.

While many women struggle to develop a conscious relationship with these qualities, each of us will have our own unique experience of them. A woman might have no trouble at all accessing anger but may have difficulty finding her genuine authority. Another woman might enjoy her sexuality with abandon but have trouble allowing herself to be disagreeable. Developing any one of these qualities is likely to help us access the others as well, but we all might start in a different place and travel a different road to wholeness. Moreover, these qualities can appear in varied ways depending on our unique personalities and talents. One woman may express the trickster through her sharp wit, while another may excel at subtle political maneuvers that get the job done. One woman's desire may express itself in a creative endeavor, while another woman may feel compelled to pursue a profession or a spiritual practice. We will all have our individual experience of learning to claim these outlaw energies. This work won't be easy. As we grow into the fullness of ourselves, there will be losses. We may lose friends. We'll likely have to consciously sacrifice some goals and dreams so that others can flourish. Most of all, we will lose the comforting but constricting smallness that has helped us to feel safe and find easy approval from others for many years. But there will be many gifts—new friends, wide new horizons filled with unexpected and extraordinary adventures, and a life infused with a sense of meaning and purpose.

Women today benefit from the remarkable gains of the women's movement over the past century or so. There have been substantial advances in women's quest for equality, and as a result, we have an enormous degree of choice and freedom regarding all areas of our lives. But throughout my years as a psychotherapist, I have seen again and again that each woman must wage an inner struggle for liberation. Whether we are accomplished professionals, stay-at-home moms, women navigating a mid-life transition, or young women just getting started in life, we will have to contend with internal forces that hold us back, cut us off from our instincts, and cause us to question ourselves.

Many of us are caught in a pattern where we compulsively seek relationship—with friends, colleagues, supervisors, and family members. Without realizing we are doing so, we orient powerfully toward connection and seek approval rather than finding a self-serving attitude. Though we may be praised for our caring, our service is usually not rewarded the way we would hope, and we become cut off from our sense of deservedness. Doing the inner work of connecting with our vital spark will help us to claim our heroine's journey, heal our wounds, and assert our personal power. It will allow us to return to the things we love, become who we were meant to be, experience the fullness of our potentials, and have our unique voice heard. Many of our most meaningful moments spring from experiences relating to love, attachment, relationship, and nurture. Personal fulfillment often requires us to be bold, assertive, and fierce. To live fully, we must develop both ways of being in the world. Integrating these two aspects will allow us to live expansively.

This book is for any woman who finds it difficult to discern what she wants or to speak up for her needs. It's for women who feel cut off from their deep source, whose anger wells up from deep inside, only to be strangled and silenced before it can be heard. It's for women who are too often tentative, apologetic, or uncertain. If you compensate for self-doubt with frantic doing, if you often feel resentful or thin-skinned, this book is for you. It's for the woman who has forgotten the wisdom of her body, a body that has grown alien to her. It's for any woman who struggles with the tension between what she knows in her gut and the story that everyone else tells her. It's for any woman who spends too much time swimming in shame because she feels as though she is either too much or not enough. It's for the woman who doesn't feel like she belongs anywhere—because she does not yet belong to herself. And it's for the woman who has struggled to hear the inner voice that speaks with quiet insistence and lets her know what is deeply right for her.

Jung noted that when we commune with ourselves, we find "an inner partner; more than that, a relationship that seems like the happiness of a secret love, or like a hidden springtime, when the green seed sprouts from the barren earth, holding out the promise of future harvest."[12] When we welcome our full self back, we can return to our aliveness and sense of being firmly planted in our own ground. We can come home to our body, its wisdom and capacity for pleasure. After a lifetime of worrying about what others think of us, of striving to please, of attending to the needs of others, we can take our own advice, laugh at our own jokes, and find ourselves rooted in our authentic desires. We can learn to hear our silence instead of needing to fill it to put others at ease.

When our fierce side shows herself, wild and assertive, expansive and true, we may demand that she behave or try to domesticate her. Then she flies away to some dark part of our soul, where she waits for us. We become convinced that she is a demon who must be held at bay, but that is only because we have refused to know her. Though she is a bit savage and uncivilized, she is also the very best of us, our brightest spark. She is waiting to return to us so we can access her wisdom, her fire, and her life.

CHAPTER 1

DIVISION: LOSING YOUR FIRE

From the living fountain of instinct
flows everything that is creative;
hence the unconscious is not merely
conditioned by history, but is the very
source of the creative impulse.

—C. G. Jung, *Collected Works, Volume 8*

We arrive in the world connected with our full potential, but most of us gradually lose access to our vital spark. No one makes it to adulthood uncompromised. All of us have parts that have been discarded and lie in life's lumber room. According to Jung, the blossoming of self-awareness that occurs as we mature necessarily produces a "division with oneself."[1] We learn to distance ourselves from essential aspects of our souls. We bury those traits that are found to be unwelcome by our families or culture. We follow the rules of convention and cease listening to the deep, instinctual voices that guided our remote ancestors. These forgotten traits, which were originally part of our fullness, fall into the unconscious and become what Jung referred to as shadow—those parts of ourselves we would rather not know.

The aspects of ourselves we lose touch with will depend in large part on our family and culture. For many of us, there was something we were not allowed to be in our families. I was never allowed to be boastful. Maybe your family ethos taught that you were never to be a burden, or rude, or lazy. Our culture also imposes expectations that shape us as we develop. In the United States, children are often taught that being outgoing and extroverted is highly desirable. Those who are slow to warm up can come to feel ashamed or inadequate. Though families and cultures require everyone to conform to norms, they generally make different demands on women and girls than they do on men and boys. As a result, women tend to lose access to different parts of ourselves than men do, and our journey to wholeness is therefore also different.

This chapter will provide a map to the territory we will be covering in this book. After briefly considering what happens to girls and young women that leaves us alienated from core parts of ourselves, we'll explore an ancient story of a woman who was able to reconnect with her fiery qualities. "Fitcher's Bird" lays out an essential template of female psychological development that the rest of the stories in this book will elaborate upon.

From Girlhood to Adolescence

How does it happen that women become cut off from their most vitalizing qualities? Though there are sex-based differences in temperament in young children—girls tend to experience more negative emotions than boys—these are small. As adolescence looms, however, boys and girls are seemingly set on significantly different trajectories. In her book *Reviving Ophelia*, psychologist Mary Pipher writes movingly about the loss of confidence that girls experience as they go through puberty.

> Something dramatic happens to girls in early adolescence. Just as planes and ships disappear mysteriously into the Bermuda Triangle, so do the selves of girls go down in droves. They crash and burn in a developmental Bermuda Triangle. In early adolescence, studies show that girls' IQ scores drop and their math and science scores plummet. They lose their resiliency and optimism and become less curious and inclined to take risks. They lose their assertive, energetic and "tomboyish" personalities

and become more deferential, self-critical and depressed. They report great unhappiness with their own bodies.[2]

Prepubescent heroines of literature and film are full of moxie and courage—think Matilda, Pippi Longstocking, or Laura Ingalls. Female protagonists at the other end of adolescence are often struggling, as is the nineteen-year-old narrator of Sylvia Plath's *The Bell Jar* or the protagonist of the 2017 film *Lady Bird*. Before adolescence, girls are often exuberant and vivacious. For some, it is as if a light goes out as they become teens. They become meek and quiet. They develop eating disorders, anxiety, or an unhealthy obsession with their appearance fueled by a desperate sense of inadequacy. Their unselfconscious joy and abandon evaporate.

By the time we have made it through the stormy seas of adolescence and found ourselves thrown upon the shores of adulthood, most of us have lost contact with some vital part of ourselves. We become so focused on pleasing or caring for others that we lose touch with parts of ourselves.

YOUNG ADULTHOOD

As we grow into adulthood, we continue to struggle with feeling self-assured. For example, research about confidence in women finds that in college women's confidence drops while men's confidence increases.[3] The word *confidence* comes from two Latin words that mean "with trust." To have confidence is to trust ourselves. We cannot fully trust ourselves if we don't have access to fiery qualities such as shrewdness, assertiveness, and desire. A lack of confidence is a symptom of being cut off from our outlaw energies.

When I was in college, I took two seminar courses with the same music professor—one on Beethoven and one on Mozart. I loved those classes. The professor was dynamic, passionate, and funny. I received top grades in both classes, and in one of them, the professor chose to read sections of my paper aloud to the other students as an exemplary effort.

He always welcomed us to visit him during office hours. A part of me longed to go. I saw my male classmates talking and laughing with him when I passed his office. But I felt shy, and I couldn't think of what I would say if I were to drop by. I had no difficulties with the material we were learning and couldn't think of any clever questions to ask him. So I never went.

In my last year of college, I considered applying for a prestigious fellowship. My high grade point average would have made me competitive, but I needed strong recommendations. I decided to ask this music professor. I approached him during his office hours and presented my request. When he realized what I was asking, his brows knitted. "You don't have anyone else you can ask?" he said irritably. "I barely know you! Haven't you made any connections with professors in the four years that you've been here? What have you been doing with your time? I wouldn't have anything to say in such a letter." He dismissed me with disdain. I slunk away, mortified and empty-handed.

I had worked hard. I had attended every class and done well on assignments and tests. I had written at least one outstanding paper. But I could not find the fearlessness and assertiveness that would have made me feel comfortable approaching this man as an equal, the way my male classmates did. Their audacity was rewarded. My agreeableness was not. I never applied for the fellowship.

As we enter the workforce, women continue to suffer from a lack of confidence, and the evidence is that this holds us back professionally. Researchers have discovered that women will apply for a job when they meet 100% of the criteria. Men, however, feel comfortable putting themselves forward when they meet approximately 60%. Studies show that men overestimate their abilities and performance, while women underestimate both, and women are much more likely to express self-doubt about their competence.[4]

Cultivating confidence requires Lilith qualities. When we can't access these, we are trapped in the mode of caring and concern, which can hold us back partly because we don't want to make others feel challenged or uncomfortable. A lack of confidence can render us timid and ineffective. The implications of this go far beyond the workplace. When we can't access boldness, authority, and a healthy sense of entitlement, we will be less able to protect ourselves, feel enlivened, or claim our power. We will have a harder time pursuing our path, nurturing our creativity, or marshalling our power to defend our loved ones. A dark but satisfying tale from the Brothers Grimm provides a rich portrait of the potential costs of being cut off from Lilith—and shows us how we can reconnect with her.

FITCHER'S BIRD

Once upon a time, there was a sorcerer who was a thief and would disguise himself and beg from house to house. One day, he knocked on the door of a house where three sisters lived. A maiden opened the door and gave him a piece of bread. With just a touch, he could compel her to jump into his basket. He carried her back to his house, which was large and well-appointed. He gave her whatever she wished for, and, at first, she was content to stay with him.

After some time had passed, he told her that he had business to attend to far away and would be gone for several days. He gave her an egg and told her to take good care of it and always keep it with her. He also gave her a key. "Whatever you do, do not go into the room that this key opens if you value your life!" he told her.

When he left, however, curiosity overtook the maiden. She went into the forbidden room, and there she saw a large basin with dead and butchered women lying in it. She was so horrified that she dropped the egg into the basin. She retrieved it immediately and wiped it clean, but the blood reappeared as quickly as she wiped it away, and no matter what she did, she could not remove the stain.

When the sorcerer came home, he immediately asked for the key and the egg. Not knowing what else to do, the girl produced them. The sorcerer immediately knew what had happened by seeing the blood on the egg.

"You have disobeyed me!" he roared. "Now you will pay with your life, and you too will inhabit the bloody chamber!"

So saying, he dragged her into the room, chopped her up in pieces, and tossed her into the basin with the others.

After some time, the man went begging again at the same house. He captured the second sister in the same manner, and in time, she met the same fate as her sister. She entered the forbidden room, dropped the egg in the basin, and was chopped into pieces.

Eventually, the sorcerer captured the third daughter, but she was smart and cunning. When it came her turn to be left alone with the egg and the key, she left the egg in the cupboard before entering the forbidden chamber. When she saw her sisters in the bloody basin, she searched and searched until she found all their parts. Then she put them all back together—arms, legs, head, and body. In this way, her two sisters came back to life.

The third sister led the other two out of the bloody chamber and hid them. When the sorcerer came home, he was delighted to find no blood on the egg. He asked the third sister to become his wife. She agreed, but said that before she would marry him, he must carry baskets of gold back to her parents' house. She then secretly put her sisters in the basket and covered them with gold.

"Don't delay!" she told the sorcerer. "I will watch you from my window and know if you tarry."

The sorcerer lifted the basket onto his back, but it was quite heavy. When he stopped to rest a bit, one of the sisters in the basket cried out, "There is no time for rest! Get going!" The sorcerer thought it was the voice of the maiden watching from the window, so he stood up and continued, but the basket was so heavy that he had to rest. When he set the basket down, the other sister cried, "I'm watching you! Get a move on!" Thinking that his bride watched from her window, he lifted the basket again onto his back and limped toward his destination.

Meanwhile, the third sister decorated a skull with jewels and other fine things. Then she put it in the window, so it looked for all the world like a beautiful maiden watching for her lover to return. Next, she undressed and covered herself in honey. She split open one of the mattresses and rolled in the feathers until she was completely covered. In this way, she disguised herself, for she looked so strange that no one could recognize her. Then she set out for home.

As she was on her way, she met the wedding guests on the way to the sorcerer's house who asked:

"O, Fitcher's bird, what are you doing here?"

"I come from Fitcher's house, quite near."

"And what is the young bride doing there?"

"She's swept the whole house clean, I know,

And now looks out on the world below."

Next, she met the bridegroom, slowly making his way back. He, like the others, asked:

"O, Fitcher's bird, what are you doing here?"

"I come from Fitcher's house, quite near."

"And what is the young bride doing there?"

"She's swept the whole house clean, I know,

And now looks out on the world below."

The bridegroom looked up, saw the skull in the window, and thinking it was his bride, he waved. But when he and his guests had all gone in, the brothers and kinsmen of the bride, who had been sent to rescue her, arrived. They locked the sorcerer and guests inside the house, then set it on fire, and everyone burned to death.

Fairy tales speak in the mysterious tongue of symbol and image, the language of the unconscious. To understand a tale symbolically, we must squint a little, soften our gaze, and sink into the story. It won't do to go too quickly or be too smart. We must take our time and let the images work on us. Then we can open ourselves up to a shift in perspective.

We start with the assumption that every element in the tale is a part of one psyche. According to that understanding, each sister is a different aspect of the young woman about whom the story is told. The sorcerer, too, is a part of her. This may be difficult to imagine at first, but it immediately rescues us from the stuck polarity of "good" and "bad" and opens up realms of psychological subtlety.

The fairy tale uses a story of relationship between a man and a woman as a symbol for the work we must do as we become more whole. Ultimately, psychological growth is an inside job—there are both rich resources and dangerous challenges in the inner world. Intimate partnerships often mirror our inner reality and therefore are a stage upon which we work out our deepest personal wounds. For this reason, many fairy tales focus on romantic couplings, and we often dream of our intimate partners. It is important to keep in mind that in both dreams and fairy tales, these relationships can be understood symbolically. They often represent dynamics at work between parts of ourselves.

The tale begins with a maiden and her two sisters, but the story does not mention the parents. The young woman who answers the door is seemingly alone and unprotected. She opens the door to the sorcerer without a thought. Her compassion and naivete make her susceptible to abduction. When she hands him some bread, she gives away her psychic energy—her power and agency—and can be compelled to jump into the basket with just a touch.

By the time they reach young adulthood, women in our culture have usually been socialized to be kind and friendly. If a strange man speaks to you on an empty subway platform, you may feel compelled to be polite and answer even though you feel uncomfortable. The cultural voice in your head telling you to be courteous may outweigh the primal warning bell that rings. When we don't feel that we have permission to say no or have a boundary, we are like the sisters who cannot adequately protect themselves from the danger represented by the sorcerer. We ignore our instincts at our peril.

Becoming Conscious

The story tells us that the first young woman was initially content to stay with the sorcerer because he gave her whatever she wanted. Hopes that we will be loved and cared for can entice us to abandon our inner knowing. We so long to be cherished that we can be persuaded to disregard our intuition. Or, we may feel helpless to do otherwise than to go along with pressures and demands. Without the fierceness needed to care for and protect ourselves, we may feel we have no choice but to rely on others and hope that they have our best interests at heart.

When the first sister is given the egg and the key and left alone, she has enough pluck to enter the forbidden chamber. This bold action indicates a desire to grow toward consciousness. We all have forbidden chambers in our psyche, things we would rather not know about ourselves or someone else. My client Laura grew up with an alcoholic father. She came to see me after realizing with shock and horror that her husband and the father of her two children had a drinking problem. Until this point, she had been able not to know what had been there for her to see. It was as if she had been given a key that she hadn't allowed herself to use. We all make such efforts not to know what is painful or inconvenient. A willingness to peer into the forbidden chamber is a healthy impulse to overcome an inner injunction not to see. The key, therefore, is also a key to greater consciousness and self-awareness.

But we should not approach such knowledge without adequate preparation. The first two sisters break one of the rules—they go into the chamber. But they follow another rule to the letter—they always keep the egg with them. Their foray into the bloody room is impulsive, driven by a healthy yet immature curiosity. They aren't aware of the magnitude of what they are up against, and blithely approach the terrible knowledge that awaits them in that room without sufficient preparation. Doing so leads to death and dismemberment.

Dismemberment is a powerful metaphor for a state of psychological dissolution. We come apart. We dissociate. We no longer experience ourselves as having a coherent sense of self. Such experiences are not uncommon. They can be caused by trauma, psychosis, drug use, or other extreme conditions. They are terrifying and can sometimes lead to a permanent state of fracture. However, they can also herald a process of profound growth and healing. Shamans in various cultures report experiences of gruesome dismemberment during their initiatory journeys. These precede an experience of re-memberment and restoration that brings with it the power to heal others.

THE THIRD SISTER

The three sisters make different choices and have different fates. Three is a number that denotes a movement toward wholeness. In fairy tales, sequences of three often imply a temporal development and give a picture of something changing over time. According to this understanding, the three sisters are all aspects of the same person but at different stages of awareness and development. Being able to fail and learn from our failures is essential to psychological growth. Video games capture this archetypal truth. We keep getting beat in the boss fight until our skills develop to the point that we win. And just as in fairy tales, we can thankfully respawn. When we are young and have not yet learned to protect ourselves, we are like the video game newbie. We behave like the first two sisters, unthinkingly giving away our energy and thereby leaving ourselves vulnerable. The third sister is an image of what it looks like to claim Lilith qualities in the interest of growth and development. To do so, she must find new ways of coping that depart from her usual ways of going through the world.

We all arrive in adulthood with a narrow repertoire of behaviors and responses that are well-honed and habitual. We have consistent strategies we employ when we are disappointed, angry, challenged, or bored. Other reactions feel impossible, partly because we may have learned that these were unacceptable. We are like a painter with a vast palette of colors to choose from, but who only ever uses a small number of hues as she fills her canvas. Learning to broaden the scope of our behavioral responses allows us to make conscious choices about how we handle things. Then we no longer rely on reflexive strategies that are merely handed to us by old, unconscious scripts. Greater consciousness can allow us to express more of ourselves and negotiate the world with increasing success. Learning from our failures allows us to learn new behavioral responses. We can try out new things—what if I do *this* this time, and not that other thing that I usually do? Just like when we become better at playing a video game, we eventually learn what mistakes not to make.

The third sister is becoming more conscious. Though she is just as susceptible as the others initially, she makes different choices early on. The third sister breaks out of habitual response patterns, and this makes all the difference. She is able to access the eight qualities we will be examining in this book. She uses her shrewdness to protect the egg while exploring the forbidden room. She disobeys the sorcerer—not just impulsively, but with consciousness and cunning. It doesn't bother her to be disagreeable. The third sister accesses trickster energy by hiding her sisters in the basket and convincing the sorcerer that she is watching him from far away. She tunes into her desire to reunite with her sisters. She harnesses her rage at the sorcerer and uses it to protect herself and her sisters. And she claims sovereignty over her body and attractiveness by changing her maiden's gown for a strange costume of feathers. She doesn't need to be sexually attractive to someone else or concern herself with presenting an appealing persona. The decorated skull indicates that her old way of being in the world where she relied on charm and beauty is deadening. She turns the tables on the sorcerer, claiming authority and ordering *him* around rather than doing his bidding. Finally, she can access her aggression and ruthlessness to protect herself, as she aids her brothers and kinsmen in burning the sorcerer and his friends to death.

THE SORCERER

The sorcerer has access to magical powers but is also a thief who disguises himself as a beggar. An ungrounded inner imperative that we center someone else's needs instead of our own can become tyrannical, an inner saboteur who steals our power and severs us from ourselves. Many women feel a constant sense of guilt because a harsh inner voice tells them that they are not enough. This can leave them exhausted and depleted. In her book *Women Who Run With the Wolves*, Jungian analyst Clarissa Pinkola Estés writes about the well-known French version of this tale, "Bluebeard." She says that the murderous husband is an image of the inner predator—and that we all have one.[5] In his current form, he cannot be bargained with, appeased, or integrated. This most difficult dark energy must be transformed by fire—a complete chemical transmutation.

The inner sorcerer can take residence in our psyches for several reasons. First, he may find a home there because we were never taught how to protect ourselves adequately as children. In "Fitcher's Bird," the three sisters presumably live with their parents, but we never see them, and no one seems to notice that the first two sisters have disappeared. We may have had parents who were absent or unengaged and who didn't see when we were distressed. In this way, we may have learned that it was not okay to address our needs. However, the sorcerer exists in the psyches of all of us, even if we haven't had early life hardship. Because of our desire to be likable and appealing, he is an ever-present danger.

BLUEBEARD

The French version known as "Bluebeard" has some significant differences from "Fitcher's Bird," and these can tell us something important about what it takes to reconnect with those qualities that empower us. In "Bluebeard," the sorcerer is a wealthy nobleman with a strange blue beard. He courts three sisters, but they all refuse to marry him because of his beard and because he has had many previous wives who have all mysteriously disappeared. At last, however, the youngest sister is persuaded to marry him because of his wealth. Sometime after the wedding, he leaves her alone with the keys to every room in the palace and instructs her to go wherever she likes—except for one small room. I'm sure you can guess what happens next. When she enters the room, she finds the bodies of Bluebeard's previous wives chopped up in a basin. She is so startled she drops the key, which is subsequently stained with blood that cannot be wiped away. The key reveals her disobedience. Bluebeard grabs her and threatens to take her into the chamber and chop her up. She stalls for a few minutes while her brothers ride to the rescue. Finally, they kill Bluebeard, and the wife inherits his wealth and eventually marries someone more suitable.

In the French version, the liberating force comes from without in the form of her brothers. We might say that the brothers are part of her psyche—an inner, freeing, masculine energy that appears at the right moment. However, even in this interpretation, the maiden does not consciously possess this positive energy. The maiden in "Bluebeard" has not yet learned to purposely claim aggression, shrewdness, trickiness, and the other qualities that allow the third sister in the Grimms' tale to save herself and rescue her sisters.

THE INNER SABOTEUR

A woman's lack of access to her agency and power can leave her victimized and helpless. This victimization can manifest in very dark ways. We may find ourselves in a relationship with someone—male or female—who feeds on our energy or is verbally or physically abusive. But there are more subtle ways to find ourselves victims of an inner Bluebeard energy.

Beth was the oldest of five siblings. Her family was poor, and she recalls feeling cold all winter because it was too expensive to heat the house adequately. Her father was an alcoholic who often became rageful and dangerous when drunk. Beth remembers huddling in a closet with her younger siblings, trying to keep out of his way. Beth did well in school and got a full scholarship to attend college, where she excelled in math and science. She completed an engineering degree and has been very successful in her field. In her twenties, Beth had a long-term relationship with a man who struggled with drug addiction. Their liaison was marked by chaos and drama. When she came to see me in her early thirties, she had not dated anyone in several years.

Beth's social life revolved around her siblings. She felt that she must be the matriarch and be strong for the family, and frequently extended herself to her younger siblings by lending them money, hosting holiday parties, and taking care of their children. She complained that her friends from college were all starting to get married while she was chronically single. I suspected this was because she reserved most of her time and energy for her brothers and sisters.

Beth first came to see me in early January, shortly after her Christmas holiday. She was depressed and depleted, though she couldn't say what was bothering her. She described the elaborate Christmas celebration she had staged for her siblings. It became clear to me while I was listening that she had done a tremendous amount of cooking, shopping, decorating, and cleaning. Her siblings, on the other hand, had behaved rather badly. Several had arrived late, and none seemed appreciative of the trouble she had taken. Only one of her sisters had helped her to clean up after the meal, and two of her brothers had made snide comments about her hybrid car and had a laugh at her expense for being "such a bleeding-heart environmentalist."

At first, Beth did not connect her post-holiday low mood with the deep disappointment and unacknowledged rage she felt toward her siblings. But when I gently suggested the connection, she grew silent, and her eyes filled with tears. Eventually, we explored how she sacrificed herself for her siblings, just as she had always done. Although her actual father had passed away when Beth was in college, an inner father—raging, cruel, and unable to be appeased—haunted her interior. He demanded that Beth perform superhuman feats and provide the warmth and love to her siblings for which she had always longed. When Beth had attempted to date in her twenties, she had found herself in a relationship with a man who carried Bluebeard energy just as her father had. Now her inner Bluebeard was keeping her to himself—out of relationships and out of life.

The inner Bluebeard severs a woman from herself. He drains her energy. He takes advantage of a woman's wish to be compassionate and compels her to put her needs aside. He leaves her off balance and doubting herself. Most of all, he makes her afraid. She may be afraid that she is doing things wrong, or that she will never be good enough. She may fear she is a bad person, or has not perceived things correctly. She may be afraid of the anger and judgments of others. And she may even be afraid that her partner will physically hurt or abuse her. When we find ourselves living in fear, we ought to wonder whether an inner Bluebeard is at work.

A WORTHY OPPONENT

Having an inner Bluebeard makes it more likely that we will encounter Bluebeard people in the outer world. Likewise, if we often find ourselves in relationships with Bluebeard types, it should cause us to wonder where this predatory force is at work in the inner landscape. When a Bluebeard is present in our lives, we can remember the lessons of "Fitcher's Bird." The third sister does not wait helplessly for rescue from without. She finds all those empowering, fiery qualities within herself and so can best her oppressor.

Our connecting feelings and attitudes—empathy, care, nurture, accommodation, and others—won't help us when we are being preyed upon. As we saw with the first two sisters, predators use our compassion and agreeableness to ensnare us. If we depend only on our connecting qualities when we come under attack, we will be left with a narrow range of options. We can passively hope that someone comes to our rescue, or we can try our hardest to be appealing so that our attacker will be moved to pity. Sometimes, such strategies work, but other times they can be fatally naive. If we can access our empowering feelings and attitudes—cunning, forcefulness, authority, selfishness, anger, and so on—we will have a broader range of strategies that we can employ.

If we don't have access to our assertive qualities and our connecting attitudes prove insufficient at protecting us, we can fall into bitterness, seeping anger, victimhood, and passive-aggressive attention-seeking. Because we haven't developed tools to defend ourselves, the world looks like a universally dangerous place. If we remain stuck in this outlook, it can calcify and become part of our character structure, setting us up for a lifetime of retreat and resentment. In contrast, when a woman develops her outlaw energies, she can become a worthy opponent rather than a victim.

FINDING OUR PERSONAL POWER

The sorcerer in "Fitcher's Bird" is not merely evil. He is powerful and wealthy, with a fine house. The sorcerer has access to riches and gives the sister a key and an egg, both potent symbols of totality. An egg images the potential for psychological wholeness that Jung termed the Self, the goal of our lifelong process of unfolding. Jungian analyst Marie-Louise von Franz noted that the sorcerer is connected with the land of the dead.[6] He knows the secrets of death and rebirth—in one version of the story, the third sister brings the others back to life using a magical balm that she finds elsewhere in the sorcerer's house. The sorcerer is an image of the possibility for psycho-spiritual growth and development within a woman's psyche. He may represent access to a transpersonal potential to which we are inadequately related, and thus it plays a destructive role in our lives. For example, becoming enthralled by belief systems, religious practices, or political movements can put us in touch with enormous archetypal forces that connect us with something greater than ourselves. Such experiences can be expansive and meaningful, but if we give ourselves over to them unthinkingly, these forces can take us into dark places and cause significant damage both in our lives and in the culture. The sorcerer's secret demand is that we claim our personal power and not surrender our critical judgment or look to others to take care of us.

Gwen's relationship with Mark was often tempestuous. He was, in fact, a kind of sorcerer—a skilled astrologer who gave frequent workshops at his home and had a loyal local following. He had overcome great hardship by holding himself to exacting standards, and rather cruelly imposed these same standards on Gwen. He did not believe in offering empathy and could be harshly critical. When he was cutting and dismissive, Gwen often lost her footing. She could not defend herself without collapsing into shrill self-pity, which would elicit more withering disdain from Mark. The result was that she was frequently unhappy but also felt stuck and unable to resolve to leave.

One week, Gwen shared with Mark her frustration over a recent interaction with a friend. Mark chastised her coldly for her attitude, which he felt was self-indulgent. Gwen witnessed herself becoming increasingly distraught as he elucidated her failings. She thought that he was mischaracterizing her, but she couldn't find a way to stand up for herself. The exchange repeated the familiar pattern that had occurred many times through the years. But this time, something subtly shifted in Gwen. When she couldn't find the words she needed, Gwen mutely walked out and drove to a friend's house, where she stayed for several days.

Gwen resisted the urge to call Mark and smooth things over as she had many times before. Instead, she allowed herself to imagine all the possibilities. What would happen if she and Mark split up? When she sat with this question, she realized that a breakup would be painful and challenging, but that she would be okay. She likewise recognized that the split would be difficult for Mark, but he would also be fine. She didn't give in to the temptation to demonize Mark or to ascribe full blame for their difficulties to him. While Gwen was grateful for the support of her female friends during the troubling days she stayed away, she found their exhortations to "dump him" overly simplistic. Somehow, she knew that the situation required a more profound transformation.

Gwen waited to reconnect with Mark until she was more centered. As usual, Mark acted as if nothing had happened, ignoring the conflict and its aftermath. But Gwen didn't simply go along this time. She told him she wanted to discuss the argument, but only when she was ready. Then, when the time felt right, she told Mark what she had been feeling before, during, and after the argument—and Mark listened. He responded to her with appropriate empathy and curiosity rather than shutting her down with sneering contempt. Gwen had become a worthy opponent, and this created new ways for Mark to engage with her.

At this time, she had a series of two important dreams:

> I am in a dark-paneled, gothic library. The devil
> is there, and a woman wants to be with him. The
> devil wants to take the woman. He doesn't, though.
> He's trying to teach her, but she's foolish and thinks
> he's trying to seduce her. The devil knows that he
> would and could kill her and thinks she's stupid.
> The woman tries to tell the devil, "Oh, I love
> you; I want to be with you," and the devil snarls at
> her. There is a tube out of which rainbow-colored
> stuff is coming out. The woman has a choice of
> jumping into the tube or being taken by the devil.
> The woman says that jumping into the rainbow tube
> will be her salvation when she knows it will really be
> her death. She's doomed. It's tragic and sad, but she
> doesn't see a way out, and maybe there is no way out.

The woman in the dream has evaded an opportunity to be taught by the devil. She thinks that the devil wants to seduce her when really, he wants her to stand her ground and show up in the contest as a worthy opponent—someone he can instruct about the ways of darkness. She has misunderstood the nature of this significant psychic content and therefore relates to it incorrectly. She thinks the options are either to avoid it by jumping into the rainbow tube or collapse into it by being seduced by it. This dream image reflected how Gwen related to many aspects of her life, including her relationship with Mark. Situations were either "all bad" and must be avoided, or they were magical and transformative but required little effort on her part. The rainbow tube represents a rigid psychological defense—an aggressive optimism that won't allow for the knowledge of darkness that the devil wants to convey.

The next night, she had the following dream:

> I've come under the influence of a dark magician, so much so that I've made an appointment to see him to become "initiated." Mark is driving me someplace, and I realize sheepishly I've made this commitment. I tell Mark, and he drives me there. I feel protected by Mark. The magician won't be able to "take me" if he's there.
>
> When we arrive, the dark magician greets us. He is very kind and gracious. There are other people with him, all dressed in robes. Mark seems comfortable joining them.
>
> I have a ring on my left ring finger that was given to me by the magician earlier. A strange bloody pattern has appeared above my finger. I wipe it away and take the ring off. A young man tells me he "looked it up" and knows the bloody pattern means I belong there.
>
> I take a bath in a large deep tub in the middle of the bathroom. I fart in the tub, and a small turd comes out. I feel divided by this—I want to show the magician and his people my disdain, and I also fear leaving anything of myself behind because they could do magic on it. So I empty the tub, look for the turd, and find a small kernel of corn.
>
> I go to find Mark and convince him to leave. He begins talking about what he'll need to give the magician as if he had struck a bargain with him. He says, "I guess he will lead the ceremony at my funeral." This frightens me, and I think Mark is under his spell.

A part of Gwen is ready to be initiated into the dark knowledge offered by the devil/magician. However, another part is still fearful.

She has misunderstood what the dark magician is offering and what he is asking of her. The blood on her finger indicates that she belongs there, just as the blood on the egg in "Fitcher's Bird" shows moral complicity and investment in the sorcerer's world. However, dream Gwen resists her initiation. She feels disdain for the dark magician and his followers. In other words, the conscious part of Gwen believes herself to be superior to the shadowy forces in the unconscious. She wants to render herself inviolable to these potent forces by making sure she leaves nothing of herself behind. She imagines it is possible to remain untouched.

Dream Gwen at first believes that Mark will protect her. This reflected how Gwen projected her darkness onto Mark so that she could continue to see herself as pure and "good." Believing that Mark possessed all the shadowy qualities in the relationship protected her from knowing about her tendency for rigidity, arrogance, and other attributes. But dream Mark can join with the dark magician and strike a bargain with him. Though this frightens dream Gwen, it accurately reflects waking Mark's fearless ability to claim his dark magician qualities in service to his psychological growth.

Intimate relationships tend to call up the primal desire to collapse into a union where we will be lovingly cared for without effort on our part. This Edenic fantasy recalls our experience in infancy, where, hopefully, we were cared for in just this manner. But once we are adults, the truth is that we must take responsibility for getting our needs met. Even in the best relationships, we cannot look to our partner to do this for us. Just like the sorcerer in "Fitcher's Bird," the devil/dark magician in Gwen's dreams demands that she claim her personal power and become a worthy opponent rather than surrender to the fantasy that someone else will meet her needs.

When we are not in touch with our outlaw energies, we unconsciously look to others to take care of us. Then we are like the first two sisters or the heroine of "Bluebeard." We helplessly wait to be rescued. Even decent people may fail us if we implicitly look to them to make us happy without shouldering responsibility for ourselves. When we can't address our needs, we are always at risk of being victims, and everyone is a potential Bluebeard.

A dramatic story from my clinical practice illustrates what it means to become a worthy opponent in stark terms. Early in my career, I worked with victims of domestic violence. In preparation for this work, I had been taught that if a man uses violence once, he will do so again, and the violence will invariably escalate. I used this information to help women assess their safety in abusive relationships and determine whether it was time to leave. A few years later, I worked in an inpatient drug rehabilitation center in a poor neighborhood in Philadelphia. The women at the center were mainly addicted to crack cocaine or heroin. Many of them had known lives of terrible poverty, trauma, and hardship. One day, a woman shared in group about how her husband used to beat her repeatedly. She was still married to him, and he no longer beat her. Her experience contradicted what I knew about domestic violence. I was curious to hear more. The woman shared that she had gotten tired of the abuse. One day, when her husband went to hit her, she pulled out a loaded gun and aimed it at him. "If you ever hit me again," she said. "I will kill you." According to my patient, the violence ceased then and there.

I'm not condoning using guns to settle interpersonal disputes, and I'm certainly not suggesting that women in abusive relationships should stay with or confront their abusers. Doing so could be very dangerous. And I don't want to diminish the true fear that any human would feel after being physically assaulted by someone they used to trust. However, the story struck me at the time—and has continued to stay with me—because it says something important about relationship dynamics. Sometimes, forcefully standing up for ourselves can bring about a profound shift. Gwen had found her metaphorical gun and stood her ground in the confrontation with Mark. She became a worthy opponent, creating new possibilities in the relationship.

EX MACHINA

The 2014 science fiction film *Ex Machina* retells the story of Bluebeard. It traces the development of two women who find their cunning, aggression, shrewdness, and other outlaw qualities and become worthy opponents.

The film begins with a young programmer, Caleb (Domhnall Gleeson), winning a coveted prize—a chance to spend a week with his tech genius boss, Nathan (Oscar Isaac), the inventor of the world's largest search engine. Caleb is helicoptered into Nathan's secluded home, which is tucked into a vast tract of wilderness. The only person there besides Nathan is a beautiful, silent young woman named Kyoko (Sonoya Mizuno), who works as his house servant. We learn that she doesn't understand English.

From the start, Nathan exudes menace. He keeps Caleb off balance with his mixture of easy familiarity, needling derision, efforts to control, and vague threats. Upon Caleb's arrival, Nathan gives him a key card and explains that it will not open certain forbidden rooms. In addition, a ubiquitous CCTV system monitors Caleb's comings and goings. As the movie progresses, Nathan becomes more threatening, and his sociopathic nature reveals itself.

Nathan introduces Caleb to Ava (Alicia Vikander), a humanoid robot with artificial intelligence that Nathan has created. He explains that the reason he wanted to bring Caleb to spend the week with him was so that he could test Ava's AI. Could Ava convince Caleb of her humanity? Each day, Caleb has a session with Ava. She is kept behind glass, a prisoner in her small apartment. Caleb is immediately taken with her, and with each session, their conversation becomes more intimate. Ava is demure and soft-spoken and moves with balletic grace. With her diaphanous body and delicate beauty, Ava is an irresistible damsel in distress.

Though Nathan monitors their conversations via CCTV, Ava cunningly triggers periodic power outages that allow them to speak unobserved for a few minutes. During one such interlude, Ava tells Caleb that Nathan is not to be trusted. She soon lets her feelings for Caleb be known and tells him that she wants to be with him.

Throughout the film, we see Kyoko in the background performing various tasks, such as cutting fish with a large sushi knife. She is a silent presence while the two men debrief Caleb's sessions with Ava, discussing questions about AI and the nature of sentience. The camera occasionally focuses on Kyoko. Can she understand what the two men are saying? In one scene, Nathan begins kissing her, and it is obvious that she is his sexual partner. He treats her as an object or possession. When Kyoko spills wine on Caleb while serving the two men dinner, Nathan reacts with verbal brutality, calling her stupid. Whether he is berating her, kissing her, or dancing with her, Kyoko passively performs whatever task Nathan requires of her. When Caleb approaches her to ask where Nathan is, she begins robotically undressing as if she is performing a routine job. She is expressionless and silent.

Caleb grows increasingly attached to Ava and distrustful of Nathan. He learns that Nathan is considering "upgrading" Ava to make a new model—a procedure that will effectively kill her. When Nathan passes out after drinking too much, Caleb steals his key card and enters Nathan's forbidden chambers. There, he finds evidence that Nathan has created—and discarded—several previous humanoid prototypes. In addition, there is video footage of Nathan treating these androids cruelly. In a scene that is strongly reminiscent of "Bluebeard," Caleb finds successive closet doors behind which hang the naked, lifeless, and dismembered bodies of these cast-off female robots. Kyoko then silently reveals to Caleb that she, too, is an android. Shortly after this, Kyoko visits Ava for the first time.

Caleb plans to rescue Ava by reprogramming the lockdown protocol so that all doors will open during a power cut. In his final session with Ava, he tells her this and directs her to cut the power at 10 pm. Nathan learns of the plan but is too late to stop it. Ava is finally free, and we see her walking through the halls of Nathan's home. Kyoko approaches her, and the camera lingers on a close-up of Ava whispering something in Kyoko's ear.

The two women are standing close together, touching one another when Nathan comes into the hallway with a weapon. He orders Ava back to her room, but she runs at him. After a tussle, he brutally knocks off part of her arm. While she is prone, he grabs her legs and begins dragging her back to her cell, but Kyoko stabs Nathan in the back with the sushi knife. Nathan smashes her across the face, apparently killing her, but Ava has had time to get on her feet. She takes the knife out of his back and plunges it into his abdomen. He staggers and then falls.

While this happened, Caleb has been locked in Nathan's study. Ava tells him to wait there, then goes into the closet of deactivated androids. Using their parts, she repairs her arm, covers herself with their skin, and emerges clothed and coiffed without any evidence that she is not human. She leaves Caleb behind, effectively imprisoned, as he desperately bangs on the door and calls for her help. In the movie's last few minutes, we see her greeting the arriving helicopter. Then we see her on a busy street, blending into the crowd.

Ex Machina follows the story of two women, both of whom Nathan creates to fulfill the needs and desires of others, but who, by the end of the film, develop their full personhood. Nathan designed Ava's appearance based on Caleb's internet pornography search preferences. He crafted her to be the perfect recipient of Caleb's projections. Ava's name is a variation of Eve. Like her namesake, she appears willing to submit to her partner. But Ava defies the expectations of both Nathan and Caleb and outsmarts them. Who was manipulating whom? Nathan designed Ava to trick Caleb, but in the end, she subverts the expectations, claims her sovereignty over Caleb and Nathan, and becomes the author of her own fate. To manipulate Caleb into helping her escape, she plays the ingenue. Sweetly seductive and flattering, she seems to be nothing more than a foil for his desires.

Kyoko's rise to personhood is even more striking. Crafted by Nathan to serve his needs for sex, a cook, and a housekeeper, Kyoko appears to lack her own thoughts and desires. She exists only in relation to others and only in the context of the services she can provide. Throughout the film, we come to understand that her mute, expressionless gaze is not as blank as Nathan assumes. We see her staring at the Jackson Pollock painting Nathan used to explain the nature

DIVISION: LOSING YOUR FIRE

of spontaneity to Caleb. We see her watching intently on the CCTV as Caleb, distraught and disoriented, slices into his arm with a razor, perhaps realizing that she and Caleb are different—and learning what a sharp object can do to a human. At this point, she seeks Ava out for the first time. "Who are you?"[7] Ava asks when Kyoko enters her space.

Ava can access ruthlessness in the interest of achieving her goals. We also come to realize that she is a masterful trickster. She has intended to manipulate all along. But Ava is as cold and calculating as Nathan. Though Kyoko comes to Ava's aid, Ava does not stop to repair Kyoko but selfishly escapes without thinking of anyone else. Ava is perhaps a warning that, as we reclaim our shadowy Lilith qualities, it is important not to lose touch with our capacity for care, empathy, and connection, lest we turn into the very thing against which we have been striving.

Like Ava, Kyoko breaks from being compulsively other-oriented and develops independent thoughts and goals. But she develops compassion for Ava and marshals aggression to stop Nathan's sociopathic plot. Kyoko ponders the deep questions about the nature of consciousness and personhood and responds out of a sense of ethical responsibility. Alone among the characters in the film, she can be in service to something greater. The ending of the film is ambivalent; though Kyoko develops a connection both to her compassionate and assertive qualities, she doesn't triumph.

HEALING THE SPLIT

Lilith was a worthy opponent for Adam. She wasn't interested in simply giving in to his preferences. That the relationship couldn't withstand her challenge says something about the perceived cost of women's self-assertion. Standing up for ourselves will likely engender conflict—not just with our romantic partners but with our parents, siblings, co-workers, friends, neighbors, and more. Many of us find such conflict uncomfortable. We value harmony and often go to great lengths to preserve peace and affinity. Yet, if we can tolerate disagreement and strife, we will be able to act from authenticity rather than from a constricted compulsion to avoid conflict.

Learning to become a worthy opponent will require that we reclaim the forbidden parts of ourselves. When facing conflict, there are times when a bold, assertive response is best. There are times when a timid appeal to mercy might be right. And there are times when using trickster energy is the most effective way to break an impasse. One mode of being in the world is not better than another. The difficulty arises when a whole range of responses and feelings has been disallowed and falls into the unconscious where we cannot find it.

We need access to connecting qualities such as empathy, kindness, and compassion, as well as assertive qualities such as cunning, aggression, and shrewdness. If we have lost touch with assertive qualities, reclaiming them will bring us back to our fuller selves. Jungian analyst Edward Edinger noted the need to accept our less likeable traits if we are to claim our potency.

> In my experience, the basis of almost all psychological problems is an unsatisfactory relation to one's urge to individuality. And the healing process often involves an acceptance of what is commonly called selfish [or] power-seeking [. . .]. The majority of patients in psychotherapy need to learn how to be more effectively selfish and more effective in the use of their own personal power; they need to accept responsibility for the fact of being centers of power and effectiveness.[8]

Healing the division within ourselves means that we take responsibility for ourselves. Doing so grants us renewed access to the animating spark of the central fire. It expands our repertoire of choices, thus broadening our world and imbuing us with increased confidence and an ability to protect ourselves. We know when something doesn't feel right and can advocate for ourselves, allowing us freedom from the demands of expectations that don't serve us. We can say no and enforce boundaries, making space for us to bring our own creative impulses forward. When we can access our connecting and assertive qualities as needed, we have what we need to live out our essential pattern and grow as fully as possible into the person we were meant to become. We have more room for joy, spontaneity, and aliveness. And the flame we came into the world with can burn its brightest.

QUESTIONS FOR REFLECTION

1. In "Fitcher's Bird," the first sister readily gives the sorcerer something to eat and this seemingly gives him power over her. Think back to a time when you gave some part of yourself away to someone who was undeserving or untrustworthy. What happened that you felt compelled to make yourself vulnerable in this way? What were the pressures—inner or outer—that encouraged this act of self-betrayal?

2. The first two sisters break one rule by going into the forbidden chamber but aren't fully prepared for this—they haven't thought to leave the egg behind. Often, growth results from repeatedly making the same mistake before we become conscious and realize there is another way of responding. Where in your life have you had to suffer many painful defeats before you grew wiser and took a new approach to a challenge?

3. The sorcerer is a complex, difficult image—capable of great harm, but also possessing wealth and access to magical powers. He may represent the possibility of a connection to a transpersonal authority, but one that can be destructive. Have you ever found yourself caught up in something that you later realized was not what it seemed at first? Maybe it was an intense personal relationship, a strong political or religious belief, or even a habit that started off healthy but became obsessive. What aspect of this experience was healing or beneficial? What can you say about why it turned dark?

4. If the first two sisters lost themselves under the influence of the sorcerer, the third sister recollects herself. She trusts her own wits and is therefore able to rescue herself and her sisters. Think back to a time when you got yourself out of a difficult situation. What aspects of yourself were important in helping you meet the challenge? Which of your qualities made the difference?

5. The third sister employs the curious disguise of covering herself in feathers. Sometimes, to turn a situation to our advantage, we have to not care about how silly or strange we might appear to others. Have you ever hidden your valuable qualities? Why did you do so? How did that work? What were the costs of doing this?

6. The story doesn't tell us much about what happens to the sisters after the sorcerer's house is burned, but in the similar tale, "Bluebeard," the wife inherits his wealth. When you have managed to work your way out of a difficult or threatening situation, what were the treasures that you gained as a result? In what ways were you stronger, wiser, or more resilient?

CHAPTER 2

DISAGREEABLENESS: FLINGING THE FROG

The opposite of a reflexive goodness is
not the bad but rather the authentic.

—James Hollis, personal communication

When I was in my twenties, I had an older friend named Terry. She was in her fifties and was a free spirit. Terry loved to cook and would invite groups of us over for delicious food on her rooftop terrace. The first time I attended one of her dinners, we had enjoyed a wonderful meal and were lingering over dessert. I was savoring a glass of wine and good conversation under the stars when Terry announced—abruptly, but with a smile—that it was time for us to go. "This has been great, but I'm ready to go to bed, so you all need to leave." Once I got over my surprise and slight hurt at being kicked out, I was full of admiration. Terry didn't have to be agreeable and accommodating. When she wanted to go to bed, she simply told us what she needed and didn't worry about our reaction. At subsequent gatherings, I was prepared for the evening to end with a brusque dismissal.

To return to ourselves and live out that which is unlived within us, we will need to defy those inner and outer voices that exhort us to be agreeable—to meet expectations of propriety and to be accommodating and likable. Research on personality traits consistently finds that women score higher than men on measures of agreeableness.[1] People who are high in the trait of agreeableness tend to get along well with others. They value harmony in relationships and are well-liked. They are quick to show empathy and care for others. They are sensitive, attuned, and trusting and tend to give others the benefit of the doubt. In general, women value cooperation and harmony more than competitiveness and aggression.

How much of this difference is due to innate versus social factors is an intriguing question. Though nurture undoubtedly plays a role, these differences are noted throughout cultures. They are stable across the lifespan, making it plausible that some of this difference is due to innate factors.[2] Coming to terms with our tendency to be agreeable may mean confronting confining stereotypes, but it may also mean facing something essential about our nature.

If a woman's tendency to be compliant and accommodating is, to an extent, innate, culture certainly reinforces it. On a recent evening at a local restaurant, I noticed two families with girls under ten. Both young girls wore t-shirts with some version of the phrase "Be Kind" on them. Kindness, of course, is a value of utmost significance. It calls on us to be generous, receptive, and compassionate. But kindness is not the same as false niceness that requires a complete capitulation to the demands of the other. And kindness is the wrong response in some situations. Exhorting young girls to be kind before they have had a chance to consolidate a stance may render them defenseless later in life.

A young woman in my practice was approached by an intoxicated man in a public park who aggressively pressured her to give him her phone number and didn't back down when she repeatedly politely declined. She was frightened because he was wielding an empty bottle, but she also felt bound by social expectations. "Did you think about shouting at him, getting up, and walking away?" I asked. "I didn't want to seem rude," she answered.

A friend went to the dentist to have a gap between two teeth addressed, but the dentist began drilling a healthy tooth instead. My friend was so concerned about not wanting to make the dentist feel uncomfortable that she never said anything and instead allowed the mistaken drilling and filling to continue. Too much kindness defangs us.

The benefits of agreeableness are significant. Being widely liked is a currency that pays dividends in social life and at work. Many a junior career has been made because of a young person's willingness to say yes to whatever is asked. Agreeable women are often the first to raise their hands when there is a job to be done, and they are often praised for their ability to get along and "be a team player." Those who are agreeable at work often wind up with positive performance evaluations, raises, and promotions—to a point.

When women are "yes people" at the office, they can wind up taking on too much of the grunt work while the juicier projects are awarded to those who advocate better for themselves. (And often these latter are men.) They can find it difficult to assert their needs and preferences and may find that others take credit for their hard work. They may be so oriented to meeting external expectations and pleasing their superiors that they give themselves away too easily.

Learning to be disagreeable is an enormous task for some women. To tolerate the other's displeasure or disapproval, to risk that another might be angry with us, to know that we have disappointed or inconvenienced someone or made someone uncomfortable can all be very difficult. Some of us are so oriented to the feelings and needs of others that we have a hard time discerning our preferences and desires. In therapy, I frequently ask someone what she would like, and the woman answers by telling me what those around her need. Although this sometimes happens with men, it occurs much more frequently with women.

We run the risk of going through the world concerned with what would make others happy while having no idea what we want. Or, we know what we want but don't feel deserving of pursuing it, especially if doing so would inconvenience someone else. This orientation can cause us to feel depleted and inauthentic. It can make us joyless and resentful without us even knowing why. And if it goes unchecked, it can lead us to be bitter. Trying so hard to accommodate others will also constellate the opposite in us. Outwardly, we may seem pleasant and appeasing, while, unconsciously, we act out the role of petty tyrant, imposing ourselves on those around us and demanding in passive-aggressive maneuvers that others give us what we have denied ourselves.

"The Frog King" is a fairy tale that guides us to embrace our authentic stance, even if it means being disagreeable. Only when the heroine responds from her center can a genuine transformation occur.

THE FROG KING

Once upon a time, a princess sat at the edge of a well, playing with a beautiful golden ball, her favorite plaything. She delighted in throwing it up into the air and catching it, but she dropped it, and it fell into the water and sank. The princess was distraught. When she looked into the well, she saw it was so deep that she couldn't see the bottom. She sat down at the edge of the well and began to weep and lament. "I would give anything in the world to get my ball back!" she cried.

As she cried, a frog stuck its head out of the water and said, "Why are you weeping?"

"Oh!" responded the princess, "You can't help me, you nasty frog! My ball has fallen into the water."

The frog offered to fetch the ball for her on the condition that she accept him as her companion and let him sit next to her, eat from her plate, sleep in her bed, and promise to love and cherish him. The princess thought that the frog's demands were nonsense and couldn't imagine that he would ever leave the water, so she quickly promised him what he asked in hopes that he would retrieve her ball.

The frog disappeared into the water and returned a moment later with the ball in his mouth. The princess quickly took it from him, delighted to have her plaything back. Then, without pausing, she rushed off back to the castle. "Wait, princess!" called the frog after her. "You promised to take me with you!"

But she ignored him.

The next day, the princess was sitting at the table when she heard something coming up the marble steps. *Squish, squish, squish!* Then came a knock at the door and a voice that cried out, "Oh, Princess! Open up, please!"

She ran to the door and opened it and saw the frog, whom she had forgotten. Horrified, she slammed the door shut and returned to the table, acting as if nothing was the matter. However, her father, the king, saw that she was alarmed and asked her what was wrong.

"There's a horrid frog outside," she said. "He fetched my golden ball for me from the water, and I promised him he could come to live with me, but I never thought he meant it. Now he is standing outside and wants to come in."

As she said this, there was another knock on the door, and she could hear the frog calling to her.

"You must keep your promise," said the king. "Go and open the door for the frog."

The princess opened the door, and the frog hopped inside and followed her to the table. She sat down and resumed eating. "Lift me beside you!" the frog called out. The princess loathed the thought of this, but her father, the king, ordered her to do it. With revulsion, she picked up his slimy little body and placed him on the table. "Now push your plate a little closer," he said to her, "so that we might eat together."

The princess was forced to comply, and when the frog had eaten until he was full, he commanded her to bring him to her bed as he was tired and wished to sleep. The princess was terrified of sharing her bed with the cold, wet frog. She started to cry at the thought of it, but her father became angry and ordered her to keep her promise. So she picked up the frog with two fingers and carried him to her room. She was so enraged at the thought of putting his slimy little body on her pillow that she flung him with all her might against the wall. "Leave me alone, you disgusting frog!" she cried.

The moment the frog hit the wall, he transformed into a handsome young prince. The princess was shocked and then delighted. The two sat up talking, and she cherished him as she had promised. Then, in their delight, they fell asleep together.

The next morning, a fine carriage arrived, drawn by eight horses and conveying the prince's servant, Faithful Henry. When Faithful Henry learned that his dear master had been turned into a frog, he had three iron bands placed around his heart to keep it from bursting from grief. The princess and the prince got into the coach to travel back to the prince's realm, and as they rode, they heard three mighty cracks. The prince at first feared that the coach was breaking, but Faithful Henry explained that the iron bands around his heart had sprung open because he was so happy that the spell had been broken.

A princess sits beside a well, innocently tossing a golden ball into the air. We learn as the tale progresses that she is spoiled and thinks only of herself. And yet there are several things present even as the tale opens that alert us to possibilities for tremendous psychological growth. The well is a potent image of an access point to the unconscious. A well stretches down into the depths, where life-giving water is found. The princess has as her plaything a beautiful golden ball. Because of its spherical shape and golden color, this ball is symbolic of the potential for psychological wholeness inherent in each of us, which Jung referred to as the Self.

Even right in the beginning, we see that this pretty, spoiled princess who is carefree and innocent has a relationship with the Self and a potential for depth. And yet her attitude toward the sacred, abiding center of the personality is too casual. She treats it like a plaything. You shouldn't toss a ball near a well. Eventually, it will fall in. She has been reckless with that which is of supreme value.

When we have been much loved and doted on, we can become careless with what is precious. A "too good mother" complex confers a sense of deservedness but does not prepare us in critical ways for the truth of the world. Innocence can make us vulnerable. It can also make us thoughtless with life's most priceless gifts.

The predictable loss of the ball in the well comes as a horrible shock to the princess. It is a kind of initiation. It wakes the princess up to the existence of her depths—the well—which she had hitherto taken for granted. It alerts her that all will not always go as she would like and that she must develop a more conscious relationship with the depths or risk losing a connection with the Self. Jung noted that a connection with the inner world is vital and that a life that is too easy and success-ful endangers this connection and makes us forget our dependence on the unconscious. In "The Frog King," the princess comes to appreciate this dependence.

When she loses her favorite plaything, she must rely on the nasty little frog. The frog symbolizes an aspect of herself that is at home in the depths and can also come to the surface. Frogs represent the mystery of transformation. They begin life as aquatic tadpoles that miraculously metamorphose into frogs that can swim in the water and walk on land. Frogs, therefore, are psychopomps, or spirit guides. Like Hermes, the only Greek god who could travel between Tartarus and Olympus, frogs can traverse the realms. The frog part of each of us has access to the inner world—those secret parts of ourselves that exist in the gloomy interior—but can also convey those contents to the wak-ing, conscious personality.

The princess's attitude toward the frog reveals a kind of hidden entitlement. Of course, the frog should get her ball and she should not be held to account. Many of us have such an attitude toward life and we don't even realize it. We somehow expect that things should go our way. When discomfort or disappointment confront us, we feel put upon, as if this were not the bargain we signed up for.

When I was twenty-eight, an important relationship failed. I was heartbroken, but I was also petulant and irritable. I didn't wish to coun-tenance the reality that things wouldn't necessarily work out simply because I very much wanted them to. Like the princess, I had known few serious disappointments in my life up to that point. It didn't seem fair that I wouldn't get what I so very much wanted. Just as the princess felt that the frog owed her, I felt that life owed me. Our egos are often childish and willful in just this way.

CONFRONTATION WITH OURSELVES

The meeting with the frog and the retrieval of the ball is an encounter with some unknown aspect of herself. And the frog part of her wants to be known, accepted, and even cherished. But after having this remarkable meeting, the princess retreats to the safety and familiarity of the castle. Jung called this the "regressive restoration of the persona."[3] After an expansive experience that challenges our narrow way of being in the world, we often retreat instead of pressing forward into the unknown. The princess would prefer to forget this encounter with the frog-like part of herself and continue to know only about her perfect world in the castle. Fortunately for her, this is not to be.

The role of the king is important and complex. The king is a rich symbol that appears in many fairy tales. The king in this story represents the organizing, law-giving aspect of the father archetype. The positive father brings order and is concerned with fairness and justice. The king in this story does just that. He is a part of our psyche that reminds us that we must honor our promises and treat others equally and respectfully. It is good that the princess has access to this energy in herself. If not, she would run away from the critical, transforming encounter that awaits her.

The inner king is, like any psychic content, ambivalent. He holds our feet to the fire and causes us to fulfill our duty, but his dictates can also leave us feeling constrained. We can become governed by collective values, lose touch with our instincts, and behave in an inauthentic manner. The inner king is the voice of the "should." When we have a healthy, robust ego, we effectively dispatch our "shoulds." We return phone calls, complete our taxes on time, brush our teeth, go to the gym, and send gifts to our children's piano teacher each holiday. If we didn't deal with these "shoulds" efficiently, we probably wouldn't function well or meet outer world goals. But, as with any king, the "shoulds" in our lives have the potential to turn into tyrants, plowing under genuine reactions and making them a servant to pale convention.

SHOWING UP

The Frog King is not interested in the princess being nice, pretty, perfect, or polite. He needs her to show up in her full authenticity, even where that is ugly or unkind. Before she throws the frog against the wall, the princess is hedging, not fully embracing the frog, but also not being honest about how much she truly detests him. From the time she first meets him, she is disgusted by him, yet she pretends. She lies to him and promises to take him with her to get her ball back. She reluctantly opens the door and lifts him onto the table because her father makes her. And she feels sorry for herself and starts to cry to avoid taking him to her bedroom. At no point is she fully present and authentic in her dealings with the little amphibian.

There is a similarity between the frog and the king. They both tell the princess what to do. But the king is interested in her meeting the expectations of convention, and the frog is interested in her meeting the deeper demands of the Self. The fairy tale eloquently shows how these things can be related. Often, the fateful encounter with ourselves occurs because we have worked to meet our duties in the external world. Jungian analyst James Hollis writes, "we each have an appointment with ourselves, though most of us never show up for it."[4] With the frog's appearance, the princess is invited to such an appointment. She skirts this encounter the same way most of us do—she avoids things, pretends it isn't happening, or goes along and fakes it. But ultimately, she connects with her Lilith core and finds what is hot and vital inside her. Doing so makes all the difference.

The frog represents an inner potential that cannot be consciously related to until she finds the fierceness to claim her authentic stance. For the princess to have conscious access to her depths, she must act according to her essential nature, not the cultural dictates of "should."

Like many women, the princess has gone through life aware of the need to please others and behave according to conventional mores. Throwing the frog against the wall is the first time in her perfect life that she does something transgressive, and this is the transformational moment. She breaks the rules. She goes against collective values and says "no" even though her father has commanded her to do otherwise. When the inner demand to be agreeable blocks our authenticity, we are stifled. A breakthrough occurs when we realize that we cannot continue to be pleasant. Then we must dare to act from our center—to fling the frog against the wall. Then the spell is broken, and we are transformed.

CONTROL

Katherine was a woman in my practice who had adopted a strategy of accommodation in the face of significant turmoil. Being perpetually helpful gave her some control in a chaotic situation. Her alcoholic father was a man deeply wounded by his own difficult upbringing. He worked only sporadically, while her mother held three jobs to keep the family fed and housed. Katherine is naturally passionate and spirited, but these qualities had to be smothered. She remembers being told not to upset her father for fear that doing so "might make him drink." Katherine was the oldest of three sisters and recalled being very aware of her mother's hardship. A few times a year, her mother's asthma would get so bad that an ambulance would come to the house and take her to the hospital. Katherine recalls being very frightened each time this happened. She dealt with the chaos and precarity at home by doing everything she could to lighten her mother's burden. She was an ideal student and unfailingly helpful around the house and with her younger siblings. She deferred her needs and desires in order to be a team player and problem solver. Katherine learned to bury both sadness and anger. She was perennially upbeat and smiling in the face of any challenge.

As it turns out, Katherine was well rewarded for this strategy. Her superior academic performance landed her a full scholarship to a top school. There, she chose to study practical subjects rather than those that interested her. Professors appreciated her helpful attitude and hard work. After graduating from college, Katherine had the opportunity to move to Europe to study, but she opted to take a job in the financial services industry to help pay for her younger siblings to go to college. Predictably, she did well in her career and easily garnered promotions. She found herself earning good money at her company even though it felt as though she had never really made a choice to be there. When she came to see me, Katherine was approaching forty. She worked full-time at a high-pressure job while caring for her two children and her aging parents, who lived nearby. She felt depleted by her work but couldn't imagine what else she would do, as she had never allowed herself to explore her interests or desires.

SAYING "NO" TO THE FATHER

One of the issues that presented itself early in our work was her unexpected rage at her father. Katherine strove to master these uncomfortable outbursts, but they slipped out despite her best efforts to be a loving and dutiful daughter. These eruptions left Katherine feeling perplexed and distraught. She did not understand them.

Katherine had not yet found a way to say "no" to the father—either her personal father or the archetypal one. In her laudable efforts to care for her family, Katherine's mother had enabled the father's alcoholism by over-functioning, permitting him to drink with few consequences. As often happens in addiction, the family was structured around the father's substance use. His drinking determined most of the family decisions—where they would live, what extracurricular activities Katherine would pursue, and how they would spend their holidays. Katherine's efforts to be helpful and put her needs aside further supported the father's passive tyranny. For Katherine, saying "no" to the father would have meant refusing to collude. She would have explored her interests and desires in college and after, instead of sacrificing these to take on responsibilities that should have belonged to her father. She would have needed to fling the frog at the wall.

Katherine felt as though the time to explore her interests was slipping away. She wanted to leave the firm where she had worked since graduating but had concerns about how that would affect her family's financial situation. Moreover, Katherine began to realize that she had recreated a similar dynamic in her own marriage. Her husband was a much better partner than her father, but he, too, had some compulsive behaviors that jeopardized the family finances and left Katherine in the familiar role of having to hold things together. At a time when she was feeling stuck and without options, she had the following dream.

> I am in a dicey neighborhood near where I grew up, and I must walk the dog, Juniper. I realize that I don't have her leash. My mother has it. I call my mother and ask her to bring the leash to me. My mom doesn't want to, but she says she will. Then the dog runs away, and I follow. The dog runs into a cave, and I am very concerned. There could be anything in that cave! As I am standing and watching, wondering what to do, a crocodile comes out of the cave, followed by Juniper. Juniper then takes the crocodile in her mouth and somehow manages to slit its throat! The crocodile is then bleeding out slowly, its arms and legs splayed. Something about it makes me think of a sacrifice. I am sad and distraught as I see the suffering of the crocodile. As it bleeds out, it begins to turn into a human until it has a human body and the head of a crocodile.

In the dream, Katherine was afraid for Juniper, a medium-sized mutt whom the family had adopted from a shelter and to whom Katherine was very attached. She was frightened to see the dog enter the cave and astonished to see it expertly take the crocodile in its mouth and slit its throat. She also felt great sadness and distress about the crocodile's death.

Juniper seems to know exactly where she is going. She knows where the cave is and what she must do there. Dogs are loyal, protective, and instinctive. They have an excellent sense of smell and can intuit danger or opportunity long before we can. They can attune to the environment around them, including the moods and needs of their owners. In mythology, dogs guard the border between the realm of the living and the realm of the dead. In dreams, they can represent a kind of straightforward, instinctual wisdom that is loyal and protective. When our ego is overwhelmed or uncertain, the dog part of us often knows what to do.

The sacrifice and mysterious transformation of the crocodile provoked strong feelings in both of us. Like all dream animals, crocodiles are images of instinct, but of a kind quite different from that pictured by a dog. Crocodile instincts are primal, blind, and unrelated. Crocodiles are an ancient species built for survival. As cold-blooded reptilian hunters, they seem to have little capacity for relationship or affection, yet mother crocodiles tenderly roll their eggs in their mouths and transport and protect their young. Since they have hardly changed in 200 million years, a crocodile in a dream might picture a part of the dreamer that needs to undergo an evolution.

The Juniper part of Katherine seemed to understand that some deep transformation needed to occur. Some ancient impulse toward brute survival needed to be sacrificed and humanized. Survival concerns had colored Katherine's childhood. She feared something terrible would happen to her mother, on whom she depended. Therefore, she spent much of her time and energy trying to protect and aid her mother. Being parentified in this way stunted her ability to develop fully as the person she came into the world to be and alienated her from the important qualities that Lilith brings. As a result, she arrived at midlife with many unacknowledged dreams, uncultivated passions, and unexplored desires.

When she had this dream, Katherine was beginning to explore new possibilities, but this felt transgressive and even dangerous. The dream shows that the conscious part of her personality still felt the need to keep her inner Juniper on a leash. It is significant that the mother has the leash in the dream but does not want to bring it back. There is an old desire to care for her mother (to keep Juniper on a leash) and an inner demand to separate psychologically from her mother (to let Juniper run). Her inner mother could hold back the healthy instincts but chooses not to. Katherine's inner Juniper overcomes any ambivalence. The dog instinctively recognizes that this primordial, survival-oriented attitude must be sacrificed.

In dreams, the animal is always sacred. In this dream, there is a tension between two different gods—two different instincts. The human dilemma is to chart a course between the demands of the gods.[5] The old principle of survival must yield to self-protective instincts symbolized by the little dog.

As the crocodile exsanguinates, it becomes human. Like the frog in the fairy tale, there is a transformation. Something that was happening at an unconscious, instinctual level is slowly becoming more conscious. Finally, it has a human body and a crocodile head. In ancient Egypt, crocodiles were worshipped as the earthly representatives of the god Sobek, the fierce deity with the body of a man and the head of a crocodile. Sobek was known as a protective god, fending off evil and safeguarding the innocent. At his main temples at Crocodilopolis, deceased crocodiles were mummified in ritual displays. Some of the mummified crocodiles have been found with mummified baby crocodiles in their mouths or on their backs, perhaps underscoring this fierce god's protective and nurturing aspects.[6]

Katherine's family had been focused solely on survival matters for several generations. Female forebearers who had dared to look for more for themselves had met unhappy fates. The ancestral story was one of required self-sacrifice and self-effacement. Like the frog in the fairy tale, the crocodile represents a divine potential that has existed in a primitive state where it couldn't be related to consciously. Both needed to be violently sacrificed before they could be transformed. By flinging the frog against the wall, the princess foreswore her niceness. Katherine had to give up the deeply unconscious, reflexive compulsion to ignore her deep desires and focus solely on survival. To do so, she had to become more connected with her vital spark.

Katherine must grieve the passing attitude. Her childhood focus on survival was a way of moving through the world that helped her persist through hardships. It enabled her to become the person she is today, and in many ways, it represents what she values most about herself—her love and care for other people. And yet that attitude has outlived its helpfulness and must be allowed to transform. The dream tells us that what it becomes is something powerful, fierce, and divine.

In her outer life, Katherine has begun the process pictured in the dream. She has become more conscious of her anger at her father. She is more aware of her habitual need to be accommodating and her desire for harmony and how these play into her sometimes sacrificing her own needs.

Katherine's excessive focus on helping and fixing was, in effect, an abandonment of herself that left her feeling depleted and despairing at midlife. Such a self-betrayal can endanger us in ways both direct and subtle. A Portuguese fairy tale that echoes many of the themes in "Fitcher's Bird" helps us to examine how this might be the case. In it, a father leaves his three daughters home alone and exhorts them to be wary. Only one of the daughters can resist the temptation to be agreeable and pleasing.

THE LITTLE MAID WHO WAS WISE

Once there was a merchant with three daughters. Their mother had died, and he was raising them on his own. He needed to travel far away on business and worried about leaving them alone. They reassured him that they would be fine in his absence.

"How can you be so sure?" the merchant asked. "I am older and wiser than you and know that many evils might come upon you. Thieves and robbers might take advantage of my absence to rob me and do you harm."

The girls promised to lock themselves in the house and not let anyone in. "Make sure you admit no one!" the merchant exhorted. They gave him their promise, and he left on his journey, but with an anxious heart.

As the merchant was leaving town, a band of robbers took note of this and determined to go to his house that night and rob it. When evening came, the leader of the robbers dressed as a beggar and knocked on the merchant's door.

"Have mercy on a poor, unfortunate one!" he called out. "It is raining outside, and no one with mercy in his heart would turn away a poor soul. Let me pass the night under your roof!"

The eldest sister peeked out from behind the curtain. "There is a terrible storm outside. I think we ought to let him in."

The second daughter also looked outside. "He is old as well as poor. Our father has always taught us to show mercy and kindness to the aged."

But the youngest daughter was more cautious. "We promised our father that we would not let anyone in. We can give him some alms without opening the door and send him on his way with our blessing."

But the two older sisters were annoyed by her presumptuousness. "Sister, we are older than you! Father always taught us to be merciful and generous with those in need!"

Despite the protestations of the youngest sister, the two older girls opened the door and invited the beggar into the house. They gave him supper and made a bed for him.

"I'm so glad we've made him comfortable for the night!" said the eldest sister.

"I think father would be concerned to see how quickly we broke our promise," said the youngest sister.

When the beggar had finished eating, he produced three apples for dessert, over which he had sprinkled sleeping powder. The elder two daughters ate theirs and soon fell fast asleep, but the youngest daughter was too nervous to eat and so frightened that she couldn't sleep a wink.

She heard the beggar get up and come into their room. He took a pin and stuck it in the foot of the eldest sister. When she didn't make a noise, he knew that the sleeping powder had done its work. So too, with the second sister. It hurt terribly when he stuck the pin into the foot of the youngest daughter, but she was careful not to move or make a sound.

The youngest sister peeked through her lashes and saw the beggar take off his coat. Underneath, he was outfitted with swords and pistols and daggers. She was terribly frightened.

She could hear him going through the house, examining the merchant's possessions and choosing items he would like to steal. Then she heard him go downstairs and unbolt the heavy door that led to the storeroom. She got up and quietly went into the next room.

There, she found his sword, which he had taken off and left on the dining room table. Soon she heard the outer doors of the storeroom unbolted. The robber had gone to call the rest of the band. She ran downstairs and bolted the inner doors of the storeroom. Now the robbers would not be able to get back into the house.

She heard footsteps outside and then loud cursing when they found the door had been closed. "It's that youngest daughter! I was suspicious of her from the first!"

"Perhaps you can outwit her yet!" said another thief.

The beggar came to the front door and knocked. "Kind lady of the house! Have pity on me!" The youngest daughter did not answer, but he kept beseeching her until she finally asked him what he wanted.

"I left my charm behind! Let me in, and I will get it. I promise I won't hurt you."

"I do not trust your promises!" said the youngest daughter.

"Pass the charm to me then," said the robber.

Now it happened that there was a hole in the door just big enough for a man's hand to fit through. It was the hole through which beggars thrust their arms when asking for alms.

"Put your hand through the door. Then I will give you your charm." She ran to get the great sword the robber had left on the dining room table. When she returned, the robber's arm was sticking through the door. She struck it with all her might with the sword and cut it off.

There were terrible screams and cries from the robbers. In their rage, they tried to break down the doors, but to no avail. The doors were strong, and they held. Soon it was daylight, and they had to run away.

In the morning, the sleeping powder had worn off, and the two older sisters were amazed to hear the story of the youngest one.

"I do not believe a word of it!" said the eldest. But when the youngest sister showed them the arm and the great sword, they knew that she was telling the truth.

When the merchant finally returned, he was delighted to find his home and his daughters safe. The eldest sisters admitted that they had broken their promise and that their youngest sister had saved them.

When the merchant had heard the whole story, he said: "After this, we must all give ear to the wisdom of this little maid. She is wise beyond her years."

As with the story of the Frog King, the father is an important and overall positive figure. He has taught his daughters to be kind and compassionate, but he is not naive and instructs his daughters about the ways of the world. "I am older and wiser than you, and I know that there are many evils that might come upon you," he tells his daughters when they reassure him that all will be well. Although he values mercy and generosity, he isn't foolish. He also values safety. He has solid doors with sturdy locks on his house, and he makes his daughters promise to use these. This father is more psychologically developed than the father in "The Frog King." He recognizes that there is a time for mercy and a time to lock the doors and let no one in.

THE SEDUCTION OF PITY

The older sisters exemplify attitudes held by many women. When in doubt, many of us default to agreeableness. In the hypothetical, the elder daughters promise to let no one in. However, when the eldest daughters are faced with a poor, old beggar in a rainstorm, their resolve is trumped by the impulse to prioritize relationships and empathy for others. This tendency toward caring for others has been reinforced by prior teaching—just as the little girls I saw in the restaurant, they had been instructed to be kind.

As in "Fitcher's Bird," the villain dresses as a beggar. When confronted with someone who needs care, we tend to let down our defenses. Pity softens our hearts and encourages us to act without regard for ourselves. But as both fairy tales note, this can be dangerous. This story highlights the moral dilemma we as women will likely face. When is it right to show mercy and compassion, and when is it best to protect ourselves, even if it means not meeting the needs of another? How do we judge whether someone is a beggar or a thief?

If the beggar were sincere, then the attitude of the elder two sisters would be appropriate. How are we to know which is which? The fairy tale images an archetypal dilemma that we must all confront. For young women, learning to differentiate between the thief and the beggar is a developmental stage we must pass through. There are many situations in which we must discern whether it is right to let our guard down in the interest of being kind, welcoming, and trusting, or whether we ought to be cold, wary, self-protective, and fierce. Most young women will have an easy time finding the former stance. Finding the latter will be an achievement.

When I was a young woman, I had frequent dreams in which this dilemma confronted me. I was eighteen and in my first year of college when I had the following two dreams.

> I was driving at night in a lonely place. I was going to
> meet a friend. There was a homeless man walking in
> the parking lot. He looked downtrodden and sullen.
> Because I needed him to move before I could park, I
> felt as if I were being pushy and causing him even
> more hardship. I felt guilty. Instead of staying in the

car, I got out to seem friendlier and to signal that I
wasn't afraid of him, even though I was. I got out and
said something to him, and then he grabbed me, and I
knew he would kill me. I was calling for my friend, but
I knew she wouldn't come in time.

A few weeks later, I had another similar dream.

This poor crumpled man was dirty with brown hair
and four eyes—two extra ones below his normal
ones, and all the eyeballs were turned up so that the
dark iris was almost hidden. At first, I was utterly
disgusted with him, but I fought against this feeling
because I felt I should feel pity. I insisted on bringing
him with me to the dining hall. I woke up at this
point, but there was a gathering sense of foreboding
as if he would turn and murder me at any moment.

I hadn't gotten the message from my psyche with the first dream,
so my dream maker turned up the volume on the second dream, providing me with an image that was much more urgent and disturbing.
The dreams were trying to communicate that, in the inner world, I was
mistaking a thief for a beggar, and a psychic death was almost inevitable. My aggressive capacity was so outlawed that it became homeless in
the inner world. I saw it as threatening and destructive when really it
would have given me the ability to navigate the new situation I found
myself in with greater authority and confidence if I could have related
to it in the right way. When we have become divorced from an inner
content, it often appears to the waking personality as dangerous and
foreign. However, it is really a lump of glowing coal, full of potential
and waiting to be fanned back to life.

The key to solving the dilemma of beggar or thief is discernment,
the ability to weigh the options carefully and arrive at a correct judgment. *Discernment* comes from Latin words that mean "to separate two

things apart." In psychological matters, discernment usually involves a process and takes time. People often enter therapy because they need a process of discernment, a place to comb through their feelings without external judgment. It is difficult to engage in discernment when we are under pressure. The daughters in the fairy tale feel a sense of urgency because the beggar is standing in the rain. They quickly default to their stance of agreeableness rather than being able to sift through the competing values.

The wise little maid in the story suggests a middle path that would offer a compromise between compassion and self-protection. Her discernment makes her cautious, and she suggests they give the beggar alms but not open the door. Her sisters sacrifice one principle for the other. Her sisters fall asleep and go unconscious to their danger, but the little maid's fierceness and cunning allow her to prevail.

PLEASING TO MEN

In the story, the little maid has earned the wrath of the robbers. She hasn't been agreeable and pliable, and the robber notes that he was suspicious of her from the start. Many women feel the need to be pleasing to men. Women often seek to position themselves wherever they find the most male approval, as this generally ensures greater safety. When men are the ones to grant access to the needed resource—whether that is money, security, power, or some other commodity—women can find themselves bending over backwards to please them. Often, these efforts to be liked can come at the expense of a woman's connection with other women.

In the fairy tale, the little maid risks being disagreeable while her sisters vie to be seen by the robber as kind and virtuous. In seeking to gain the approval of the beggar, the older sisters disregard the little maid's warning and chastise her for her lack of charity. They assert their superiority over her and criticize her caution. Where men control access to power and resources, women can perceive one another as rivals, thus undermining female solidarity. When we see other women only as rivals, we tend to feel insecure and to doubt ourselves. This makes finding our inner fire much harder.

The 1991 film *Raise the Red Lantern* directed by Zhang Yimou is a devastating depiction of how women's need for male sanction can turn them against each other. The film is set in 1920s China. Songlian (played by Gong Li) is just nineteen and has been to university, but her father has died and there is no more money. Her stepmother forces her to marry a wealthy man. She becomes his fourth mistress and enters a household that is ruled by the master's capricious desires. Each day, a ritual occurs in which the master announces in which house he will spend the night. His chosen companion for the evening is treated to her favorite foods, sensual massages, and an elaborate ceremony in which beautiful red lanterns are lit throughout her apartments. Whoever is not selected that night is treated less well by the servants and must defer to the wishes of the master's chosen companion. The women, therefore, are pitted against one another in a relentless competition for the few petty niceties they are allowed. Songlian is never sure whom she can trust. The women seek to harm or undermine one another. At the end of the film, as the master marries yet another young concubine, we see Songlian drifting aimlessly through the compound, apparently having gone insane.

When we are young, we see ourselves as we imagine a man might see us and ask ourselves, *Do I measure up? Am I thin enough? Pretty enough?* We carefully monitor what we reveal about ourselves and try to be appealing and nonthreatening. It may be a cliché that men feel threatened by intelligent, accomplished women, but it is a cliché that has been borne out in at least some research.[7]

In college, I attended a party where several of us stood around talking. The men in the group were unapologetically sharing their accomplishments. I observed the men as they did this and noticed that the women in the group were all relatively quiet. The achievements of the men were admired and celebrated by all of us. Then, one of the men who had been talking and sharing the most suddenly fixed his eyes on me and looked me up and down. He reached out and took my wrist and looked at it admiringly. "Look how thin you've gotten!" he said, encircling my wrist with his fingers. "You're looking great!" I remember thinking to myself, *And there it is in a nutshell. Men are admired for their achievements, for being bigger. Women are admired for their appearance and for being smaller.*

Part of learning to be disagreeable involves getting past our need to be appealing. Growing older helps. The animated film *Howl's Moving Castle* begins with an introduction to Sophie, a plain-looking young woman who eschews time on the town with her coworkers to stay in the hat shop working late. As the other young women leave, the discussion turns to the dashing wizard Howl, who has a reputation as a seducer. He is said to tear out a woman's heart—but only pursues beauties. That Sophie sees herself as plain and undeserving of a man's attention is emphasized at the film's beginning. We see her try on a hat and briefly strike a fetching pose in front of a mirror before becoming crestfallen at the image of herself that she sees reflected. When her sister warns her about the dangers of Howl, Sophie insists she is completely safe since Howl only targets beautiful girls. Sophie's sister remarks on her tendency to put others first. "It's your life, Sophie. Do something for yourself for once!"[8]

Shortly after this, a witch turns Sophie into an old woman. She is now portly and bent with gray hair. Since the spell also prevents her from being able to talk about her curse, Sophie quickly realizes she cannot stay with her family any longer. So she ventures into the Waste alone, where she finds Howl's castle walking about. Cold and in need of a place to stay, she lets herself in and sits by the fire. "I'm sure Howl won't eat the heart of a shriveled old lady like me," she tells herself.[9]

With Sophie's transformation into an old woman, an inner shift has also occurred. She is no longer timid and excessively agreeable. She is determined, cunning, and pushy. Once inside Howl's castle, she immediately begins bossing around Calcifer, the resident fire demon responsible for the health and vitality of the castle and of Howl himself. Howl's assistant—and later Howl himself—are surprised that Calcifer immediately takes her direction. Now that she is connected with her own vital spark, the fire demon is no match for her. Being old and ugly renders her less self-conscious about her perceived failings. When Howl returns, she is unabashed. "Who are you?" he asks her. "You can just call me Grandma Sophie," she says. "I'm your new cleaning lady." As an old woman, Sophie is crusty and unafraid to cause offense. "Well," she says to herself, "one nice thing about getting old is nothing frightens you."[10]

As women age, we may find ourselves like Sophie, freed from the burden of having to be appealing and attractive. Then we can step comfortably into our disagreeableness. We are liberated to say what we think, push for what we want, and pursue our desires. Like my friend Terry, who kicked us out of her dinner parties when she was ready for them to be over, we can be generous—offering our friends beautiful meals—but also attend to our own needs because we don't worry too much about being likeable.

For many women, being liberated from the need to be agreeable is one of the greatest gifts of growing older. The poet Dorothy Parker captures this in her witty 1926 poem.

INDIAN SUMMER
In youth, it was a way I had
To do my best to please,
And change, with every passing lad,
To suit his theories.
But now I know the things I know,
And do the things I do;
And if you do not like me so,
To hell, my love, with you![11]

Many of us have a strong, innate impulse to be appealing and agreeable. Our pliability is laudable, but if we are to stay connected with our soul, we will need to have the capacity to sometimes be dreadful, objectionable, or offensive. The vigor and conviction that allows us to fling the frog against the wall or sever the arm of the robber can help us pierce the barriers that have been built up over the years between us and our vital, authentic selves. When the fog of false niceness clears, what confronts us is our truth. Our fiery self may make us uncomfortable. She isn't coy or demure. She is earthy and animal, coarse and chthonic. She is unlovely and unpleasant. But she is full of vitality and integrity. She cares about us and our unfolding and isn't concerned with what others might think. When we claim our outlaw energies, we become loyal friends to ourselves. We know the things we know and do the things we do and can prioritize the unique needs of our own souls.

Questions for Reflection

1. The princess in "The Frog King" promises to bring the frog home if he finds her ball, but she really has no intention of doing so. Where in your life have you naively thought that you could get something for nothing? When have you felt that you had been treated unfairly by life because you didn't get your way? What did you do about this? What did you learn?

2. The princess is forced to keep her promise by her father. She must suffer the confrontation with the frog part of herself. When have you been forced to acknowledge something about yourself you didn't want to know? What did you learn as a result of this confrontation?

3. The princess finds the frog disgusting but continues to try to please her father by taking it to her bedroom. It isn't until she lets loose her rage that she expresses her true feelings and flings the frog at the wall. When have you chosen authenticity over agreeableness? Was it difficult to do, and, if so, why? What was the result in the end?

4. In "The Little Maid Who Was Wise," the eldest sister is moved to break her promise to her father when the beggar knocks on the door during a storm. Sometimes, our pity or concern for another blinds us to potential dangers. Where in your life have you been seduced by pity in a way that later proved potentially harmful? What was it that made you so susceptible to the plight of the other person so that you chose unwisely?

5. The older two sisters in the story are compelled by their desire to be charitable. We might imagine that they were focused on appearing kind and virtuous. Our society generally rewards kind and virtuous behavior in women. Has there been a time recently where you can identify that you were swayed in a certain way because you wished to seem kind, generous, or big-hearted?

6. The little maid picks up the big sword and cuts off the robber's arm. This is a little like flinging the frog at the wall. Sometimes, we have to get in touch with our capacity for violence in order to set a firm boundary. Have you ever had to be very stern—perhaps even to the point of using physical force—to protect yourself? Were you surprised that you were able to do so? What did you learn about yourself from this encounter?

CHAPTER 3

Shrewdness: Getting Over Innocence

One always learns one's mystery at
the price of one's innocence.

—Robertson Davies, *Fifth Business*

W hen I was eleven, my mother let me save up to buy a sterling silver puzzle ring that I had been coveting. I loved it. When I had a chance a few weeks later to take it off and show how to dissemble and reassemble it for a group of older girls I looked up to and admired, I was thrilled. I felt lucky to have been included in the invitation to spend the afternoon at Melissa's house. Though she was just one year older, she seemed much worldlier than I was. She had blonde hair, and her parents were divorced. She lived with her mother in a small house that was pleasantly cluttered with interesting things. A glass jar of sourdough starter sat on the kitchen windowsill and bead curtains hung between the rooms. Her mother had taught her how to back up the car and turn it around in the driveway. I was in awe of this adult skill. When I had finished the demonstration of my wonderful new ring, Melissa asked me if she could borrow it for a while. I readily handed it over, happy to have excited her interest. She disappeared to another room but rejoined us shortly. As we got ready to leave some time later, I asked Melissa to return my ring.

She denied that I had given it to her, suggesting that I must have misplaced it. I knew that this wasn't right, but Melissa's friends all backed her, of course, and I felt powerless to contradict her assertion. I never got that ring back.

When I handed my ring over to Melissa, I was too naive and trusting. I wasn't able to access my gut instincts about what might really be going on. Shrewdness is the ability to see things as they are, not as we wish they were or think they should be. The dictionary tells us that *shrewd* means "having or showing sharp powers of judgment, astute." The term was taken from the small rodent, the shrew, which has a long, pointed snout and tiny eyes. It originally meant "evil in nature or character." To this day, the word *shrew* has two meanings. It refers to the small mammal, but it also means "a bad-tempered or aggressively assertive woman."

This one word, then, reveals a deep cultural truth. Women with sharp powers of judgment are considered bad-tempered or aggressively assertive. To avoid being a shrew, a woman mustn't be too shrewd. Don't see what there is to know. Remain innocent and naive. Yet when we can't access our shrew(d)ness, we risk being unable to protect ourselves.

Frequently, we know more than we let ourselves believe. We may have an awareness of something but be invested in not knowing it for some reason. We let our need to remain innocent shut us off from this knowledge that otherwise might be available to us. Jungian analyst Mark Winborn has made the point that analysts in training can have difficulty accessing their own wisdom because they are reluctant to confront others or raise issues that may make their patients uncomfortable. It can be startlingly illuminating to pause during a fraught interaction—clinical or personal—and ask yourself the question, "what do I know right now?"[1] Often, the answer that comes back to us in these moments is surprising and full of wisdom.

When we can't claim what we know, we lose access to shrewdness and can become trapped in an innocence complex. This can impact us in small ways such as when I lost my ring, but it can also have more serious consequences. If we are unable to imagine that others might not have our best interests at heart, we open ourselves up to being taken advantage of by peers, partners, and even institutions.

I once worked in a hospital social work department. My supervisor had been the head of the department for over twenty years. She had never married or had children. Her job had been her life. When the hospital hired a new administrator who was focused on cutting costs, she was fired without warning, given half an hour to clear out her desk, and escorted off the premises by hospital security. After devoting her entire career to the hospital, she was not even given the opportunity to say goodbye or enjoy a send-off by colleagues who might have expressed appreciation for her contributions. Evidently, my boss had assumed that she could trust her employer to look after her. Her faith had been misplaced, and the job that she had depended upon for her livelihood, purpose, and community had been taken away from her without warning late in her career.

Being too trusting can be perilous. In "Bluebeard," the heroine had a funny feeling about her suitor—something was off about him. However, she let her instincts be overruled. Our culture frequently demands that women silence their inner voices, especially when they whisper truths that others find inconvenient. When we comply with these demands, we turn away from the strength and power that would come with greater consciousness. "To forbid a woman to use the key to conscious self-knowledge strips away her intuitive nature, her natural instinct for curiosity that leads her to discover 'what lies beneath' and beyond the obvious," notes Clarissa Pinkola Estés. "Without this knowing, the woman is without proper protection."[2] An inability to access our shrewdness can leave us vulnerable to being preyed upon by those who most certainly do not have our best interests at heart. When we haven't developed our powers of sharp judgment and discernment, we leave ourselves open to being victimized and manipulated.

The term *gaslighting* comes to us from the world of cinema. The 1944 film *Gaslight* portrays a particularly insidious form of psychological abuse in which a seemingly genteel Victorian man seeks to convince his heiress wife that she is crazy so that he can steal from her.

When he leaves her alone, he lowers the gas lights in the house and then denies that he did so that she begins to doubt her own perceptions and sanity. When we put our trust uncritically in others while abandoning our shrewdness and discernment, we give them the power to cause us to question the integrity of our own mind.

When we are over-identified with being innocent, we can be blind to the world around us in a way that leaves us unprotected and easily victimized. The well-known tale of "Little Snow White" starkly illustrates this truth. This familiar story shows us the danger of being too innocent and demonstrates how we can get past our tendency to remain naive and childlike. The original Grimms' version contains several minor but significant differences from later versions that are more familiar.

LITTLE SNOW WHITE

Once upon a time, a beautiful queen sat by the window sewing while snowflakes fell. The window had an ebony black frame, and as she sewed, she pricked herself with the needle and drew three drops of blood that fell on the snow. The red blood looked so beautiful on the white snow that she thought, "If only I had a daughter with skin as white as snow, hair as black as ebony, and lips as red as blood!" Soon thereafter, she gave birth to a little girl as white as snow, red as blood, and black as ebony, and she named her Snow White.

The queen was very beautiful and very vain. She owned a magic mirror that she consulted every morning.

"Mirror, mirror, on the wall,

Who's the fairest of them all?"

The mirror would answer:

"You are fairest of all, O Queen!"

And the queen's heart would be soothed to know that she was the most beautiful woman in all the land.

However, as the queen's little daughter grew, she became more and more beautiful until one day, when the queen asked the mirror her customary question, the mirror responded differently:

"You are passing fair, tis true

But Snow White is fairer far than you!"

The queen was seized with great envy, and from that moment on, she hated her daughter. She found she could have no peace while her daughter surpassed her, so she called a huntsman and instructed him to take Snow White into the woods, kill her, and bring back her lungs and liver as proof. "Then, I'll cook them and eat them with salt," she told the huntsman.

The huntsman did as he was told and led the child into the forest, but when it came time to stab her with his knife, he found he couldn't do it. Little Snow White promised to run deeper into the forest and never return. The huntsman told himself that wild animals would likely eat the child in any case. On his return, he killed a wild boar, cut out its lungs and liver, and gave those to the queen. She boiled and ate these with salt and thought she had eaten Snow White's organs.

Meanwhile, Snow White ran deeper into the forest. At last, she came upon a little cottage that belonged to seven dwarves. They were not at home, and she let herself in and looked around. She took a bit of food from each of their seven plates, and a drop of wine from each of their seven cups. When she grew tired, she tried each bed, and the seventh was the coziest so there she fell asleep.

When the dwarves returned from the mines, they noticed that someone had been eating from their plates, drinking from their cups, and sleeping in their beds. Then they found Snow White asleep in the seventh bed and were overcome with her beauty. When she awoke the following day, she told the dwarves her story. They took pity on her and offered to let her stay if she would keep house for them. "When we go to the mines," they told her, "you will be here alone. You must watch out for the queen, for she will know to look for you here!"

The queen now believed that she was once again the most beautiful woman in the land, but the next morning, the mirror told her otherwise and revealed that Snow White was alive and living with the dwarves. The queen was furious.

Enraged, she disguised herself as a peddler, sought out the dwarves' cottage, and knocked on the door.

"Open up, my dear! I have pretty wares to sell!" she cried.

Snow White looked out the window. "What do you have for sale?" she asked. The old peddler woman took our silk laces of rich colors.

I can certainly let this old woman in, thought Snow White when she saw the beautiful laces. She looks honest enough.

Snow White opened the door and purchased the laces. The queen offered to lace her up properly, and Snow White consented. But the queen pulled the laces so tight that Snow White could not breathe and fell down as if dead. Then the queen hurried away.

When the dwarves returned that night, they were shocked to find Snow White lying as if dead. They quickly loosened the laces, and the girl revived.

"It was certainly the queen who sold you those laces!" the dwarves warned her. "You must be more careful! Do not let anyone into the cottage!"

Back at home, the queen was once again satisfied that she was the most beautiful woman in the land, but the next day the mirror revealed that Snow White was still alive. Again, the queen was furious. She created a different disguise for herself and returned to the dwarves' cottage with a poisoned comb. This time when she knocked on the door, Snow White responded that she wasn't allowed to let anyone enter. However, the queen took out the comb, and when Snow White saw how shiny it was, she thought to herself that this wasn't the same old peddler woman. She opened the door, let the queen come in, and bought the comb.

"Come, let me comb your hair!" the queen said. No sooner had she pulled the comb through Snow White's hair than the maiden fell down as if dead. When the dwarves returned that night, they removed the poisoned comb and Snow White revived. As before, they exhorted her not to let anyone in.

Once again, however, the mirror alerted the queen that Snow White had survived. When she heard this, she was so outraged that she began to tremble. "Snow White shall die!" she exclaimed. Then she shut herself a secret chamber and crafted a beautiful red apple filled with deadly poison only on one side. Finally, she disguised herself as a beggar woman and returned to the dwarves' cottage.

"I can't let anyone in!" Snow White said when the beggar woman knocked at the door.

"Suit yourself!" said the queen. "But wouldn't you like at least to try a bite of my beautiful red apple? Look, we'll share it!"

The queen cut the apple in two, saving the reddest part for Snow White, for that was the half that contained the poison. When Snow White saw the queen enjoying her half of the apple and saw how red and juicy the part offered to her looked, she couldn't resist. She let the queen pass the apple through the window and ate it hungrily, whereupon she fell down and was dead.

When the queen returned home and consulted the mirror, it confirmed that she was once again the fairest in all the land.

The dwarves rushed to revive Snow White when they found her upon their return but could not. They laid her on a bier and wept and wept. They meant to bury her, but she looked more alive than dead, and her cheeks were so pretty and red. So they made a glass case and put her in it so that they could admire her. They always left one of the dwarves at home to watch over her. Time passed, and Snow White remained in the glass case. She did not rot. She lay as if sleeping, as beautiful as ever.

One day, a prince was riding by and asked to stay the night at the dwarves' cottage. When he saw Snow White, he was so overcome with her beauty that he begged the dwarves to give her to him and promised to take care of her and hold her in the highest regard. The dwarves took pity on him and gave him the glass coffin. He had it carried back to his castle and placed in his room, and he would sit day upon day by the coffin gazing at her, and if he were away from her, he would become sad. So he made his servants carry her from room to room so she would always be near him. At last, the servants became angry about this, and one servant opened the glass case and lifted Little Snow White angrily into the air. "Why must we go to so much trouble on account of a dead maiden!" he said and shoved her roughly back into place.

As he did so, however, the bit of poison apple lodged in her throat popped out, and Snow White revived. She went immediately to the prince, who was overjoyed to see Snow White alive and well, and a wedding date was set immediately.

Snow White's mother was invited to attend. When she arrived, she was given iron shoes that had been heated in the fire. They burned her feet, but she had to keep dancing in them until she was burned to death.

An initial image sets the stage and highlights that this story will be about innocence and shadow. The whiteness of the snow indicates purity, the blackness of the ebony represents shadow and darkness, and the redness of the blood symbolizes passion, sexuality, and the life force. It is significant that Snow White's name only encompasses the first of these three attributes, yet she contains them all from the beginning.

In this tale, innocence and shadowy Lilith qualities are split. The queen embodies all of the dark attributes. Like Lilith, she is anything but maternal and is capable of killing and eating her child. On the other hand, Snow White has no *conscious* relationship with any negative qualities. She is pure and innocent.

But Snow White's ebony hair and blood-red lips point to her shadowy, Lilith qualities that are evident early in the tale. She steals the dwarves' food from their plates, and her vanity makes her susceptible to the queen's enticements when the latter comes to sell the laces and the comb. Snow White's capacity for concupiscence is symbolized by the red apple—a potent image of sin and temptation. The apple has red cheeks, as does Snow White. Flushed cheeks can be a consequence of emotional and even sexual arousal.

The tale makes clear that the problem is *not* with vanity, lust, or aggression per se. These qualities have their place. They only become a problem when we either become identified with or possessed by them, as is the case for the queen—or when we are so cut off from them that we can't even see that we have them, as is the case for Snow White.

OPENING THE DOOR

One of the notable elements of the story is Snow White's naivete in repeatedly opening the door to her mother, even though the dwarves have warned her against doing so. She doesn't seem to learn, and is infuriatingly willing to let her evil mother back in. Her naivete shows an almost willful desire not to know or acknowledge the possibility that someone might want to hurt her. She is irritatingly stuck in an innocence complex.

There are many reasons why we might find ourselves held fast by an overly innocent worldview. Admitting that others might not always have our best interests at heart can challenge our fundamental beliefs about the world. When this is the case, we may find that we prefer to cling to comforting illusions. We may be invested in seeing ourselves as pure and naive. Maybe being virtuous and innocent is an important part of who we think we are. Finally, remaining innocent also absolves us from taking responsibility for ourselves. If we are ignorant of what is going on around us, we can't be expected to face it and deal with it. We then expect others to care for and protect us.

Clinging stubbornly to innocence and refusing to claim our shrewdness and allow ourselves to know what we know keeps us in a childlike, self-absorbed mindset that prevents us from coming to grips with our fate. When I was in analytic training, I participated in a case colloquium that was run by a senior analyst. To progress in training, I would need to do well in this colloquium, but I have always been a good student and I imagined that this analyst would like me and approve of my work. When he wasn't immediately admiring but instead challenged me brusquely, I was thrown off and became defensive. This reaction, of course, only served to make him more hostile toward me.

My initial response was to feel both self-righteous and sorry for myself. When I was able to bring more self-reflection to the situation, I could see that my innocent, good-student complex meant that I had been very focused on wanting this analyst to like and approve of me. I hadn't even considered what the situation might feel like from his perspective. In fact, I came to understand that he was somewhat intimidated by the task of leading this colloquium. He felt unsure of himself and afraid of being exposed. My eagerness to show how smart and competent I was didn't endear me to him, it threatened him. When I was able to take my focus off my solipsistic needs for affirmation and consider his perspective, I could see that he needed reassurance and admiration from us. Attuning to this fact and responding appropriately shifted the dangerously negative dynamic that had been developing. I received adequate feedback and was allowed to advance.

When I was too focused on my own needs in this relationship, I was a bit like Snow White. Like the fairy tale heroine, my obstinate naivete belied an unconscious entitlement that the world should treat me a certain way. The analyst who led the colloquium was clearly not the same as Snow White's murderous mother, and yet both Snow White and I suffered from a lack of agency in our situations because we were overly naive in our expectations that we would be loved and well-treated, and because we lacked an ability that would allow us to take into account the perspective and motivations of the other.

TRAUMA

Experiencing trauma early in life can also affect our ability to develop shrewdness, leaving us more susceptible to future woundings. A consideration of the dynamics of trauma can deepen our understanding of the fairy tale. The Scottish psychoanalyst Ronald Fairbairn noted that abused or neglected children have two choices. They can either believe that their parents don't love them and that they are alone and defenseless in a frightening world, or they can assume that they are deficient, unworthy, or bad, and therefore deserve the treatment they are receiving. The second belief is far less frightening because it gives us a sense of control in a chaotic and terrifying situation. We think that if we just work harder and try our best to be good, our parents will love us. If the problem is with us, there is still the hope that we can get what we need because we can work to fix whatever is wrong. However, this belief sets up a dynamic familiar to many of us. Although we have no reason to expect that anything has changed, we go back to the same disappointing relationship or situation, hoping that this time something will be different. Such an attitude has poignantly been called "relentless hope."

I once worked with a man in his late fifties whose eighty-year-old mother had been harshly critical of him her whole life. He would pick her up from her retirement community every week and take her to the grocery store. He admitted to me that he had a barely conscious hope each week that *this time* something would be different. She might soften and express her love or at least appreciation. Instead, week after week, the outings were the same. She was irascible and withering, showing nothing but disdain and impatience for her son, just as she always had. His irrational hope that she would change made these encounters even more painful.

Perhaps we can imagine Snow White suffering from relentless hope fueled by a stubbornly naive belief that, deep down, her mother had to be good, that her mother must love her. Just like my client who continued to approach each weekly trip to the grocery store unconsciously hoping for a redemptive gesture, Snow White kept opening the door, hopeful that this time the wares her mother bears would be welcome gifts.

I, TONYA

The dynamic of relentless hope is movingly depicted in the 2017 film *I, Tonya*, which is based on the life of Olympic figure skater Tonya Harding.

Tonya's stubborn hope that her mother would show herself at last to be loving had left her unable to access her own wisdom—and shrewdness. While she clings to the naive hope that she can gain her mother's love, she cannot truly claim her power. Throughout the film, we see Tonya's mother, LaVona (played by Allison Janney), verbally berating and physically abusing Tonya (played by Margot Robbie). In one scene, LaVona beats her small daughter repeatedly with a hairbrush. In another scene, she casually pushes Tonya's chair over with her foot. The abuse is cruel and unrelenting, but we see Tonya hoping for repair and redemption throughout the film. For example, at her wedding to Jeff, she sees her mother watching her from across the room. Tonya straightens her dress and approaches her mother with a shy, expectant smile, clearly hoping for a warm and conciliatory encounter.

LAVONA: I don't know what to tell you. [*Tonya smiles at her mother who takes Tonya by the shoulders.*] Marrying the first idiot who said you're pretty. You fuck dumb. You don't marry dumb. [*LaVona heads to the food table. Tonya stands there, stunned.*][3]

In a pivotal scene toward the film's end, Tonya sits inside, sewing sequins on a skating costume. Reporters surround her home, hoping to get a glimpse of Tonya amid the scandal after the attack on fellow figure skater Nancy Kerrigan. Tonya's husband, Jeff, has been implicated in the attack, and the world wants to know whether Tonya herself was involved. Tonya is a prisoner in her own home, without support or friends. There is a persistent knock at the door. When Tonya finally answers it, it's LaVona. Like Snow White, Tonya cannot resist her mother's knock. We see Tonya deliberate silently for a moment before pulling her mom inside. In the awkward silence that follows, LaVona says the first kind things we have heard from her.

LAVONA: I like your hair pulled back like that. Makes you look young.
TONYA: I'm twenty-three, mom.
LAVONA: You seem like you're holding up good. Fuck 'em, you know?

TONYA: I know.

LAVONA: I never did like that Jeff.

TONYA: Mom.

LAVONA: I'm not here to say I told you so. I'm not.

TONYA: Why are you here?

LAVONA: I want you to know . . . I don't know. I'm on your side. I want
you to know. [*Tonya watches her. LaVona looks away.*]

LAVONA: Big crowd out there. A lot of people support you. [*Tonya is
silent.*] You've done good. I'm proud of you. [*Tonya wells up.*][4]

Throughout this exchange, the vulnerable, lonely Tonya responds
to her mother's half-hearted expressions of warmth with a suspicion
that quickly melts into desperate longing. Here, at last, is proof that
her mother really does love her. She has been waiting her whole life
to hear her mother tell her she was proud of her. Tonya rushes into
her mother's arms, her eyes filled with tears. LaVona tries to hug her
back but can't manage it. While Tonya embraces her mother, full of
emotion, LaVona quietly asks her if she knew about the attack. Tonya's
affect suddenly changes. The spell has been broken. She searches
LaVona's coat until she pulls a tape recorder from LaVona's pocket.
Tonya throws her mother out of the house, and we learn that the two
have no further contact.

The antidote to relentless hope is to become more intimate with
our outlaw energies, such as selfishness, aggression, and vanity. Once
we know about our potential for darkness, it will be much easier
to recognize these qualities in others. Snow White's task, therefore,
involves getting to know her shadow. Luckily, the dwarves can help
her with this. Dwarves are earthy creatures who work underground in
the mines. They know how to maneuver in darkness. In several other
versions of the tale, such as one from France called "The Stepmother,"
Snow White takes refuge not with little men who work in the mines
but with a gang of thieves.[5] The heroine then finds some protection
from undeveloped parts of herself that have a relationship with earth-
iness, cunning, and transgression.

GETTING PRODDED AWAKE

Next to naivete and stubborn innocence, Snow White is characterized by passivity. Like some women, Snow White makes her way through the world by appealing to others for help and relying on her beauty. She begs the huntsman to spare her life, and he does so partly because of her beauty. She places herself at the mercy of the dwarfs, who take her in because of her beauty. Eventually, the prince takes her on as a cumbersome project because she is so very beautiful.

Her long sojourn in the glass coffin emphasizes the theme of passivity. Like Sleeping Beauty, a prolonged state of rest seemingly brings about her transformation. But, during her somnolence, something important happens to Snow White. She has been digesting that bit of poison apple she received from her mother. Psychologically, we might understand that she has been metabolizing her own capacity for darkness.

It is fitting that her resurrection is brought about by the irritable servant. Save her vicious mother, the servant is the only person in the story to feel some justified annoyance at her passivity and helplessness. She's nothing but a burden to him, and at last he musters his aggression enough to rough her up a bit, releasing her from her frozen state.

We can be jolted out of a self-pitying attitude by a rough brush with honesty. In graduate school, I became depressed after a relationship ended. Although my inner life was filled with turmoil and melancholy, I functioned well enough in outer life—until statistics. This class did not come easily to me; I failed the first few assignments and did poorly on the midterm. I became petulant and resentful, as if the universe had done me a foul turn by simultaneously imposing this statistics class on top of this unfair breakup. I wasn't just struggling in the class; I felt sorry for myself for struggling.

I visited the professor to seek extra help but was sulky and resistant. He reflected this to me forthrightly, and it caught me up short. Here, too much tenderness or understanding would have impeded my growth. I needed to be handled roughly to prod me back into a state where I could take appropriate responsibility for myself.

Shortly afterward, something princely and active roused itself in me, bringing about a shift in attitude. I realized that I could go on feeling sorry for myself or figure it out somehow. If I chose the former, I would likely fail the class. No one was going to come to my rescue. So I shifted my studying tactics. This required being a bit shadowy. The professor had forbidden us from studying together (he felt we would learn the material better if we studied by ourselves), but I began to see that transgressing this prohibition was my only hope. Several of us formed a study group, and as we discussed it together, the material started to make sense. In the end, I did well in the class and even made a lasting friendship in that study group.

At the tale's end, Snow White finally gets rid of her sweetness and innocence and takes in a necessary bit of her mother's darkness. Not only is Snow White ready to partner with the princely qualities in herself, but she also can behave aggressively when needed. The final scene of the tale is the wedding—a symbolic image of union with her own princely qualities and a claiming of her aggression as she metes out punishment to the queen.

INNOCENCE AND THE TRAP OF SELF-SACRIFICE

Suzanne was a woman in my practice who had always found her self-worth through being kind and serving others. She had grown up the youngest of three siblings with an alcoholic father, and by the time she came along, the family was in a state of increasing chaos and dysfunction. The middle brother, Carl, had been born with cerebral palsy due to an obstetrical accident. He was in a wheelchair and needed a lot of care. Her parents divorced when she was eight, and from then on, there were fewer resources. As her mother became increasingly absent and overwhelmed, Suzanne found a place for herself in the chaos as Carl's caregiver. She was always by his side. The adults around her praised her for being so helpful. Meanwhile, the extended family focused much of their support on Suzanne's eldest brother, Tony. For a while he lived with Suzanne's wealthy grandparents, who took him sailing in the summer and sent him to boarding school in Europe.

When the three grew to adulthood, Suzanne stayed close to home and continued to be very involved in Carl's care. She worked as a nurse practitioner, married, and had two children. But things always somehow seemed harder than they should have been. Her marriage was not a good one and ended in divorce. Although she was bright, talented, and hard-working, she was often on the outs with her colleagues.

Meanwhile, Tony moved to New York and worked in the financial services field, where he did very well. He rarely involved himself in family difficulties. Suzanne did the heavy lifting when it came time to care for their aging parents. She felt resentful about this, but somehow she continued to hope that her efforts and value would be recognized and appreciated. As with Snow White, relentless hope characterized aspects of Suzanne's life.

Suzanne fought against the feeling that life had treated her unfairly. She was like Snow White; she had defaulted to being kind and empathic since childhood when she found a role for herself as her brother's caregiver. Though her love for her brother was genuine and admirable, the adults around her had allowed her to sacrifice herself and her childhood because it made their lives easier. As is the case for many of us, Suzanne's martyrdom was welcomed.

BITTERNESS

These early experiences shaped Suzanne's orientation to life. Catholicism and Quakerism informed her spirituality, and she practiced what she preached, often putting the needs of others ahead of her own. Unconsciously, she expected this strategy to pay off. In her innocence, she assumed that her hard work and self-sacrifice would be seen, appreciated, and repaid, but that's not what happened. Instead, people routinely took advantage of her, and as the years went on she developed a slightly bitter edge and a sense of simmering rage that others could sense. Suzanne sometimes had interpersonal difficulties at work, and it was my impression that others were responding both to an unconscious understanding that Suzanne would not defend herself adequately and an awareness of her bitterness. It was a bad combination that invited contempt.

Bitterness is the shadow side of innocence. Because wide-eyed naivete leaves us open to exploitation and attack, we will likely become bitter if our innocence remains untempered by shrewdness, which gives us the tools and knowledge we need to establish effective boundaries. If we do not develop the discrimination needed to identify potential threats, it can seem like the world is against us. As a result, we close ourselves off from life and become brittle. In this way, stubborn innocence breeds paranoia. Because we can't tell friend from foe, eventually the whole world looks like it is out to get us. By contrast, maturing out of our innocence gives us the wisdom we need to defend ourselves when necessary, leaving us free to experience the world in an open-hearted way.

Like Snow White, Suzanne possessed the needed outlaw qualities from the start but had an inadequate relationship with them. For example, when she felt particularly sidestepped in a family situation with her adult children, she could become rageful and punishing. When she felt isolated at work, she found herself making barbed comments at team meetings or even helping herself to excess office supplies. The healthy feelings of deservedness that got cut off early now came back and expressed themselves "sideways."

MOURNING THE FANTASY

Suzanne's task was to work her way out of her innocence complex where she expected that if she were just "good," the world would treat her correctly and reward her. This task required forging a conscious relationship with shadow so that she could access shrewdness.

A critical moment occurred when her niece became engaged. Born some ten years after Suzanne's youngest child, Dora was Tony's only child, and Suzanne had worked hard to be a loving and connected aunt.

Suzanne made a point to go to New York every year on Dora's birthday to take her to a Broadway show. She also invited Dora down for a weekend every year before Christmas, and the two would bake cookies and see the holiday display at Longwood Gardens. Dora had loved to spend time with her aunt when she was little, but Tony and his wife always seemed subtly disparaging of Suzanne and discouraged Dora's attachment to her. "I remember calling her a few weeks before her thirteenth birthday to tell her I had gotten tickets to see *Mamma Mia* on Broadway," Suzanne told me. "She was irritable and distant and told me she wouldn't be able to make it." Dora seldom wanted to spend time with her aunt once she was a teenager, but Suzanne never faltered. She continued to keep in touch with Dora and sent small presents for her birthday and Christmas. Suzanne was happy to learn of Dora's engagement and looked forward to participating in the wedding and other festivities.

Then Suzanne ran into an acquaintance in the neighborhood who was friends with her brother. This person casually mentioned an upcoming engagement party to be held in Manhattan. Suzanne was stunned as she had heard nothing whatsoever about these plans. Suzanne had not been invited. What happened next was crucial. She was able to witness herself turning away from the truth. A part of her—the Snow White innocence part—insisted that this couldn't be true. "I don't think that's right," she told this person. But another part of her took in both the casual betrayal by her brother and niece—just another in a long line—*and* her tendency not to know something painful. This moment helped her to see her lifelong pattern of hiding an uncomfortable truth from herself to maintain a belief that the world was an essentially good and fair place. Because she had done many months of painful work to accept and integrate her shadowy qualities, she could see her brother's selfish and cruel behavior for what it was.

Suzanne could mourn the fantasy that her hard work and sacrifice on the part of others would be rewarded and appreciated. This paved the way for her to claim her shrewdness, a canny awareness of others' limitations and flaws. Then she could protect herself when needed while cultivating an open heart.

KNOWING OUR DARKNESS

We must all sacrifice the innocence of childhood if we are to live fully. Such a sacrifice can be painful because, as we saw with Suzanne, it can mean allowing ourselves to know that we have not been loved and cared for in the way we should have been. It also requires that we admit to ourselves that we can do bad things when we would rather not know this about ourselves. It can be frightening to become aware of our power for destruction. However, being shrewd means sacrificing an overly innocent attitude so that we can see what is before us. This includes being able to perceive in a clear-eyed way our own capacity for greed, aggression, selfishness, and cunning. Being alert to our shadowy qualities will make us less vulnerable to being victimized by those qualities in others. "Knowing your own darkness," Jung remarked, "is the best method for dealing with the darknesses of other people."[6]

We all have the ability for selfishness, hardness, and even cruelty. If we cling to our innocence complex—if we refuse to allow ourselves to become acquainted with these capacities—we increase the likelihood that these shadowy qualities will enter our lives unbidden, making an appearance in ways that are beyond our conscious control. You might find yourself making a cutting comment to a friend who inspires envy or responding to your spouse's questions with outsized irritation. But being cut off from our dark qualities can cost us in more direct ways as well. If we don't forge a conscious relationship with our capacity for selfishness, greed, or aggression, we won't be able to harness the protective, positive, and growth-promoting features of these qualities. There will be times when attending to our needs will require us to put ourselves first or hurt or disappoint someone else. Cultivating shrewdness means that we welcome an awareness of these dark qualities within ourselves and don't shrink before the knowledge that we, too, are capable of selfish or even morally ambiguous acts.

VALUING OUR GIFTS

Becoming wise to shadowy qualities in ourselves and others is one-half of what it takes to develop shrewdness. The other half requires us to see and claim our gifts fully. Too often, we have trouble recognizing our strengths. If we have an inkling of them, we discount them, perhaps afraid of making others uncomfortable. The modern American fairy tale *The Wizard of Oz* features Dorothy (Judy Garland), a gingham-clad girl from Kansas, who, like Snow White, must become aware of her capacity for darkness and learn to own her talents and gifts.

From the beginning, we see that Dorothy is capable of aggression—she is companioned by her dog, Toto, who boldly barks at the wicked Miss Gulch (Margaret Hamilton). Nevertheless, these aggressive, protective instincts present a problem for Dorothy, as they do for many girls and women. Toto has a habit of going into Miss Gulch's garden and chasing the old woman's cat. When the movie opens, a crisis point has been reached because little Toto has bitten Miss Gulch. This is a symbolic image of Dorothy's untamed, self-protective instincts. We also see Dorothy's aggressive capacity displayed upon her arrival in Oz—albeit unconsciously. She unwittingly drops her house on the Wicked Witch of the East. Though seemingly an accident, Dorothy's great destructive power is in evidence, and the citizens of Munchkinland know it. Glinda arrives in her ball of light and asks immediately, "Are you a good witch? Or a bad witch?"[7] Glinda correctly presumes that Dorothy is powerful and has the capacity to be destructive.

But Dorothy doesn't know her power. She is too accustomed to seeing herself as innocent and good. "Who, me?" she asks in response to Glinda's question. "Why, I'm not a witch at all! I'm Dorothy Gale from Kansas."[8] When the Wicked Witch of the West confronts her about having killed her sister, Dorothy replies that it was an accident. Yet Dorothy becomes the rightful owner of the powerful ruby slippers because she dispatched the Wicked Witch of the East.

As Dorothy travels to see the Wizard, the Wicked Witch of the West hounds her, hoping to get the ruby slippers. When the witch imprisons her and threatens to kill Toto, Dorothy immediately offers her the slippers.

"That's a good little girl!"[9] the witch responds as she reaches for Dorothy's feet. But the slippers cannot come off the girl's feet while alive, and the witch gets zapped when she touches them. Dorothy's aggression and power manifest through the action of the shoes, while she consciously denies this part of herself.

"Oh, I'm sorry!" Dorothy says. "I didn't do it! Can I still have my dog?"[10]

Dorothy apologizes to the witch, denies her own power again, and behaves naively, expecting the witch to play fair and keep her word.

In a pivotal moment, the witch sets fire to the scarecrow and Dorothy quickly throws water on him. Some of the water splashes on the witch, and she begins to melt.

"Who would have thought a good little girl like you could destroy my beautiful wickedness?"[11] the witch cries as she disappears into nothingness.

Dorothy is identified with being a "good little girl" and is consistently surprised by her own potency. She is stuck in an innocence complex and has not developed the shrewdness required to know her own darkness and her own fierce strength and power. When the Winkies, who work for the witch, express shock that Dorothy has killed her, she again disavows her agency. "I didn't mean to kill her, really I didn't," she replies.[12] But like Snow White before her, Dorothy can overcome her innocence and acquaint herself with her capacity for aggression and destruction. She requests and is granted the witch's broomstick and carries this with her back to Oz. Her claiming of the broomstick symbolizes the integration of some of the witchy powers.

Like Snow White, Dorothy has power and agency that she doesn't at first recognize because she is trapped in an innocence complex. A common theme in both stories is that the heroine becomes the object of envy and cannot protect herself from this because she cannot imagine that others would want to hurt her.

ENVY

If we are unconscious of our gifts, we cannot protect ourselves from poisonous envy. Envy is a powerful, destructive force. If you think back to when someone was envious of you, you may be able to recall the palpable sense of malice in the field between you. Envy is no joke. It is a powerful emotion that can provoke ugly, spoiling reactions in those struck by it. It can motivate criticism and attacks, both outright and covert. It is the subtle word in the staff meeting that means we are passed over for the promotion, or the lie that spreads discrediting or condemning mistruths about us.

When we have a gift that we do not recognize or claim, we are more susceptible to attacks of envy from others. The ruby slippers are a potent image of a sparkling talent or trait that belongs to us but that we have not yet learned to claim or wield. Other people can see this about us, but if we cannot see it ourselves—if we go through life being overly modest and sweet, underestimating ourselves and our abilities, then we will readily become a target for others. Cultivating shrewdness can help protect us against this vulnerability because we allow ourselves to acknowledge our gifts that might provoke envy.

I recall the first time I met my client Alison after speaking with her on the phone. She arrived for our initial appointment, and I met her in the waiting room. When I saw her, I was taken aback. She was statuesque, with an elegant posture and figure. She had a classic beauty and a gorgeous smile. Her hair was perfectly coiffed, and she sported a neat manicure. Her clothes were fashionable without being showy. My first reaction was to feel intimidated and acutely self-conscious of my comparatively unkempt appearance.

Alison's mother had been a cold, controlling woman who rarely showed her children any warmth and was harshly critical of every aspect of Alison's appearance. When our needs do not get met as children, we internalize this as shame and self-hatred, and Alison suffered from terrible self-loathing that found expression in her feelings about her appearance. She couldn't stand to see herself in any reflective surface. An accidental passing glimpse in the rear-view mirror could

plunge her into despair. Appointments at the hairdresser were fraught·
as she feared she would hate the result and be dropped into a vortex of
shame and self-disgust.

In addition to being beautiful, Alison was bright, funny, and
warm. She had a sparkling personality that made her instantly likable.
Yet she often found herself the target of mean-spirited aggression
from other women. She had a group of friends with whom she used
to get together for dinner monthly, but she became aware that they
were gossiping behind her back, and she was gradually ostracized.
She was deeply hurt by this and could not understand why it had
happened. Throughout our work together, something similar happened several times, and each incident was entirely mysterious for
Alison. We discussed how she managed to find her harshly critical
and rejecting mother out in the world and to recreate aspects of her
childhood experience unconsciously.

I suspected that envy was part of the mix. Alison's mother was a
woman who set a great store by her appearance. Though Alison couldn't
imagine that her mother felt envious of her, it was not hard for me to
suppose that this overbearing, critical woman may have, like Snow
White's mother, had a hard time watching her daughter grow into her
beauty while she aged. Did her mother feel envious of Alison's beauty
and youth? I thought of my reaction to Alison the first time I saw her.
Did Alison possibly provoke envy in other women underscored by
the feelings of inadequacy and intimidation I had experienced upon
meeting her?

Because Alison was unaware of her beauty, she couldn't fathom
that anyone might envy her appearance. So Alison went through life
a little bit the way Dorothy went through Oz—bearing a bright and
shiny gift for all the world to see, while she could not acknowledge
it. And if you can't fully acknowledge that thing about you that is
special and draws admiration from others, then, like Dorothy, you are
always going to be at the mercy of those who would like to take that
thing from you or who would enjoy seeing you fail or have something
bad happen to you. Developing shrewdness strengthens our ability

to protect ourselves from envious attacks because we become aware of our gifts and can anticipate others' reactions to them rather than remaining stuck in self-deprecatory innocence and naivete.

When my children were small, I was friends with a woman named Maura who had a son the same age as mine. She was bright, ambitious, and funny, and suffering from an incurable disease that would eventually be fatal. While I was working away on my career as a writer and analyst, Maura had to take time off to undergo various treatments. One day, Maura casually shared something about my son that was very hurtful. It was a scathing indictment of him—and of my parenting—that she had heard from a mutual acquaintance. For good measure, she followed it up with her own withering assessment of my son. I was stung. I admired and trusted her. As the mother of one of my son's good friends, I felt she knew and appreciated him. Her sharing this with me caused me to doubt myself and my parenting. It also felt gratuitously hurtful. There is no doubt that she intended to wound, and the weapon had hit its mark. A few hours later, I developed terrible back pain. When I asked my mother several days later if she thought I was doing an adequate job of parenting, I broke into sobs.

And then, something quite surprising happened. A day or two later, I woke up in the morning, and it was as if I had been spontaneously transported into Maura's body. I experienced the agony of knowing that I would likely not see my child grow to adulthood. I could feel the rage bubbling up in me that fate had robbed me of that opportunity. My feelings toward Maura instantly clarified and softened. I was sure beyond any doubt that her attack was motivated by envy—and who could blame her? Not only was I able to focus on my career—something she longed to be able to do—but I had no specter of mortality looming over my time with my child. In that instant, my parenting insecurities were assuaged because I understood the real motivation behind her criticism. I forgave Maura but I also knew that I had to become cannier and not take my safety for granted in the relationship.

PROTECTING OURSELVES FROM ENVY

Through my years in clinical practice, I have found that many women have trouble protecting themselves from envy. Doing so involves developing shrewdness—we must be aware that someone could be envious of us. Many women underestimate themselves and their accomplishments so that, like Alison, it doesn't even occur to them that they might incite such an emotion. We must also be careful of needing approval from those who might feel envious of us. Doing so gives them power over us that they can use to knock us down a peg. Maura's critique stung me partly because I already felt insecure about parenting and looked up to her. I wanted her approval, and she implicitly understood this and used it to hurt me.

One must be careful about where one throws one's pearls. We shouldn't hide our gifts; in any case, some gifts cannot be hidden. But we ought to be savvy about sharing news of good fortune. Indiscriminate boastfulness may invite envy. When you find that you are the object of envy, you must meet it with cool confidence. When others are envious of us, it won't do to be "nice." You can't placate envy by trying to win the envious one over. Some women respond to envy with self-deprecation. Self-effacing comments in the face of envy may seem like a good strategy for calling off the attack, but they seldom work. Instead, such a strategy opens us up to further assaults and makes us more vulnerable. Knowing your worth, feeling confident in yourself, and being conscious that others are seeking to bring you down will help you to steer clear of the harmful effects of such an attack.

A feeling of guilt or unworthiness may make it difficult to protect ourselves. Whatever our gift—be it good health, success, or wealth—we probably came by it (at least in part) due to luck. If we are beautiful, intelligent, or talented, we were lucky to have been born with such attributes. Even if we worked hard to get where we are, fortune likely smiled on us along the way. We may not, therefore, feel deserving of our gifts. The lack of deservedness can invite us to feel as though we need to downplay our gifts, give them away, or work hard to elevate the person feeling envious. Of course, compassion for those less fortunate is admirable. But we also need to feel deserving to claim our gifts, whatever they are, and however we have come by them. Accepting our good fortune is part of opening our hearts to the disallowed parts of ourselves.

We mustn't be naive about the world. Alison had trouble recognizing her beauty because she had been deeply wounded in childhood. Being raised in a family where we are loved and adored can make us vulnerable in a different way; it can lead us to take for granted that others will love and cherish us as a matter of course. While having such an expectation can powerfully influence our lives in a positive direction, it can also predispose us to be overly naive. It can make it difficult for us to realize that others might not take such delight in our triumphs and talents as our loving parents did.

BECOMING WISE

An impulse to protect ourselves from envy runs deep. Many cultures have injunctions against certain behaviors lest one incite the envy of the gods. For example, Jewish customs discourage giving baby gifts to expectant mothers. This stems from ancient fears that celebrating an unborn child may attract evil spirits. Such worries are embedded deep in our psyches, and we may have been taught to hide our gifts early to avoid making others feel bad or inspiring envy. Such messaging from our caregivers can cause us to become disconnected from our talents, again leaving us naive and vulnerable.

It is normal for young children to go through a stage that psychoanalysts call *primary narcissism*. If you spend time with young elementary school children, you will see that they think very highly of themselves. They will tell you confidently that they are the best artist or the fastest runner. Our parents must handle this sensitively when we are in this developmental stage. Young children must have these positive feelings about themselves mirrored and affirmed—to an extent. Too much affirmation of a child's perceived specialness can turn this normal, healthy childhood narcissism into the more malignant kind we see in some adults.[13] However, repeatedly shaming a child for thinking or speaking well of herself can inflict a lifelong wound. The world is a harsh place, and most of us will get our overestimation of ourselves cut down to size quickly enough. Having a little warm space where we can see ourselves as special for a time and have that belief reflected in the eyes of our parents allows us to integrate a positive sense of ourselves. If we were made to feel ashamed of our normal, healthy, positive esteem for ourselves when we were young, we learned that we must split off feelings of pride and self-regard. These feelings become tinged with shame and go into the shadow. We lose our conscious relationship with them.

If we are to develop shrewdness, we will need to reclaim the ability to feel unabashed positive regard for ourselves. Feeling good about ourselves in a realistic, grounded way helps us protect ourselves. While part of shrewdness involves having a clear-eyed appraisal of our weaknesses and limitations, it also calls for a practical appreciation of our abilities. We value our worth and recognize our strengths and accomplishments. We don't need to shout this from the rooftops, but we also don't need to hide it. Valuing ourselves will take practice if we have been schooled for a lifetime to be modest and unassuming. There are practical steps we can take.

Permission to Celebrate Ourselves

As women, we tend to undo our accomplishments. Hannah started a landscaping business after taking several years off to stay home with her children. Within the first year of operation, the company scored some significant wins, and she was profiled in a regional magazine. She was delighted to share this with me, but quickly passed over it to discuss new challenges. I slowed her down. I had sat with her throughout the incubation of this business. I had been with her through the time that it was just an idea and through the doubt of the early days. I'd seen the setbacks and the temporary despair. I'd witnessed the risk, hard work, and fear that she would never make it. I had been with her on a journey to climb a high peak. Finally, we stood at the summit, looking out over a vast expanse. It was as if Hannah shrugged her shoulders after a short minute and said, "Okay. Enough of that! Now we have to figure out how to get down."

Not allowing ourselves to acknowledge our successes keeps us from being able to see ourselves and our situation clearly. In other words, it keeps us from being as shrewd and savvy as we could be. When we reach a milestone or enjoy a major accomplishment, we need to allow ourselves to steep in it and take it in rather than skipping over it. We can do this by celebrating and honoring the achievement consciously. How one does this doesn't matter as long as the intention is there. You might open a bottle of champagne, buy a cake, or throw a party, but taking an hour off to walk in the woods or creating a small celebration ritual works just as well. Permit yourself to return to pleasant thoughts about your accomplishment throughout the day. If you monitor the flow of your inner dialogue, you may find that you pull away from positive thoughts. For many of us, engaging in positive reverie about our accomplishments feels forbidden or even dangerous because it seems self-centered. But allowing ourselves to bask luxuriously in our achievements—at least briefly—is key to reclaiming our sense of boldness, which in turn helps us to be shrewder when dealing with others.

Taking in our accomplishments on the internal level is much more important than crowing about our latest wins on social media or talking about them with friends and family. Sharing our successes publicly inevitably puts us in the precarious position of looking for feedback. Instead of focusing on our victory, we may monitor our social media post to see how many likes and comments we get. And, of course, when we expose our achievements to the world, we risk inciting envy. The point is to develop a deep appreciation for ourselves and our triumph. After all, we know better than anyone the amount of work that went into it. With this solid self-appreciation, we can choose wisely with whom we share our accomplishments. If we have an accurate appraisal of ourselves, we can fend off attacks brought about by envy and pragmatically assess our strengths and weaknesses.

When we develop shrewdness, we become clear-eyed about ourselves. We don't have illusions of our innocence or purity. We have a realistic appreciation of our strengths and gifts. We have a sense of our capacity and potential. We also become clear-eyed about the world. Our instincts speak to us, and we listen to them. We allow ourselves to know what we know. We see whom we can trust and whom we ought to hold at arm's length. This knowledge enables us to maneuver with greater freedom because we can perceive potential threats in time to head them off. It also helps us become acquainted with our destiny. When we sacrifice an overly innocent attitude, we confront the truth about ourselves, connect with our essential nature, and discover the pattern we came into the world to live out.

Being shrewd doesn't mean becoming pessimistic or nihilistic. On the contrary, real wisdom makes it easier to open our hearts to joy. "It is by no means difficult to be a blind idealist, nor a cynical realist," according to Marie-Louise von Franz. "But it is difficult and desirable to see, without illusion, reality as it is and yet to nourish the inner flame and keep it high."[14] Becoming shrewd won't make us closed off and suspicious. Instead, it will open the world up to us, allowing us to renew our connection to our source, to the central fire.

QUESTIONS FOR REFLECTION

1. In "Little Snow White," the queen is envious of her beautiful daughter. Envy between mothers and daughters is not just the stuff of fairy tales. Are you aware of how your mother may have envied you? How do you think she dealt with her envy? How did her envy affect you? If you are a mother, have you ever felt envious of your child? What were you envious of, and when did you become aware of the feeling? Were you surprised by this feeling? How did you handle it?

2. Envy is a major theme in the story. Think about your life right now. What about you might others envy? Often, when others have malice toward us and we don't understand why, it is because they envy us. Where in your life might you be the object of envy right now? How might you be able to protect yourself?

3. The huntsman and the dwarves are kind to Snow White because she is so beautiful. If we have a quality such as beauty that makes other people like us immediately, certain aspects of life may come easily for us, but this can mean that we don't develop other aspects of ourselves. What qualities do you have that win people over easily? How conscious of these qualities are you? How much do you rely on these traits?

4. One of the most striking aspects of the story is how readily Snow White opens the door each time the queen appears. Where in your life have you been overly trusting or naive? How did you eventually learn not to be so innocent? Why do you think it was so difficult for you to learn that you shouldn't put your faith in something or someone?

5. Snow White's transformation comes during a prolonged, death-like sleep. This can be an image of passivity or even depression. You may have suffered through a fallow period of your life—perhaps it was one in which you actually slept a lot. Looking back at such a time, what are the indications you see now that a process of change was underway even while things looked lifeless? How did such an experience help you to transform?

6. The irritable servant plays an important role in the story. He is not charmed by the beautiful maiden who has become such a burden. When have you been treated roughly in a way that woke you up or restored your sense of agency? When have you gotten sick of your own passivity or lethargy and jostled yourself awake? What were those experiences like?

CHAPTER 4

Trickster: Opening to the Unexpected

The possibility remains that the
unconscious may reveal itself in an
unexpected way at any time.

—C. G. Jung, *Collected Works, Volume 14*

Being a trickster requires audacity and boldness. I recently witnessed a trickster moment in a local post office. The line was long and moving at a glacial pace. There was only one worker at the counter. People in line shifted their weight, their feet aching. Mothers trying to occupy small children looked weary and exasperated. Then, an ordinary-looking middle-aged woman nearby turned around and whispered to us not to be alarmed. She began a spot-on impersonation of someone having a psychotic episode. She started talking loudly to herself in an agitated tone. The room grew quiet, and those further away from her who hadn't heard her whispered warning looked decidedly uncomfortable while those closer tried to suppress our smiles. In a moment, a second employee appeared at the counter, and the line sped up! What would have happened if one or several of us had politely asked the worker behind the counter if another staff person could help? I doubt it would have been effective. If we had shouted and been rude, things would likely have deteriorated. But this woman's brazen ploy worked—and it made me smile.

Once we have cultivated shrewdness, we will have a sober view of ourselves, other people, and the situations in which we find ourselves. Shrewdness helps us see what is what. When we see a situation with clarity, we can be more choiceful about how we respond—including opting to use our cunning or wiles to address a challenge indirectly. Trickiness and guile give us more options for how to deal with situations. As we grow up and become used to following rules, we may lose contact with our capacity for spontaneity, playfulness, liminality, laughter, and transgression. These traits are a human birthright and are enlivening and vitalizing. Trickster energy can be bold, playful, and sneaky. It compensates rigidity and hubris. The trickster invites us not to take ourselves too seriously. In mythology, the trickster is a figure who subverts normal rules and defies convention. He points out society's failings and renews the culture. He travels between the realms, often able to go where others can't. He makes space for uncomfortable truths to be exposed.

Trickster invites us to play. We delight in thinking up pranks to play on our family and friends that will make us all giggle. Trickster encourages us to bend the rules and see unique opportunities for solving problems. It prioritizes ends over means and often requires that we transgress the normal bounds and expectations. When we access trickster cunning, we are deliberately sneaky and skillfully deceitful. We manipulate a situation to achieve our goals. Trickster energy invites us to think strategically and put the desired outcome ahead of relationship values such as empathy and kindness. Cunning is an outlaw energy that can help us connect with our desires and protect ourselves and those we love.

Many of us grow up learning that we must work hard to achieve our goals, and while this is a valuable lesson, it can lead us to believe that we cannot ever hope for anything good to come to us without long labor. For many of us, working hard and following the rules is a daily, unconscious negotiation with the universe. It's as if we are saying, "I'll do my bit over here, and, in return, please don't annihilate me." If this is the bedrock assumption according to which we operate, any departure from the straight and narrow may bring with it a fear that we will be punished.

TRUST

A trickster attitude allows us to confront our fate with insouciant confidence. Trickster is the god of shortcuts and clever ideas. The trickster finds a solution that no one else has found yet. Trickster teaches us that cunning and a bold attitude sometimes win the day better than hard work and a rigid, rule-bound approach. To be wily and sly is to be in command of our agency. We aren't waiting for someone else to solve our problems and can be wildly creative in coming up with a solution.

Trickster energy contradicts the belief that toil is required to be successful. Trickster makes something from nothing. Where there was only empty air before, trickster finds a way to create a business, discover a novel solution, or gain the upper hand in a surprising move. One of my favorite trickster tales from childhood was "Stone Soup." Soldiers returning home from war come to a village where no one is keen to offer them food. They build a fire and begin boiling a large pot of water into which they put a stone. When the curious villagers ask what they are making, they explain that they are making stone soup. They assure the villagers that it will be delicious and only needs a bit of carrot, a pinch of onion, and a handful of beans. Each villager willingly brings whatever they have, and that night the entire village enjoys a delicious bowl of stone soup together.

To make use of the trickster, however, we must trust ourselves and the universe. Feelings of shame and inadequacy get in the way of the self-trust needed to access the trickster. In my first year out of college, I was a history teacher and dorm parent at a girls' boarding school. One day, I left my suite to make coffee in the tiny dorm kitchen, only to find my door locked upon my return. I thought I had been careful to leave it unlocked, but apparently, I had made a mistake. My energy was taken up by self-reproach. How could I have been so careless? I was ashamed. I had to use the dorm phone to contact campus security and ask someone to come and let me in. In the meantime, I waited in the common area, where the girls discovered I had locked myself out of my room. I was humiliated. They smirked and were full of disdain as perhaps only fifteen-year-old girls can be.

As you can imagine, I was meticulous afterward not to repeat this mistake. Subsequent times that I left my room without my keys, I checked and double-checked that the door was not locked. And yet, one day, the same thing happened. This time, however, I had a very different attitude. I was confident that the fault was not mine, and this allowed me to think creatively. I slipped my plastic faculty ID card between the jamb and the locking mechanism, and the door slid open. By being a bit tricky, I had saved myself time and humiliation. But I had been unable to access that attitude while feeling mired in shame for my perceived deficiencies.

We often don't like tricksters. We think they took the easy way. We resent their apparent effortless success, their arrogance, their pluck. We see them get ahead based on subterfuge and ruses and think to ourselves that it isn't fair. If we find ourselves having this reaction, it may be an invitation to us to get in touch with our own cunning. Where are we laboriously and fruitlessly following rules when a strategic intervention might move things forward?

PROTECTING OURSELVES

Perhaps the fundamental element of trickster energy is a bedrock belief that we are the final authority on ourselves. As a result, there is a healthy suspicion of outside experts and a confidence that, in the last analysis, we can trust ourselves more than anyone else. This attitude is powerful and liberating.

I knew an American man who worked for an NGO in an African country. He was there during a period of significant civil strife. He was in the capital city during an uprising when a truck full of a dozen young local men came to his office and demanded that he go with them. My friend was an astute observer of human nature and quickly realized that he was in significant danger. However, he also saw an opportunity. He correctly perceived that the young men had no plan. They were swept up in the day's general chaos and acting impulsively. My friend knew that his behavior could shape their response. He projected as much calm as he could. He began talking and joking with them and thanked them for making sure he got home safely. The young men did indeed drop him off later unharmed. In a moment of real duress and fear, my friend had not assumed that someone else would come to his rescue, nor did he assume good intentions on the part of his captors. Instead, he used trickster energy to direct their intentions subtly.

Here, by way of contrast, is another story. Like the rest of the world, I watched the events of September 11, 2001, with horror and fascination. One detail that I learned later stood out for me. After the north tower fell, many in the south tower started to leave but were told to return to work by employers and security guards. This story made me shudder. Trust in authority can override our deep instincts, sometimes with tragic results. Trickster energy doesn't rely on others to keep us safe. It is, in this sense, profoundly optimistic. It says, *I know I can take care of myself.*

The famous Middle Eastern tale of "One Thousand and One Nights" is an especially charming version of a female trickster tale where the protagonist must use her wits to keep herself safe.

One Thousand and One Nights

King Shahryar discovered that his wife had been unfaithful to him. In retribution, the king vowed to wed a new virgin every day and to have her beheaded the next morning. When the vizier could find no more virgins of noble birth, his daughter Scheherazade willingly offered to marry the king. Once the couple was together in the king's chambers, Scheherazade told a story, and the king listened, enrapt. He listened the whole night to her tale. But Scheherazade stopped in the middle of her story, explaining that the sun was coming up and she would need to finish the next night.

The king wanted to hear the rest of the story so badly that he chose to let her live for one more day. The second night, she finished her first story and began another tale, this one even more exciting than the first. Again, the king lay awake all night listening, and again she stopped in the middle of the story as the sun began to rise. In this way, she tricked the king into letting her live for one thousand nights. Only then did she tell him that she had no more stories, but by this point, she had given him three sons and he had fallen in love with her.

Scheherazade has a great deal of confidence in her ability to evade a seemingly inexorable fate through the use of her cunning. Her clever ploy works, and she not only survives—she becomes queen. The story shows that trickery can sometimes work where other approaches fail. The hard-hearted cruelty of the king cannot be assuaged by appeals to mercy or even threats of force. Just when things look hopeless, a clever ruse carries the day.

Trickster is the energy that sees a way forward even when all seems lost. In the 2020 Bosnian film *Quo Vadis, Aida?* a woman uses her wiles to try and save her family. The film takes place in Srebrenica on July 11, 1995. Aida Selmanagić is a schoolteacher who has been working as a translator for the UN's Dutch Battalion. She is married and has two sons, one seventeen and the other a bit older. Aida is shrewd. As the film opens, she is translating during a tense meeting between the Dutchbat commander and the mayor of Srebrenica. Bosnian Serb forces under the command of Ratko Mladić are attempting to capture the town, which had been declared a UN safe zone. Through Aida's translations, the UN commander promises the mayor that there will be airstrikes if the Serbs don't withdraw, but we can see in Aida's eyes that she doesn't quite believe what she is saying. There have been many broken promises before.

When the promised airstrikes do not materialize and Mladic's troops overrun the town, thousands of refugees flood the fenced, guarded UN compound where Aida works. The first several thousand make it inside, but the Dutch soldiers close the gate, leaving tens of thousands of people pressed outside. Searching desperately for her family, Aida learns that one of her sons has made it inside the base, but her husband and second son remain outside. When appeals to the Dutch to allow them in don't work, she uses her wits. Ratko Mladic has asked for three volunteers to meet with him to negotiate the fate of the civilians. No one wants to go. Aida convinces the Dutch to let her husband go as one of the negotiators. She finds him among the crowd and brings him inside the compound, her other son following along with him.

The family has now been reunited inside the base, but this momentary experience of relative safety does not last long. Armed Serbian troops demand to be let in the base under the pretense of checking to make sure there are no soldiers inside. The Dutch capitulate, making it clear who is really in charge. Aida is not naive as to what this means. She removes her family from the throngs of civilians and hides them deep within the compound, among the offices of the Dutchbat officers. When she learns that a list is being made of UN personnel who will be allowed to leave when the Dutch withdraw, she bribes her colleague with a cigarette to have her family's names added. She tries to make UN identification cards for her husband and sons to make it easier for them to leave. When each of these ruses fail—the Dutch take her family's names off, and the ID card machine is broken—Aida tries more and more desperate tricks. She begs a worker to let her family hide in his vehicle; she asks if her family can be stowed among the gear the Dutch are packing up; she hides her family in a shipping container inside the base; she lies to the junior officer who insists her family isn't on the list; and she begs the doctor to take her family with him in the convoys of wounded who are leaving. "I'll shoot them in the foot," she offers.[1] When all else fails, she begs. In the end, all of her efforts are to no avail.

Though Aida is not successful, her attitude throughout the film embodies trickster energy. While one son falls into a paralyzing panic and her husband collapses into apathy, Aida never gives up. When direct efforts to save her family fail, she tries anything, including lying, sneaking, and hiding. Though she hopes that Dutchbat will help her protect her family, she never blindly trusts that they will.

WHERE DESPERATION MEETS PLAYFULNESS

Trickster responses are often borne from desperation. We resort to using tricks when we are powerless or when all other avenues have been exhausted. A trickster solution is always the preferred method for the disenfranchised or dispossessed. Without other, more direct ways of accessing power, artifice and deception become the primary way the oppressed gain advantage. Stories in which the heroine employs trickster ruses tend to be dark. In "Fitcher's Bird," the third sister uses trickiness to expose the sorcerer and rescue her sisters. Aida resorts to tricks when all other options fail. In real life as well, we might notice ourselves resorting to trickiness in desperate situations.

While I was working for an international relief and refugee program in the former Yugoslavia during the 1990s, a female friend and I were alone in a house when soldiers armed with Kalashnikov rifles intimidated our guards and demanded to enter. In the ensuing encounter, it wasn't clear what these men wanted of us. They herded us into a bedroom and had us sit on the bed, all the while with their rifles trained on us. I was momentarily paralyzed with fear, and it seemed possible that we were either going to be raped or executed or both. At a moment when all of this seemed to hang in the balance, my friend looked up at our captor and said simply, "Deutschmark?" This one word altered the interaction, changing a potentially dangerous assault into a mere robbery. At gunpoint, we emptied our wallets, removed our jewelry, and even offered them the keys to our UN-registered vehicles. Like the aid worker in Africa, my friend was resourceful enough to see that she might be able to influence how things went, even with a gun pointed at her. While these exchanges were taking place, my friend saw her opportunity to escape. She was able to run from the house and our attackers followed her. She made it to safety, and I was able to secure the door again until help came.

That so many stories of the female trickster center around using one's wits to protect oneself or one's family points to women's vulnerability. Because of our physiology and our role in human reproduction, women are susceptible to male violence. In "Fitcher's Bird" and "One Thousand and One Nights," the heroine must use her wits to guard against a predatory man. The tales highlight the potential for sexual victimization and the importance of a woman using guile to keep herself safe.

Though trickster stories may begin as desperate and dark, they may also be playful and humorous. This is true both in fairy tales and in real life. Sometimes, the trick turns a dark story into a lighthearted one, as is the case in "One Thousand and One Nights." At other times, playfulness and guile are used to solve a less urgent situation, such as dealing with a long line at the post office. Trickster tales involving male heroes are frequently full of charm and comedy. The trickster hero often profits from a delightfully improbable adventure, as in "Puss in Boots" or "Jack and the Beanstalk." Many trickster stories feature female protagonists, but most show the heroine using her wits to save herself or someone else. Examples of stories featuring playful female tricksters who use their wits not just for self-protection but to pursue adventure and riches are harder to find, but there are a few. One of my favorites is the English tale "Molly Whuppie." The tiny heroine uses her trickster wits to protect herself and her sisters against great odds, but she also uses trickery to enrich their lives. Even though she is facing down a giant, her cunning is full of playfulness.

MOLLY WHUPPIE

A couple had too many children and couldn't feed all of them, so they took the youngest three and left them in the wood. The three children walked through the night, tired, hungry, and frightened. Then, at last, they saw a light and walked toward it until they came to a house.

The children knocked at the door, and a woman answered. They begged to be let in and given something to eat, but the woman explained that her husband was a giant who would eat them and that he would be home any minute. But the children begged and begged and promised to stay only for a moment, so she let them in and gave them milk and bread.

Just then, however, the giant came to the door. "What is this I smell?" he said in a dreadful voice. "Who is here?"

The giant's wife explained that the children were tired and hungry and begged him to let them stay just the one night and not touch them. The giant said nothing but sat down to eat his dinner.

The giant and his wife had three children of their own, and the three human children were going to stay in the bed with the giant children. The youngest of the human children was named Molly Whuppie, and she was very clever. She noticed that before the children went to bed, the giant placed necklaces of gold on his children and necklaces of straw on herself and her sisters. While everyone else quickly fell asleep, Molly Whuppie stayed awake. Then she exchanged the gold necklaces and the straw ones.

In the middle of the night, the giant grabbed each of the three children with the straw necklaces and beat them with his club until they were dead, thinking he had killed Molly Whuppie and her sisters. But, of course, he had killed his own children. When the giant went back to bed, Molly woke her sisters. The three of them slipped quietly out of the house. They ran and ran until they came to a large house. It just so happens that a king lived there. Molly told the king her story. "You did well," he said. "But you would do even better to go back and steal the sword that hangs above the giant's bed. If you do this, I will marry my eldest son to your eldest sister." Molly said she would try.

So Molly went back to the giant's house. She crept in quietly and hid under the bed. The giant came home, ate an enormous dinner, and went to sleep. When he was snoring, Molly stole from under the bed, climbed up, and took the sword from the wall where it hung over the giant's head. But it rattled as she got it down, and the giant woke up. Molly ran and ran, and the giant chased her until they reached the Bridge of One Hair. Molly could get over it, but the giant couldn't. He cursed and yelled at her that she would be sorry if she ever came back, but Molly kept running. She gave the sword to the king, and Molly's eldest sister married the king's eldest son.

"You've done well, Molly, but you could do even better," the king told her. "If you steal the purse full of gold that lies beneath the giant's pillow, I will marry my second son to your second sister." Molly said she would try. Back she went to the giant's house, and once again, she climbed under the bed and waited until the giant was sleeping. Then she came out from under the bed, slipped her hand under his pillow, and drew forth the purse. She started to run, but the giant woke up and came after her. She ran as fast as she could, but the giant was catching up with her. When they reached the Bridge of One Hair, Molly could cross it, but the giant could not. The giant raged and cursed her, but Molly just kept running. She gave the purse to the king, and Molly's second sister married the king's second son.

"You're a clever girl, Molly, but if you would do even better, steal the ring the giant wears on his finger," said the king. "Do that, and I'll marry you to my youngest son." So back Molly went to the giant's house and hid under the bed. She waited until the giant was snoring. Then she pulled and pulled at the ring on his finger. But just as she about had it off, he woke up and grabbed her. He stuffed her into a sack and sewed it up tight, then went to the woods to find a thick stick to use to beat her to death. While he was gone, Molly cried out, "Oh, if you could see what I see!" The giant's wife was intrigued and asked what Molly saw. Molly didn't answer but merely said, "Oh, if you could see what I see!" The giant's wife grew more curious and insisted that Molly tell her. "Get a pair of scissors and cut a hole in the sack so you can come in and see." The giant's wife cut a hole in the sack and climbed inside. Molly climbed out and sewed up the sack with the giant's wife in it. She didn't have to wait long for the giant to come home with a huge stick that he used to start beating the sack. The giant's wife called out, but the dog was barking, and he couldn't hear her. He beat her and beat her until she was dead. Then Molly ran out of her hiding place. The giant saw her and chased her, but he could not cross the Bridge of One Hair. Molly married the king's youngest son and never saw the giant again.

The story begins with a terrible scene of destitution and lack. The family is so poor that they must turn out their three youngest children. Many of us may have grown up in families with psychological—if not financial—poverty. Perhaps our parents were too busy with their worries to have much time for us, especially if we had many siblings. Being brought up in a very large family can constitute a kind of neglect. While there are certainly families who manage to raise many children with adequate love and warmth, I have had numerous adults in my practice who come from families of six, seven, or even ten siblings. Chaos and lack often marked their childhoods.

There can be a surprising upside to such an upbringing, which we see in this story. People who have not received a lot of nurturance growing up can sometimes realize early on that they must be responsible for themselves. As a result, they don't suffer from an illusion that the world will look out for them, and they become very adept at caring for themselves. They can come by shrewdness easily.

Molly isn't too trusting. She pays attention and notices things, such as when the giant gives different necklaces to the children. When her sisters go to sleep, Molly stays awake. She does not allow herself to become unconscious of what is happening around her, and she doesn't assume good intentions on the part of the giant. Having a bit of healthy skepticism about other people's motives helps us keep ourselves safe.

In the first part of the story, Molly behaves like many trickster heroines, using her wits to save herself and her sisters. After they reach safety, however, something a little different happens. The king makes an offer to Molly, creating an incentive for her to return to danger to try and gain a reward. Molly goes back voluntarily to the giant's house, taking a risk to reach for more. In this, she is like her fellow giant-conquering hero Jack of beanstalk fame. Like Jack, Molly isn't satisfied with just being safe. She knows the giant has access to great riches and is willing to risk claiming more for herself.

The Bridge of One Hair is an important and curious image. In a similar Scottish version of the tale, the heroine makes a bridge out of a single strand of her own hair. She can cross, but the giant cannot. This detail emphasizes Molly's smallness in contrast to the giant's great size. Again, the trickster attitude helps us to turn our weaknesses into an advantage.

SEEKING MORE

Grace grew up in a family where no one had time for her. Her father was an alcoholic, and her mother was overwhelmed with the demands of raising kids and wrapped up in her troubles. Neither of Grace's parents had gone to college. Though her mother was supportive of Grace attending university, she could not offer any help navigating the college selection or application process. Her mother didn't take Grace on college visits, but when a friend's family visited a prestigious university a few hours away, Grace went along. She was amazed by the campus with its stately historic buildings. She was overwhelmed with the sense that this was part of a wider world full of new possibilities. Some part of her knew she belonged there.

Grace applied and was accepted, but she was too scared to see how much it cost. Her mother and father never asked. Grace vaguely knew that the school would be too expensive, but she couldn't risk being told that her family couldn't afford it, so she said nothing. Her mother wrote a check for the small deposit required to hold her spot, and Grace proceeded to prepare to go to school in the fall. As the move-in date grew closer, she became increasingly afraid of what would happen when the bill came due, but she kept her secret. She arrived on campus on a hot, late August day with her mother and a car full of her things. When they checked in, they were directed to the bursar's office, and it was here that Grace's mother learned for the first time what the price tag at this renowned university would be. At that point, Grace's mother was no longer in a position to prevent Grace from going, and arrangements were made to allow her to apply for loans and enroll. Grace did well in college and eventually attended graduate school. Her urgent gamble—directed from the guiding center of the personality—paid off.

Grace's deep, inner sense that it was her destiny to escape the small world of her dysfunctional family led her to use trickster energy to make this happen. Like Molly, her smallness and seeming insignificance within the family turned out to be an asset. Her mother didn't focus on Grace and her college experience, so she completely overlooked the need to attend to the cost. Grace instinctively knew this and kept it hidden.

Grace's cunning was borne out of desperation. Like Molly, she had little power and few resources. She had only a fervent desire for more, the audacity to brave the unthinkable, and the cunning to try something a bit daring. Both Grace and Molly escaped by a hair's breadth. In either case, things could have gone the wrong way, but they didn't.

A MORAL GRAY AREA

Trickster stories come in an endless variety of types, but one common theme is that the trickster hero or heroine is willing to subvert conventional values in service to growth and life. For example, Molly deceives the giant into killing first his own children and then his wife. In addition, Molly doesn't hesitate to lie, steal, or engage in violence when needed. This seemingly immoral behavior serves the larger goals of protection and thriving. This is the hierarchy of values that Lilith invites us to hold. Could we believe in ourselves to the point where we would be willing to bend the rules? Could we let our unfolding matter that much to us?

So it was with Grace's subterfuge. Some part of her yearned for a larger, more expansive existence, but to reach for more, she had to engage in ethically questionable behavior. This moral ambiguity is part of what makes trickster energy so difficult to access for many women. Being the trickster will require that we break the rules. Grace was not used to lying—and she certainly lied by omission. She also wasn't used to demanding much, and in her desperate deception, she was demanding a great deal. She was asking her parents and the university to provide financial help. But she was asking for something significant on the psychospiritual level as well. She was asking for support as she sought to spread her wings to fly.

Borne from desperation and a lack of other options, a trickster response can be the thing that saves the day and even opens up vast new horizons as it did for Grace. Sometimes being a trickster means taking a playful attitude to what seems a hopeless or desperate situation. Playfulness and humor can help dissolve obstacles or loosen up a situation that has been characterized by too much rigidity. The trickster is close kin to the fool, and when we play tricks, we may make another look foolish or take that role on ourselves. We don't worry about looking foolish, and instead delight in the freedom that foolishness allows.

Lucille Ball's early life was full of struggle. Her beloved father died from typhoid fever when the comedian was three years old. Other early tragedies meant that her family had little money. As an acting student, her teachers bluntly told her that she would never succeed. Ball's early career was characterized by roles in B movies. She was almost forty, and stardom had eluded her.

Then, Ball convinced studio executives to cast her real-life husband Desi Arnaz alongside her in a television show, and *I Love Lucy* was born. It made television history. It paired an all-American woman with a Latin husband, and it was the first show to be filmed in front of a live studio audience. When complications emerged around the show's production, Ball and Arnaz formed Desilu Productions, and Ball became the first woman to head a television production company.

Ball later headed Desilu by herself. In addition to *I Love Lucy*, Desilu was best known for *Mission: Impossible* and *Star Trek*. Ball's genius at physical humor, her incredibly expressive face, and her fearlessness to take on any antics no matter how silly made *I Love Lucy* one of the most watched and beloved television shows of all time.

Ball's character on the iconic television show is a perfect trickster. She's not interested in being bound by conventional expectations. Her husband, Ricky, announces that he wants a wife who will bring him his slippers in the evening and raise his children, but Lucy wants to be a star. She never stops trying to find a way to break into show business. She isn't afraid to break the rules, dissemble, or sneak to get what she wants. When she learns it will be too expensive to ship home a log of fancy cheese from Europe, she decides to disguise it as a baby. Unfortunately, she is seated next to a nosy new mother who wants to compare notes about the infants.[2] In earlier cultures, the trickster was known as the "delight maker," and *I Love Lucy* is delightful, indeed.

Ball appears to have embodied some of this same bold spirit in her life as well. There have been rumors that Ball could be a difficult woman. Richard Burton wrote in his diary that she was a "monster of staggering charmlessness and monumental lack of humour."[3] Trickster energy isn't nice. It is bold, playful, and expansive. It takes risks and is always looking for the unseen angle, the unexpected chink in other people's defensive armor. Ball's daughter, Lucie, remembered that her mother always liked to joke when socializing.

One of my mother's favorite things to do, when a small group of people was involved in some ordinary conversation, was to wait until one of them left the room and, as soon as she returned, blurt out, convincingly, "Here she is now! Why don'tcha tell her to her face?" This was always followed by frozen silence, and then she'd howl (with that depth-of-the-sea laugh she had) to see the look on the poor soul's face, who for one horrible moment thought someone had been saying terrible things about her when she was gone.[4]

The playful trickster is more interested in turning things on their head, seeing things in a new light, upsetting the apple cart, and getting a laugh than caring for other people's feelings. It is wild, audacious, and raucous.

DISCERNMENT AGAIN

Trickster energy is always morally ambivalent. Grace's desperate and unwitting use of trickster energy was in service to her growth and unfolding. When is trickster energy in service to growth or renewal, and when is it in service to something darker? When employing trickster energy, discernment is required. It is best to use it consciously, choosing a trickster mode of dealing with a problem because we know it has the highest likelihood of success in a situation characterized by too much stuckness. For example, the woman in the post office knew exactly what she was doing. Playing the trickster can become a tool in our psychic toolbox—a choice we can make. It ought not to be a primary way of moving through the world.

When we resort to trickster methods to resolve an impasse or solve a difficult problem, we temporarily set aside values such as fairness, empathy, and relationship to prioritize our safety or pursue larger goals. When Grace unintentionally employed cunning to get herself into college, she responded to her soul's deep demand rather than attending to the needs of her family. If we can't sometimes set aside what others require of us and fervently take hold of our own wants—if we can't access our vital spark—we won't be able to nurture the precious thing that wants to come into the world through us.

If we grew up learning always to be "good" and follow every rule, we might have lost touch with trickster's vivifying and renewing energy. This may have dropped out of conscious awareness where it waits to be rediscovered. Author Lewis Hyde has remarked that trickster represents "sacred amorality."[5] When the trickster impulse arises from the guiding center of our soul, it will always be in service to something larger. Hyde continues: "When he lies and steals, it isn't so much to get away with something or get rich as to disturb the established categories of truth . . . and, by so doing, open the road to possible new worlds."[6] Grace wasn't trying to see what she could get away with. She was in desperate pursuit of her destiny.

Trickster energy is always a bit shadowy, but it is always full of life. It is mischievous, animated, and provocative. It invites us to break taboos and defy expectations. It is full of renewing potential and shows up in service to that which is sacred. It can help us protect ourselves, but it can also help us create a more spacious vision of ourselves and our life. And it brings with it the spirit of fun and playfulness that is vital to our sense of aliveness. Trickster embodies the unexpected thing that arises without warning from the unconscious, bringing with it a new perspective and new opportunities. Trickster is exuberantly unafraid to flout the rules and so is a fundamental aspect of our inner flame, our vital spark.

QUESTIONS FOR REFLECTION

1. Scheherazade must have had great confidence in her abilities since she wasn't afraid to marry the king. When we have strong faith in our abilities, we can take on problems that look daunting to other people. Cunning and trickery are powerful resources that can help us feel confident even in very difficult situations. When has your trickster ability helped you to navigate a difficult situation?

2. Molly Whuppie comes from abject poverty—her parents have turned her out because they don't have enough food. This leaves Molly and her sisters vulnerable, and they quickly find themselves in a giant's house. However, Molly relies on herself. She stays awake when the others go to sleep. When have you "gone to sleep" in a potentially dangerous situation? When have you, like Molly, been the one to stay awake?

3. Molly and her sisters make it away safely, but Molly learns that she can earn good fortune if she returns. When have you been able to face your fears? What helped you to do so? What happened when you faced your fears, and what did you learn from this experience?

4. Molly is able to best the giant repeatedly in part because of her small size. We may be small in size, or small in terms of how much psychological space we allow ourselves to take up. Being small in either way is often a disadvantage, but Molly uses it to her advantage. How have you been able to get the upper hand in a situation because you turned a weakness into a strength?

5. Molly's tricks result in the violent death of the giant's children and then his wife, even though she herself never resorts to violence directly. Molly simply engineers things so that the giant suffers from his own sins. Where have you seen an opportunity to allow someone to experience the natural consequences of his or her actions? Were you able to let that happen? Why or why not?

6. Molly must first steal the sword above the bed, then the bag of gold under the pillow, then the ring on the giant's finger. Each item is more intimate to the giant and requires closer contact. The more we face our fears, the more rewards we gain, until we receive the ultimate boon. Molly is much more ambitious and fearless than we would imagine, given her difficult beginnings. How have you prevailed over difficult circumstances? In what way has hardship helped you to become more resilient?

7. Trickster energy can be playful, fun, and delightful. It combats rigidity and too much seriousness. How do you make room for it in your life? How could you add more?

CHAPTER 5

DESIRE: EMBRACING LIFE'S FIRE

> We are out there on the high wire of all of
> our possible futures, and we belong there.
> The gods want us there because they want
> something more of us than the comforts
> and certainties of our timorous egos.
>
> —James Hollis, *Hauntings*

When Frances Gumm was just two years old, she attended a singing performance of the Blue Sisters—three girls between the ages of five and twelve. When the youngest of the trio stepped forward and began a solo, her older sister recalls that Frances was transfixed. "When it was all over, she turned to Daddy and—I'll never forget it—said 'Can I do that, Daddy?'"[1] Little Frances was born with a desire to sing. She made her own solo debut not long after this event, and eventually became known to the world as Judy Garland, one of the most beloved singers of the twentieth century.

In the most primal sense, desire connects us with life. Evolution has gifted us with appetites that ensure our continued survival. We enjoy food, sex, activity, and becoming attached to one another. Fulfilling these urges is deeply pleasurable and satisfying. We would do them for their own sake, but by engaging in these activities, we also fulfill the biological imperative that sustains us and our species.

Similarly, we may feel compelled by deep, urgent longings that come from within and make an irrefutable demand upon our soul. Perhaps we feel the urge to create a garden or learn another language. We cannot silence a profound yearning to travel or live near water. "Your desires," according to the Kabbalists, "are God's promises to you." This beautiful statement asserts that our deep wishes are seeded in us by the transpersonal. Something larger than us knows our secret purpose, and desire pulls us toward it.

Desire is one of the great engines that drives psychological growth and development. It is one of the clearest expressions of our vital spark. It is a force that moves us out over the threshold of complacency and into life. It calls us forth to our destiny. And yet we may have been discouraged from honoring or even knowing our desires. We are told they are selfish, grandiose, foolish, or unbecoming. As women, we are particularly susceptible to becoming cut off from knowing what we want. Perhaps we don't even know that we don't know what we want. Many women develop a pattern of ignoring their own needs and wishes, both large and small. Because women often orient to caregiving, our wants and requirements can easily become overlooked. Ignoring our desires can leave us feeling depleted and resentful. When we neglect our desires, we do not have access to the life-giving energy of the central fire. Learning to listen for the insistent prodding of our heart's desire later in life is vital to seeking those glowing coals beneath gray ash.

OUR INNER PATTERN

Getting in touch with our authentic desires is critical for us to engage in life as fully as possible. I'm not referring to superficial ego appetites. A heartfelt desire arises from a deep place. It comes folded within us, a secret kernel we carry when we are born. It may seem irrational or at odds with what we've always expected from ourselves. It nags. We put it away and tell ourselves not to be ridiculous, but it keeps coming back.

The heart's desire is always a thing of spiritual significance. Whether we wish for great love, a farm at the bend of a river, or fame and glory, our heart's desire usually speaks of a yearning for the transcendent and reaching for our destiny. One of Jung's central ideas is that psychological development unfurls mysteriously toward an ultimate goal. He referred to this as *telos*, a Greek word meaning "end." According to this understanding, we all have an innate goal toward which we strive, even though we may not realize it. The metaphor of an acorn provides a way to imagine this inner pattern. An acorn is small enough to fit into the palm of our hand yet contains everything needed to unfold into a giant oak.

Jung has much to say about the need to tend to the blossoming of this innate goal, which he termed *individuation*. "Individuation . . . is that one becomes what one is, that one accomplishes one's destiny, all the determinations that are given in the form of the germ; it is the unfolding of the germ and becoming the primitive pattern that one was born with."[2] When we live according to this inner pattern, we are becoming the oak we came into the world with the potential to be. When we are not living according to this pattern, life may feel stale and empty. We sense that something is wrong. We may find that we are full of secret resentments. Jung speaks about this in vivid, metaphorical language in one of his lectures.

> If you fulfill the pattern that is peculiar to yourself, you have loved yourself, you have accumulated and have abundance; you bestow virtue then because you have luster. You radiate; from your abundance something overflows. But if you hate and despise yourself—if you have not accepted your patten—then there are hungry animals . . . in your constitution which get at your neighbors like flies in order to satisfy the appetites that you have failed to satisfy.[3]

To live our pattern, we must listen to desire. If the desire wells up from deep within, it will usually guide us home. This doesn't mean we should trust any strong urge, and it is not an excuse to set aside responsibilities to current relationships and commitments. Rather, a strong desire is an invitation to listen to ourselves and approach this yearning with curiosity and compassion rather than shame and judgment. What is the longing really about? What is it asking of us?

The Iranian fairy tale "The Pink Pearl Prince" illustrates the significant growth that can occur when we identify and claim our desire. In the story, the meaning of the desire is at first obscure, but the heroine trusts it and never wavers.

THE PINK PEARL PRINCE

A rich merchant in Persia had three daughters, Razia, Fawzia, and Nazneen. One day, the merchant called his daughters to him and told them that it was time for him to make the holy pilgrimage to Mecca, and he asked the daughters what gifts they would like from the Holy Land. Razia asked for diamond earrings, and Fawzia wanted a diamond pin. Nazneen asked for a pink pearl. "If you do not get it for me, I will not allow you to enter the house," she told him.

The merchant set off on his journey. After many days, he reached Mecca. Once he had finished his religious observance, he bought gifts for his daughters. He quickly found the diamond earrings and the diamond pin for his two eldest daughters, but he could not find a pink pearl for Nazneen.

He planned to travel home by boat, but the ship could not sail no matter how the crew tried. Finally, the captain announced that the ship could not get underway because someone on board had failed to keep a promise. The merchant realized that he was the source of the problem. He disembarked and began searching once again for a pink pearl. He finally met a man who informed him that the Pink Pearl was none other than the king's son.

The merchant went straight to the palace, sought an audience with the prince, and told him the whole story. The prince gave the merchant three boxes to take back to his daughter. The merchant boarded the ship once again, and this time it sailed without trouble.

When the merchant reached home, his daughters greeted him warmly. He gave the diamond earrings to Razia, the diamond pin to Fawzia, and to Nazneen he gave the three boxes. But the merchant bore resentment against Nazneen for her demandingness. After giving her the boxes, he threw her out of the house. "You have caused me much trouble," he said. "Be gone and let me not see your face again."

Tearfully, Nazneen left home, carrying with her the three boxes. She walked for miles and miles. At last, exhausted, she set her burden down. "I wonder if what is in these boxes is the cause of my banishment," she said, and she opened the first box. Miraculously, a palace arose in front of her. When she opened the second box, an entourage of servants appeared and carried her into the palace. All was glittering and beautiful. She allowed herself to explore the castle and enjoy all she saw. She was in no rush to open the third box, wanting to save the surprise for later.

After some time had passed, she thought to herself that she should open the third box. When she did so, a beautiful bridge appeared that arched over a clear stream. Upon the bridge rode a handsome youth astride a splendid horse. It was none other than the Pink Pearl Prince! He greeted Nazneen and warned her that if she shut the lid of the box while he was on the bridge, he would die. Nazneen and the Prince then went on to enjoy the palace together. They were deeply in love.

Meanwhile, Razia and Fawzia missed their younger sister and went out on foot to seek her. After a long journey, they came upon a beautiful palace and decided to rest there for the night. It was none other than Nazneen's palace. When they knocked on the door, the servants admitted them, and Nazneen was delighted to see her dear sisters. Her sisters were treated well by the servants, and they explored every inch of the palace. Fawzia found two open boxes and one that was shut. She opened the shut one but found nothing inside, so she closed it again. After some time, the sisters left for home with many rich gifts.

Nazneen had not seen the Prince for many days. She opened the box, but the bridge did not appear this time, and neither did her lover. She surmised what had happened and grew afraid. She ran outside, not knowing what to do. After some time, she sat beneath a tree. There, she overheard the conversation of two birds perched in the branches above her. "The oil of the hair of the demon who sits at the base of this tree will be good for the Pink Pearl!" one said.

Nazneen knew bird language. She at once found and killed the demon and took some oil from his hair. Then, posing as a doctor, she traveled to the palace of the Pink Pearl Prince. The Prince's mother called the doctor in, explaining that her son was sick unto death. Nazneen rubbed the Prince all over with the oil, and he was restored. The King and Queen were overjoyed to see their son alive and well. They wanted to reward the doctor. Nazneen asked only for the betrothal ring and necklace.

She sped back to her own palace with these gifts. There, she opened the third box, and the bridge again appeared with the Pink Pearl Prince riding upon it. Then she took the betrothal necklace and put it on her neck, and the betrothal ring on her finger. The Prince asked where she had gotten these from, and she related the whole story to him.

Nazneen and the Prince were formally engaged. Their wedding was celebrated with great joy, and the two lived happily ever after.

Nazneen's story has some obvious parallels with "Beauty and the Beast." In the well-known French tale, the older sisters ask for expensive items while Beauty asks only for a single rose. It may look as though Beauty's request is the humblest, but it isn't really. It is much like Nazneen's request for a pink pearl. Neither the rose nor the pink pearl are ordinary items, but rather represent that which is of supreme, transpersonal value. Neither Beauty nor Nazneen is satisfied with the common fate, even if diamond encrusted. They both dare to want more, and in both cases, their wish causes a challenge to the father.

We might understand that Razia's diamond necklace and Fawzia's diamond pin are the desires that come from the ego, while the pink pearl is the want that springs from the guiding center of the personality that Jung called the Self. The image of a pearl in the Biblical passage from Matthew also images the thirst for something of transcendent value. "The kingdom of heaven is like a merchant seeking beautiful pearls, who, when he had found one pearl of great price, went and sold all that he had and bought it."[4] When we recognize something truly precious, it is worth everything we have.

In both this Persian tale and in "Beauty and the Beast," the father in the story encounters hardship as he tries to meet his daughter's request. In both stories, the father is a merchant focused on commerce in the material world. He takes a too-casual attitude toward the unconscious. In our tale, the father boards the ship homeward without fulfilling his promise, but you cannot cheat the Self. If we try to press forward with our ego goals without giving the needs of the soul their due, we will find that the winds of life are not favorable to our journey.

EXILE

Nazneen eventually gets the thing she asked for, but she is exiled as a result. Banishment is a common theme in similar tales and underscores an important psychic fact. Pursuing our heart's desire will demand that we leave the safety of convention and risk everything. She who follows her heart's desire will be required to leave childhood comfort and seek her fortune in the wider world. We cannot pursue our destiny without leaving behind the smaller, familiar version of ourselves.

This profound psychological fact has been portrayed many times, but one of the most well-known examples is in the Dickens novel *Oliver Twist*. Fate has selected Oliver as the boy who requests more food when the children finish their meal of thin gruel.

Child as he was, he was desperate with hunger, and reckless with misery. He rose from the table; and advancing to the master, basin and spoon in hand, said: somewhat alarmed at his own temerity:

"Please, sir, I want some more." The master was a fat, healthy man; but he turned very pale. He gazed in stupefied astonishment on the small rebel for some seconds, and then clung for support to the copper. The assistants were paralysed with wonder; the boys with fear. "What!" said the master at length, in a faint voice. "Please, sir," replied Oliver, "I want some more."[5]

Oliver's boldness does not pay off. He is beaten, isolated, and exiled, given to the first person who would take him, the undertaker, Mr. Sowerberry. Thus, we see that Oliver's journey begins in the underworld with the dead. When he comes into conflict with the other apprentice, Oliver runs away to London, where he finds himself part of a different kind of underworld—that of Fagin and his gang of thieves and criminals. Oliver's adventures take him from one misfortune to the next, but ultimately they lead him to his destiny—a reunion with his true family.

Beauty and Nazneen face a similar underworld journey upon first being exiled due to expressing their heart's desire, though Nazneen's is short-lived. Beauty must go to live with the terrifying monster, and Nazneen must wander alone and friendless. The motif underscores the psychological reality that our desires will initiate us and that the first step of any initiation requires a leave-taking of the familiar and a katabasis, or journey to the underworld.

TRANSGRESSION

Seeking our heart's desire is always transgressive. To do so, we must defy conventional dictates, disappoint parents' wishes, and contend with the inner and outer voices that insist that we stay put and meet the demands and expectations that others have placed on us. Seeking our heart's desire often feels selfish for many women.

Although Nazneen finds her heart's desire with relative ease by fairy tale standards, he is tragically taken from her. The sister who shuts the box is symbolic of a limited or overly concrete way of seeing the world—that part of us that thinks our dreams might be too big and impractical and should therefore be boxed up. Such attitudes can cause us to doubt and betray ourselves as we quest after our desires. Significantly, the remedy involves the oil from the hair of a demon. Healing our relationship with our deepest desires will require a little demonic Lilith energy.

Nazneen has a mysterious knowledge of this prince; she knows he is for her. The prince can be understood not as an actual outer relationship but as an inner energy that exemplifies higher aspirations. Thus, the marriage with the prince is a kind of inner wedding, a claiming of oneself. She displays a positive attitude toward this inward quest by her treatment of the miraculous boxes. First, she is not dismayed that she receives boxes in place of the pearl that she requested. Then, she takes her time to open the third box. She wants to enjoy the first two for a while. The unconscious rarely delivers its gifts in packages that we would expect. Nazneen's openness shows she is willing to receive the gifts the unconscious offers.

Many times, we may go out into the world in search of our heart's desire with some clear picture of what we want. That image draws us forward just as the vision of the Grail inspired King Arthur's knights to pursue their quest. We imagine the kind of person we want to marry, the kind of house we long to live in, or the kind of career we believe would make us happy. Having such a goal is a powerful inducement toward life, yet we rarely have our wishes fulfilled precisely in the way we pictured them. Retrieving the glowing coals from the ashes will require that we accept the gift being offered, even if it initially disappoints or seems other than what our ego had planned.

An odd detail introduced later in the story is that Nazneen knows bird language. When and how did she learn this? I suspect that this ability relates to her mysterious knowing about the Pink Pearl Prince. Knowing bird language is akin to being able to attend to the subtle promptings of our intuition. When we know bird language, we allow ourselves to know things we didn't even know that we knew.

FORGOTTEN DESIRE

Carol was a woman in my practice who was a gifted artist. Carol grew up as her mother's confidante. Even when Carol was a child, her mother would frequently complain bitterly about her unhappiness in her marriage. In addition, Carol's younger brother had a chronic health condition that took much of her parents' attention. Once when her parents were at the hospital for several days with her brother, seven-year-old Carol was left with a younger aunt whose boyfriend molested Carol. She remembers not wanting to say anything because she worried that her parents had enough on their minds. Thus, Carol learned several things early on—stay small, don't draw too much attention to yourself, and take care of others. As she grew older, Carol spent hours sketching in a notebook. She filled page after page with images that arose from her rich fantasy life. However, she never took her drawing beyond the private pages of her sketchbook.

Carol resisted formal art training, preferring that her drawing be part of her inner world. After graduating, she got married and had three children. Carol's marriage was, in many ways, a continuation of the survival strategy she had developed. The unconscious bargain that the couple struck was that he would manage the money and other practical matters, and Carol would care for the children. This arrangement allowed Carol to stay small and protected, but it also left her in a childlike position. Carol continued to draw and sometimes took the odd painting class, but her art remained an unanswered question in her life.

Then she had a remarkable dream that shook her to her core and whose effects rippled through her life and changed it forever. She told me this dream several years after she had it when she first entered treatment with me.

I'm in my old high school in a classroom on the
top floor. The sun is setting, and it is the last class
of the day. It's also the last class of the semester, the
final review. This is the final lesson that will pull
it all together. My teacher is a bright, passionate,
younger woman whom I admire immensely, and
the subject is one I am deeply interested in. She is
speaking in front of the class. My classmates are all
crowded around her, vying for a closer position and
her attention, calling out. I'm sitting at the farthest
table away in the back left corner. I'm watching my
classmates and despairing that I can't be like them.
From here, I can't hear what my teacher is saying.
I'm straining my eyes, but I can't see the board.

Suddenly, I see Peter across the table from me, a
boy I knew in grade school. He's a young man now
with a beautiful smile and bright dark eyes. He
moves his notes toward me so that I can see them.
The "notes" are a drawing of concentric circles with
geometric and natural patterns. When I see it, a
wave of understanding washes over me. This IS the
lesson. I copy the drawing, but when I look at mine,
it is a circle with a hawk flying toward the left. In
the hawk's eye, I see countless other birds, all flying
left, each with a red ribbon in its talon. Then class
ends, and I stand up to leave. I'm grateful to Peter.
I thank him but feel embarrassed and awkward.

Out the door, my classmates all turn to the right
and head down the stairs. I turn left and walk down
the long hall. It leads to stairs, down into darkness
and more halls. The school is darker and emptier as
I go. I always go down and to the left until I can't go
farther. This is the far wing of my grade school. A set
of glass doors leads outside. It is a dark night, and I

don't know what to do. I'm paralyzed with anxiety and fear. Suddenly I realize that Peter is coming along behind me. I don't want him to see me. I feel so ashamed and back quietly into the shadows.

Peter passes me. He is a tall man now. He's at the door and about to leave and hasn't seen me. I feel relief! That was a close call. But as he puts his hand on the glass doors, he turns around, and our eyes meet. He does know I'm here. I'm shaking, feeling so small. But his smile is warm and kind, and he offers me his hand. I step toward him and take it.

As we cross the threshold out into the night, something floods through me. There is a connection between our hands like an open conduit. Across it, all the shame and fear I'm holding, all its roots, all my history, everything about me, flows into him. He sees it and witnesses it all. I can feel him considering it openly, lovingly, knowingly, and without judgment. It turns a circle between us and when it returns to me everything has changed. Longstanding painful inner things come back in a new light. They realign and find their right places. Nothing has changed but everything, everything is different.

Carol woke from the dream with a feeling of profound love. She remembers feeling crushed that she had to come back to waking reality. The dream highlighted how full of shame and fear she had been and how she had spent her life in hiding as a result. For Carol, the dream experience of being seen and accepted by Peter was profoundly healing. Over the next few years, she thought about the dream all the time. "It was an island where I could go to get a tiny piece of that feeling of healing and acceptance—and the sense that there was something bigger and divine."

During this time, she was raising her children and working at a small home business making hand-printed gift cards that she sold online. She bought herself some inexpensive pens and a little sketch-book. She found herself tracing circles on the pages using cereal bowls and making delicate, colorful mandalas that she described as "self-therapy." Carol had no idea that, at a time of significant psychic turmoil, Jung drew intricate circular patterns—mandalas—which he understood as an expression of his soul's yearning to return to its center. Though she spent time drawing every day, she didn't think of herself as an artist. She shared her work with no one.

Two years after she had the dream, she was back in her hometown visiting her parents on the Fourth of July and unexpectedly glimpsed Peter, the boy from the dream.

"I remember everything about that day. I hadn't seen Peter since we were thirteen. I had no idea where he was or what he was doing. I saw him, but he didn't see me. I panicked. I needed to get away. I was watching the fireworks over the harbor, but all I could think about was getting out."

The following day, she woke up and picked out ratty, oversized clothes that she felt would hide her well. Later, she took her children to a café—and Peter walked in. While she was figuring out how to slip away, he approached her and said hello. Carol remembers that she fell into a kind of altered state. She found it difficult to speak and answer his questions about what she had been doing and why she was back in town. "It was as if I had been dropped into a dry well," she recalls.

As they talked, he told her he was working as an artist and invited her to visit his studio, which was a few blocks away. Carol had had no contact with him since middle school and had no idea that he had pursued a career in art. That afternoon, Carol and her family visited Peter's art studio in an old Tudor-style building in the center of town. Peter and his wife showed Carol the paintings, drawings, and sculptures that he was working on or had recently completed. At one point, the group was seated around a table covered with drawing after drawing of mandalas—layer upon layer of intricately patterned circles that looked just like the images in the dream. Carol was stunned. Carol felt awkward and awful when her husband boasted that she was also an artist. She remembered that Peter had been cute, athletic, and popular in middle school—all the things she wanted and could never be. Now, he was working as an artist in a beautiful studio with a significant catalog of work.

Carol floated through the day as if she were in a dream. "I felt as though I had dropped down so deep that I couldn't come back up and talk to other people. It was as if all this water came into the well and knocked down the stuff I had built inside me. This inner wall got washed away. Once it had tumbled down, there was a new openness."

On the car ride home, Carol struggled. The dream had been so important, and now she had reconnected with the actual person, and here he was doing the exact thing that she thought she could never do, even though she remembered being better at art than he was in middle school. She was having urgent, burning feelings of jealousy. Peter had devoted himself to art, while Carol had let her interest in art languish in the penumbra. She felt pangs of wild regret. If Peter could do it, couldn't she? "I had come in contact with a vision of what I most wanted, and it was so different from what I was doing. And I finally just blurted aloud in the car to no one, 'You can't stop me!' I had this incredibly intense reaction, and it was full of life. I realized I hadn't been living."

Six months later, she felt more alive. Inside, there was a flow of energy that had never been there before. She remembers singing and dancing in the kitchen, and she started drawing voraciously. "I was so happy. I felt so free. I remember standing at the sink washing the dishes; everything was so beautiful. It was like being in love. I was so happy to be here. And everyone noticed it."

Reconnecting with Peter catalyzed the healing potential of the dream. Carol found that she wasn't holding back in social interactions. Her allergies and migraines cleared up. And she started painting.

"I can do this!" she found herself thinking. Carol committed herself to art. She began an intensive study of drawing and painting. She joined a local artists' cooperative and began showing and selling her art.

As with Nazneen, Carol faced setbacks and difficulties. Her husband was supportive, but he sometimes felt threatened by her new passions and the changes in her personality. Like Nazneen, Carol had to give up aspects of her former life. Her relationships with friends shifted, and she had less time to spend with her children now that she was getting busy elsewhere. At times, these changes filled her with sadness and guilt, and she wondered if she was doing the right thing. She had to integrate some fiery, assertive energy to declare her commitment to her heart's desire against these important, competing claims.

As Carol committed further to her art, she continued to feel challenged by what was being asked of her as she pursued her heart's desire. At times, she was full of doubt and couldn't see the way forward. During one such period, she had the following dream:

> I'm in a sunny place. There is a circle of people. I am
> standing slightly to the side. A man has a fishbowl full
> of thousands of small, folded slips of paper. He puts
> his hand in to pull one out, and I know immediately
> that it will be mine. He pulls out a paper and reads the
> number 4D. It is my number. I step forward. Another
> man has a clear container filled with mud and sludge.
> He is pouring it into my hands. A large golden ring
> falls into my cupped hands among the mud.

The dream is a clear statement of an encounter with her destiny. She recalled that she was very anxious in this dream. She did not know what would happen when her number got called or what the mud contained. When we claim our heart's desire, we will be asked to face the unknown. Doing so will require courage.

When she was young, Carol's destiny to become an artist had been split off and exiled to the dark forest of the inner landscape. While Carol was busy getting into the outer world, her unlived life waited quietly. It didn't allow her desire to die. When the time was right, it placed that desire before her in the form of the remarkable dream and the synchronicities that followed.

THE POWER OF DAYDREAMS

It is a tremendous gift to have a deep knowing of our heart's desire. Though we may suffer because of unfulfilled longing, an awareness of desire drives and guides us, often providing us with an important ordering and structuring principle. We know our priorities and may have an easier time making big life decisions as a result. Pursuing our heart's desire can feel like a quest, which is often exciting and filled with purpose even when it is fraught.

Many people who come into therapy lack a clear awareness of their heart's desire. Coming to know what we deeply want may be in part a matter of temperament. Some of us were simply born with strong drives toward self-actualization. Others of us may feel content to drift along. Both of these temperaments come with advantages and disadvantages. One is not better or more right than the other.

However, some of us may have a niggling sense that there is something we're meant to be doing but we don't know quite what it is. Such an experience can be accompanied by feelings of ennui, emptiness, or chronic disappointment with life. Knowing our deepest desires requires an ability to listen to ourselves. Some of us were never asked what we wanted when we were children. If our parents needed us to be a certain way or want certain things, our ability to attune to the desires that well up from deep within may not have had a chance to develop.

People who have a hard time knowing what they deeply want are often subtly dismissive of their inner promptings, though they are usually not aware that they are doing this. If you are yearning to get in touch with your deep desires, notice what appeals to you, even if it seems silly or you don't see how it could be important. What has energy for you? In what direction do your thoughts drift when you have nothing on your mind?

We met Katherine in an earlier chapter when she dreamed of the transforming crocodile. Katherine grew up in a family in which there wasn't a lot to go around. By the time she was sixteen, she was earning money to pay for her own clothes so that she would be less of a burden to her parents. When she graduated from college, she got a job close to home and helped support her parents instead of pursuing a graduate degree overseas. When she came to me at thirty-nine, Katherine had been in a career that paid well, but that she had never really chosen. Because she had always been focused on survival concerns, she had never been able to take time to imagine what she might like. She felt that she was meant to do something else but didn't know what that would be. She was feeling some despair that the time was passing and that she would never have the chance to discover that which she came into the world to realize.

Katherine had never been encouraged to give free rein to her imagination about what she might want to do or become. If our lives are overly constrained by hardship or trauma, we may have a difficult time feeling as though we have permission to get in touch with our deep desires. Children need their parents to have rich and wild imaginations for them. Such imaginations get unconsciously passed along as permission to dream big. Financial hardship can curtail such imaginations, but it doesn't always; likewise, wealth and ease do not guarantee them.

Katherine and I spent time together pondering what shape her future might want to take, but our progress was slow. Then, one day, she mentioned that she had noticed herself daydreaming and was concerned that she was using these fantasies as a way to escape from her daily life. When I inquired about the content of these daydreams, Katherine was forthcoming. "I see myself getting a PhD in a foreign city, like Madrid or Brussels," Katherine told me. "I imagine that I am doing important research and writing in a field like political science. I'm working with brilliant colleagues, and we are making a difference!" In these fantasies, instead of using her professional skills to help other people work through their problems, she was pursuing answers to her own fascinating questions. Her daydreams were also filled with color-ful details about her life in this new city.

Katherine had been dismissing these daydreams as irrelevant or self-indulgent. She was worried that they were distracting her from her real life, but I disagreed. The fantasies were providing us with rich information about what she would find genuinely exciting. Daydreams usually feature those things that we are lacking in our "real" life. They tend to show us what is missing. If our days are full of adventure and busyness, we might daydream about curling up in front of a fire with a book. Katherine's daydreams of studying in a foreign city didn't mean that she needed to leave her children and enroll in a PhD program in Dublin. They did suggest, however, that she needed more of something in her life—more exploration, more learning, and more engagement with deep questions of her own choosing. Our discussion about her daydreams led us to ask whether graduate school might be in the cards for her. It wasn't an option she had let herself seriously consider before because it didn't seem practical. Now, it was at least under conscious consideration—and Katherine found herself genuinely excited by the idea.

A part of Katherine had had a pretty good idea as to what she wanted, but she hadn't let herself know that she knew because that thing felt impractical or off limits. Like Nazneen, a part of her had per-haps always known what she truly wanted but this part had become split off. It was as if her true desire had been simply buried some time ago. The same week that Katherine told me about her daydreams, she related the following dream.

> There is something wrong with my house—maybe
> an electrical issue. A man comes to help me. Maybe
> he is an electrician. We are walking around outside
> the house and there are several construction vehicles
> there, entirely blocking my street. The workers are all
> women and they have dug up the sidewalk in front
> of my house. I look into the trench that they are

digging. I see pipes and some standing water. They explain that there is a woman who has been missing and they are looking for her. One of them tells me that I might think that the issue with the house is a big deal, but that the real issue is here. I think to myself that the woman must be dead if she has been buried underground, but they tell me that they heard her so it's clear she is alive. I offer to help them look for her. They tell me I should first see a picture so that I will know what she looks like. To see the picture, I will need to go see my friend Gary. I find him, but he explains that he doesn't, in fact, have the photo. I will need to go somewhere else to find it. I wake before seeing the photo, but I somehow know that when I see it, it will be a picture of me.

Katherine's deep desires have been buried, but they aren't dead yet! Even better, there is a team of hard-working women determined to uncover her, and Katherine herself is willing to help. Katherine shared that Gary was an acquaintance who had an intellectual and philosophical side, but who was trapped working as a lawyer to pay the bills and support his family. He had tried various compromises, including working as an attorney for a nonprofit, but he was still largely dissatisfied. Dream Gary couldn't help her. The dream was encouraging her to have a much more expansive imagination about her future beyond making small compromises that felt practical.

JEALOUSY AND SHAME

Carol's destiny expressed itself to her as bitter jealousy at first. When we have been split off from dreams and desires, jealousy often reintroduces them to us. We may have a dream that features someone who appears to have everything we want while we feel forlorn and utterly alienated. Or, like Carol, someone in the outer world carries these desires for us, and our jealousy of that person introduces us to ourselves. The emotions can be acutely painful. We feel we have had a glimpse of our heart's desire, but we can't imagine ever reaching it. Such an intense experience of jealousy can be helpful to us. It shines a bright light on what we most want in the world. If you ever have trouble finding your heart's desire, you must ask yourself, "of whom am I most jealous?"

When we investigate what stands between us and claiming our heart's desire, the answer is often shame. We are ashamed to admit what we long for because it seems too audacious of us to want it. My interview for a Jungian training program represented the culmination of years of effort in pursuing my heart's desire. I had received a master's degree, studied in a Jung seminar, completed years of analysis, and passed a preliminary interview. Like my metaphorical journey, my travel to the site of the final interview had been long and arduous. I arrived late in the evening at the Denver airport, and from there, I traveled to Boulder, Colorado, where the training organization was holding its semi-annual conference. It was close to midnight when the shuttle finally dropped me off at the hotel. When I entered the lobby and saw signs for the Jungian conference, I was overwhelmed by a crippling wave of shame. What was I doing here? Who was I to think I could belong? If I could have turned around and walked out at that moment, I might have done so.

FEELING LIKE AN IMPOSTER

In 1978, psychologists Pauline Clance and Suzanne Imes published a paper entitled "The Imposter Phenomenon in High Achieving Women." Since that time, their observation that bright, competent women often feel as if they are frauds has entered mainstream culture, where it has become known as "imposter syndrome." Although men can suffer from feeling like an imposter as well, the phenomenon is associated mainly with women—especially successful and talented women. The eminent author Maya Angelou once remarked, "I have written eleven books, but each time I think, Uh-oh, they're going to find out now. I've run a game on everybody, and they're going to find me out."[6]

Imposter feelings can get in the way of our taking our desires seriously. You might wonder, as I did, whether it isn't laughably impertinent of you even to imagine aspiring to some of your ambitions. If you find that imposter syndrome stops you from taking steps toward your heart's desire, it can be helpful to label it for what it is. Naming these painful feelings of fraudulence as imposter syndrome can leach some of their energy away because we know that they don't necessarily reflect reality. Instead of listening to the chiding remonstrances of imposter syndrome, we can recall our accomplishments and talents. Remembering that only capable, gifted people tend to experience imposter syndrome can also tame these sabotaging feelings.

Imposter syndrome is really just an experience of shame—the shame and vulnerability we feel when we have allowed ourselves to be big. Brené Brown describes the wretchedness we feel after showing ourselves fully as a "vulnerability hangover."[7] Shame often divorces us from our longings. Nothing leaves us feeling quite so vulnerable and exposed as our naked desire. To admit what we most yearn for is to reveal our soul. We fear our inadequacy and unworthiness will be on display for all to see, and this fear can cause us to turn away from what we most desperately want. So we deny our desires, sometimes even hiding them from ourselves. It helps to remember Lilith's steadfast self-confidence. You are equal to anyone, she reminds us, for you are made of the same clay. Her voice can help us to embrace our deepest yearnings. It can help rekindle our vital spark.

QUESTIONS FOR REFLECTION

1. In "The Pink Pearl Prince," Nazneen makes a highly specific request of her father. She seems to know that the pink pearl is her destiny, without even fully understanding what it is. Many people can relate to knowing early in life that there was something they

yearned for, even though they couldn't know why or perhaps even put words to it. Perhaps they had an early intimation of something that needed to come through them. When in your life have you felt an ineluctable yearning for something? What did it feel like? How did you respond?

2. Nazneen's sisters seek material riches, but Nazneen's desire connects her with something beyond mere wealth. When we aren't in touch with our desires, we can tend to fill up any emptiness we feel with food, shopping, alcohol, smartphone use, or other things that numb us. Where in your life have you made use of addictions and compulsions instead of listening for your heart's desire? How are you doing that in your life currently?

3. Nazneen's father's boat cannot sail because he has not kept his promise. When we don't keep our promises to ourselves, life's winds will not fill our sails. How have you failed to keep your promises to yourself?

4. Nazneen is thrown out of the house when her father returns. Questing after our heart's desire can make others feel uncomfortable, as it may challenge their choices. How have you been received when you have followed your desires?

5. Nazneen's present consists of three boxes. This is likely not what she was expecting, and yet she receives the gifts graciously. Sometimes, we are longing for something in particular, but life offers us a different gift. Where have you received your heart's desire in an unexpected form? How long did it take you to recognize the gift that life was offering? What did you do to accept it and make room for it?

6. Nazneen is able to save the prince because she knows bird language. This is something akin to being attuned to our intuition and helps

explain why she knew to ask for the pink pearl at the beginning of the story. How do you make room to listen to your intuition? Perhaps you can write down your dreams or write in a journal. When has your intuition guided you toward a solution that your conscious mind would not have found?

CHAPTER 6

Sexuality: Loving Yourself

This is your body, your greatest gift, pregnant
with wisdom you do not hear, grief you thought
was forgotten, and joy you have never known.

—Marion Woodman, *Coming Home to Myself*

Many women have experienced a profound wound to their
sexual selves. Women's bodies are often on display for the
benefit and pleasure of men. As women, we may feel constantly judged.
Are we pretty enough? Thin enough? How do our bodies measure up?
Do men find us attractive? For many of us, a healthy appreciation of
our bodies and their ability to experience pleasure becomes blocked
by crippling insecurity. Women often tune in to the needs and wants
of their partners so much that their own more subtle desires can easily
get ignored. Listening to the cues from our bodies about what is pleasurable can become one of those things that remains undeveloped in
a woman's life. It waits to be discovered, integrated, and owned in a
conscious relationship with ourselves.

For many women, the focus of sex is on being attractive and
pleasing to their partner. Some of this is due to simple differences
between male and female sexual responses. Male sexual pleasure is
relatively straightforward, while a woman's response to sexual stimu-
lation and arousal is much more individual and mysterious. It often
takes women decades to know their bodies and enjoy sexuality on

their terms. As a result, we tend to focus on meeting the immediate demands of our partner's sexual fulfillment. Taking the time and space to explore what we would like may not rise to the level of priority.

Lilith demanded mutuality in her sexual relations. She wasn't willing to be subdued and lie under her husband. She asserted that her right to pleasure in sexual encounters ought to be just as important as her husband's. She was unabashed in her pleasure-seeking.

WAKING UP TO PLEASURE

The welling up of sexual desire is one of the purest, most embodied expressions of our vital spark. It is eros, or the universal principle of connection manifesting itself primally through our physical being. Sexual urges express our longing to be in the world, in our bodies, and in deep communion with one another. They are an incarnation of our deep love affair with life itself. Sexuality is profoundly personal. What excites us is often wild and weird and can vary greatly from what we see on television, in the movies, or in pornography. Our sexual fantasies are our own, for us to keep private or share as we choose. They are our own secret language of sensual, embodied delight.

Coming to appreciate her body and beauty for herself and not because it is pleasing to a man may require a woman to reconnect with previously cut-off outlaw energies. This was the case for my client Emily, a woman I worked with for many years. Emily was a college philosophy professor of some eminence and accomplishment. She had been married to her husband for almost thirty years, and the couple had two grown children. During our work together, sex had rarely been a topic of discussion—until one day. Emily took her customary place opposite me on my couch, but her usual smile and greeting were absent that week. "Something has happened," she announced. She was perturbed.

Emily began describing her relationship with a young student. Lilian had transferred to the university where Emily taught after an eating disorder caused her to take several semesters off from college.

Emily recalled that she noticed Lilian immediately. "She was sitting at the back of the seminar room. I remember thinking that I had never seen her before. There was something about her gaze. She looked so serious and sad but also somehow more *alive*, more *there* than any of the other students in the class."

Lilian's intensity and searing intelligence immediately struck Emily. Lilian began coming to every office hours session, and Emily soon found that she looked forward to seeing her. According to Emily, Lilian's plight as a new student struggling with mental health issues captured her. "I remember thinking that it's no wonder she wasn't making friends easily. The other students aren't on her level. She has one of the keenest minds I've ever seen." Emily confessed to me that she was aware at some level that Lilian was becoming dependent on her and that their connection was emotionally exceeding the bounds of a normal student/professor relationship, but she was too invested to pull away.

Lilian began to confide in Emily about personal things. She shared that her anorexia had become acute when her girlfriend broke up with her. The relationship had been Lilian's first love, and its ending plunged her into despair. A period of intense loneliness and suffering began. Emily found herself compelled by the younger woman's story.

Emily shared with me that she had always had scrupulous boundaries at work. She was an engaged and caring professor but never became overly involved in a student's life. With Lilian, those boundaries became shaky. When Lilian was especially distraught one day, Emily gave the younger woman her personal cell phone number. The two began a lively habit of texting daily. When Lilian asked for a meeting to discuss her final paper and Emily couldn't fit her in during her usual office hours, she offered to meet Lilian for lunch.

"Some part of me knew I had let things get too far," she told me. "But I could also see that our connection was helping her. She was growing more confident and comfortable. She started making friends and even joined a club." As much as their friendship may have been helping Lilian, it was also doing something for Emily. She admitted that she had never felt something like this before. "I think about her all the time," she told me. "I just feel deeply alive because she is in my life."

It had become customary for the pair to meet alone weekly during Emily's office hours, which were scheduled late in the day when the department was mostly empty. The two would sit in big leather-backed chairs while the setting sun shone into Emily's office. Lilian would talk, and Emily would mostly listen and reflect. One such afternoon, Lilian confessed that she was in love with Emily and was physically attracted to her.

Emily told me that Lilian's confession had touched her and that she recognized that her feelings for Lilian were something of a similar nature. But she had gently explained to Lilian that, although she was extremely fond of her, any relationship between them would be impossible for many reasons. She also told Lilian honestly that she was no longer a sexual person. Emily had gone through menopause some years before. As far as she knew, that had brought about the end of her interest in sex. However, when Lilian left after this tender exchange, Emily was astonished to realize that she had become quite sexually aroused.

"Nothing like that had ever happened to me before. Never." She recalled that in all her years dating men, having sex with men, and being married to a man, she had never felt spontaneous physical arousal to this degree. She was shocked by her body's capacity for awakening when, for several years, she had been without any sexual feelings at all. She confessed that there had been little intimacy with her husband— sexual or emotional—for many years. "I don't think I realized it before," she said, "but I think I've been very lonely in my marriage."

After the confession, her feelings for Lilian intensified, and boundaries continued to crumble. She noticed, to her great shock, that she became sexually aroused whenever she was in Lilian's presence. She brought her confusion about this into our sessions. Feeling juicy and alive again was wonderful, but what did it mean? Was she a lesbian? Had she been one all along? Should she leave her husband and be with Lilian? Our work created a space where she could wonder about these things and explore possibilities in her imagination without acting on them.

Her love for Lilian was profound and sincere, if somewhat inexplicable. There were times when she was so swept away by her deep love and desire for Lilian that she thought of overturning everything in her life to be with her young student. However, when she was a bit more clear-eyed, she could see that acting on these feelings would not be wise. It would mean losing her career for which she had worked very hard. It would mean losing her marriage and risking her relationship with her adult children. And she knew the affair would not survive in the harsh light of everyday reality where trash must be taken out and bills must be paid. It would be a betrayal of what Emily saw as her sacred duty to teach and mentor. Above all, it would be a betrayal of Lilian. Even though Emily had not crossed any physical boundaries, her violations of the student/professor limits had been damaging. Emily was aware that the experience had been confusing and destabilizing for Lilian, and she felt profound regret that she had caused her young student more suffering. She knew that any further transgressions would significantly wound Lilian.

Emily eventually managed to steer the relationship with Lilian into a blossoming mentorship and friendship without the heated romantic and erotic components. But she was left wondering what the experience meant. For Emily, her love for Lilian was a profound awakening to her own attractiveness and sensuality. She had never thought of herself as pretty. Seeing herself through Lilian's eyes had given her the gift of feeling beautiful. To be attractive to Lilian felt utterly different from being attractive to anyone else. "If a man expressed interest in me, it always made me more insecure and nervous because I expected that he would eventually find me inadequate. With Lilian, that fear of inadequacy doesn't get provoked in that way. We are confident and comfortable in our mutual attraction in the fantasies I have of us being together."

For Emily, the shared love and attraction with Lilian helped heal a profound wound to her sexual self—a wound she hadn't even known existed. "I didn't know it could feel like this to be attracted to a person or to have a person be attracted to me." Though she had rarely discussed sex in her previous treatment with me, she now shared that she had always found sex rough and impersonal. All that changed with her attraction to Lilian. Emily told me that fantasies involving her younger student were tender and gentle. "In my imagination, sex with Lilian is beautiful," she told me. "Sex has never seemed beautiful before."

Emily experienced sexuality with men as tinted by shame and inadequacy. Her newfound ability for pleasure and passion, discovered just as the sun of her sexuality was setting, allowed her to find a very different way of being sexual. A dream she had around this time underscored this.

> I'm in a house with many rooms. Lilian is spending
> the night. I bring her into my bed, and we have sex
> right there. She pleasures me until I have an orgasm,
> and then we are in each other's arms. It feels good to
> be tangled up with her. Then she leaves, and I get up
> to go with her. I touch her arm and ask her if she is
> okay. She answers that she is very happy. She takes my
> face in her hands, looks me in the eye, and tells me
> that it was beautiful, meaning giving me an orgasm
> was beautiful. This feels good to hear and like an
> antidote to deep shame. We embrace and it feels so
> good to hug her.

Emily shared with me her experience—that no matter how much a sexual encounter with a man might begin as a mutual exercise in enjoyment and pleasure, it always ended up being about the imperative of his orgasm. Like many women, Emily didn't orgasm through penetrative sex. When her husband attempted to give her an orgasm, it often took a long time, and she felt tense and pressured, so she often stopped him from even trying. Therefore, her sex life had always been somewhat unfulfilling. Through the luxuriant fantasies she had of Lilian and the genuine love they shared for each other, Emily was discovering for the first time her ability to experience her sexual feel-ings on her own terms.

VIRGINITY

In many stories and traditions, virginity has long been a symbol of unbroken psychic wholeness. Though the common definition of the word refers to someone who has not had intercourse, we can understand the concept symbolically to be much richer. Psychologically, a virgin belongs to herself. Jungian analyst M. Esther Harding was a prominent articulator of women's psychological experience and wrote eloquently on the symbolic meaning of virginity.

> In the same way the woman who is a virgin, one-in-herself, does what she does—not because of any desire to please, not to be liked, or to be approved, even by herself; not because of any desire to gain power over another, to catch his interest or love, but because what she does is true. Her actions may, indeed, be unconventional. She may have to say no, when it would be easier, as well as more adapted, conventionally speaking, to say yes. But as virgin she is not influenced by the considerations that make the nonvirgin woman, whether married or not, trim her sails and adapt herself to expediency. I say whether married or not, for in using this term *virgin* in its psychological connotation, it refers not to external circumstances but to an inner attitude.[1]

Zeus's long-suffering wife, Hera, usually appears in Greek mythology as the jealous goddess seeking to punish her husband's many paramours. But one story about her tells of her visit to the magical spring at Argos known as Kanathos. By bathing in this spring, she restores her virginity, her original sense of belonging to herself. Mythologist Christine Downing relates Hera's renewal to the experience of "late-blooming lesbians," who finally come to belong to themselves sexually, perhaps after decades of being with a man.[2]

When I shared this myth with Emily, it resonated deeply with her. Her love and attraction for Lilian had been a renewing font that restored a long-forgotten sense of wholeness and sole jurisdiction over her body and her desires.

Emily spent many months lightly holding the question of her sexual orientation. She and I discussed that it wasn't uncommon for middle-aged women to suddenly discover an attraction to other women and "switch teams." Was this her story? But in the end, Emily's attraction wasn't about sexual orientation. Emily recognized that this remarkable glimpse of sexual verdant springtime amid an otherwise mellow autumn seemed confined to her special connection with Lilian. She came to see it as an exquisite gift that allowed her to become more intimate and loving with her body and her sense of pleasure and desire. "It has taken me until now," she said. "But I have finally fallen in love with my body." This discovery was full of sweetness, but there was some bitterness too. She had never known in waking life the delicious reciprocity she experienced in her fantasies and dreams of being with Lilian.

Eventually, Emily reflected that she had always felt disappointed by her husband's selfishness during their intimate encounters. As time passed and Emily's feelings for Lilian mellowed, she could see too that Lilian had, of course, been selfish in her way as well. Sexual intimacy can bring up powerful fantasies of being tenderly cared for, of having all our needs met by our partner. But it may be that the deepest, most satisfying love we will find will be that which we can give to ourselves. Emily had been unconsciously waiting for her husband to give her something, and when he didn't do it, she looked for that need to be met in her relationship with Lilian. But she was never going to find what she was looking for in either of those places.

When the heat of her feelings for Lilian had cooled, she once again found that her aging body no longer became aroused or desired the release of orgasm. Emily didn't miss sex or sexual desire. But she did still yearn for the juicy flow of eros. And she found it in some surprising places. Emily had always been a practical, no-nonsense type of person who hadn't invested much in grooming or self-care, but now she began to change how she treated her body. When she needed new sheets, she spent a little extra money and bought some that were especially soft. She indulged in some fragrant body lotion and enjoyed smoothing it on her skin after a shower. She started to take weekly baths, and found she liked to drink aromatic tea throughout the day instead of her standard decaf coffee. Her newfound enjoyment of simple sensual pleasures surprised her. "Who would have thought that these things would matter to a dried-up crone like me?" she laughed. But they did.

If you find that you feel a longing for more embodied aliveness, it might help to remember that there are many ways this can manifest in a woman's life. A luscious experience of sexual pleasure—either with a partner or by ourselves—is one obvious way, but cherishing our bodies and treating them reverently in a manner that rewards all the senses is another. Try stopping throughout the day and asking yourself, *What does my body want? What would feel good to it right now?* We spend so much time numbing ourselves to our bodies' needs through overworking, overeating, or overusing technology, alcohol, or drugs that we may have lost touch with the vibrant animal alive in our form.

For Emily, sex between a man and a woman had an inescapable element of conquest and surrender, whereas sex between two women seemed to offer an experience of profound mutuality. Such deep communion is part of what we yearn for in sexual experiences. It is what Lilith sought from Adam when she asserted her equality. While it is available to us in heterosexual relationships as well, women may have to learn to demand it. The story of the loathly lady dates to the Middle Ages and offers a surprising answer to our craving for mutuality.

THE WEDDING OF SIR GAWAIN AND DAME RAGNELL

King Arthur was out hunting with his men in the forest when a marvelous hart happened by. The king alone followed him, stalking his quarry stealthily until he was far from where he left his men. Skillfully, he raised his bow and hit the hart squarely. Then was Arthur able to slay his quarry. But at that moment, a well-armed knight approached him.

"King Arthur, I am glad to find you here alone and unarmed! You have done me wrong, giving away lands that rightfully belonged to me, and now I will kill you!"

This knight's name was Gromer Somer Joure. Arthur reasoned with him; it would be dishonorable for the knight to kill him then and there. Gromer Somer reluctantly agreed to let Arthur go on the condition that he return in twelve months, alone and unarmed as he was now. In that meeting, Arthur would need to tell Gromer Somer what women desire most. He would forfeit his life if he could not correctly answer that question.

Once back at court, Arthur was despondent, for he knew that he had only postponed certain death. Sir Gawain noticed the king's preoccupation and begged him to unburden himself. Arthur, therefore, related the whole story to Gawain, who immediately announced his intention to help the king discover the answer to this mysterious riddle.

"We'll leave in the morning," Gawain told Arthur. "I will ride in one direction, and you ride in the other. We'll ask every man and woman we meet to tell us the answer to this question. Surely, we'll come on the right answer within the year."

And so they carried out this plan, asking every man and woman they met what women most desire. Some said that women love to be well-dressed. Others said that they love to be courted. Some said they love a lusty man who will embrace and kiss them. Finally, after eleven months had passed, Arthur and Gawain met back at court. They both had a large book full of answers but were no closer to solving the riddle—and the year was almost up.

Arthur decided to ride into the forest and look for answers one last time. While he was riding alone, he met a hideously ugly woman. Her face was red, and her nose was running. Her mouth was wide and full of large, yellow teeth. Her watery eyes bulged out of her head like large balls. Her back was curved, her neck was thick, and her middle was as round as a barrel. The scant hair on her head was matted and greasy.

Yet she was seated upon a horse that was bedecked in finery. She rode up to Arthur and told him she alone could deliver him from death.

"What do you mean?" asked Arthur. "How could you be helpful to me?"

The ugly woman explained that she knew the answer to the riddle and would tell him if he could promise to wed her to Sir Gawain.

"What a cruel fate for Gawain to be married to you! I know he won't want to say no. But I've never seen such an ugly woman, and I don't know what to do."

"It doesn't matter that I'm ugly," the woman replied. "Even an owl finds a mate. Now go to Sir Gawain. Tell him that Dame Ragnell awaits his answer. This is your only chance."

"I cannot speak for Sir Gawain," Arthur said. "But I will tell him my predicament and leave the matter in his hands."

It was with a heavy heart that Arthur revealed his predicament to his most trusted friend and knight, Sir Gawain. As Arthur predicted, his friend willingly agreed to marry the ugly woman to save the king's life. And so Arthur rode back to the wood the next day and delivered the news that Dame Ragnell was to become the wife of the handsome and brave Sir Gawain.

"Now I will tell you the answer you seek," the ugly woman said.

"Some think women want to be beautiful or have lots of sex. Some think we want to be flattered and charmed. But they don't understand. What all women—rich and poor—desire is sovereignty. Now when you tell this to Sir Gromer, he will be furious, for he will have to let you go!"

It happened that not long after was the date that Arthur had promised to return to the place where he had first met Sit Gromer and to fulfill his promise. Sir Gromer was waiting for Arthur just as he said he would, and as Dame Ragnell predicted, Sir Gromer was enraged when the king produced the correct answer. But he kept his word and let Arthur go.

Then it was time for the wedding of Sir Gawain and Dame Ragnell. Arthur begged the loathly lady to allow the nuptials to take place quietly, with no witnesses, but she would have none of it.

"I will wed openly or not at all, for otherwise, I should be shamed," she said. And so she rode to court side by side with the king. The people were amazed to see her ugliness, and not a few shed a tear to think of kind, good Sir Gawain as her lifelong bedfellow. But Sir Gawain came forth willingly and took her hand.

And so Dame Ragnell arrived at the church in front of all the court dressed in great finery, but the beauty of her clothes only served to accentuate her extreme ugliness. And after she was married, everyone hurried to the nuptial feast. Dame Ragnell sat alone, eating great quantities of all the food. She was coarse and uncouth, cutting her meat with her long fingernails and allowing the juices to run down her chin.

Only when the meal was over and it was time for the newlyweds to retire to the bedchamber did Sir Gawain seem a bit downcast. He dragged his feet and was reluctant to go. When they were both undressed and in bed, Sir Gawain lay stiffly on his side of the bed.

"Why don't you show me a little courtesy on our wedding night, husband?" said Dame Ragnell. "Kiss me, at least."

"I will do more than that, my lady," replied Gawain, and when he turned to her, he saw that she was the most beautiful creature he had ever seen. Sir Gawain cried out and asked who she was, and she confirmed that she was his wife. He embraced her then, and as you might imagine, they made great joy.

"Sir," she said, "I am under a spell, and my beauty will not hold. You must choose whether I shall be beautiful by day and ugly by night, or beautiful by night and ugly by day."

"Ah!" exclaimed Gawain. "That is a hard choice. To have you beautiful by night only would make me sad and ruin my reputation, but to have you beautiful by day would make the nighttime cold. Choose what you think is best, dear lady. I put the choice in your hands."

"Thank you, dear husband, for by giving me the choice, you have broken the spell! I shall now be beautiful both day and night!" Then they rejoiced indeed.

The following day, Sir Gawain and his bride were slow to rise as they enjoyed themselves greatly. Arthur's men began to worry. They were afraid the ugly woman might have done away with Sir Gawain and resolved to go and check on him. Imagine their surprise when they saw the good Sir Gawain and his beautiful wife lying happily in each other's arms! Dame Ragnell explained that her stepmother had cast a spell that deformed her, and that Gawain had delivered her by granting her sovereignty.

There is something comical yet poignant about the king and his best knight setting off on a journey to learn the answer to such a simple question. The two men take a remarkably ham-fisted approach to learning the mysteries of women's desires. They've turned it into an academic research project, complete with ponderous volumes of notes. That it takes such a monumental effort and should be so hard to discover says something about the unbridgeable distance between men and women, especially in the bedroom. A woman may feel that her lover has acquired ideas about female sexual desire and functioning that seem remote and theoretical, having nothing to do with her particular body or tendency for pleasure. Many women complain that men often persist in strange ideas about what women find pleasing even after being shown otherwise. Each of us has our own very personal experience of pleasure. What matters is sovereignty and the ability to know and decide for oneself.

SEEKING MUTUALITY

Whitney was a woman in my practice who was frequently disappointed in her sex life with her husband. "I am looking for intimacy to be a real encounter between us. I want to feel his presence and connectedness to me in that moment," she told me. As Whitney had explained to her husband, such an immediate and tender connection would be the starting point for playful exploration and mutual pleasure. Instead, she found his approach to sex to be mechanical and disconnected. No matter how often Whitney asked her husband for more romance and play, she felt sexual arousal for her husband was a bit like flipping a light switch. "He's just on. And when he's on, he thinks I'm naturally on too." Unfortunately, Whitney often found it easier to go along with her husband's desire for sex even when she hadn't had the lead-up she would need for the experience to feel mutual and pleasurable. "It's the end of the day. I'm tired. Sometimes, I just want it over with."

There is perhaps no part of life that is as fraught with disappointment as sex. In few other areas do we feel so vulnerable or nurse such tender hopes for mutuality and connection. Though there are couples who have positive, reciprocally enjoyable sex much of the time, I suspect that they may be a minority. Few couples are well-matched in terms of their level of desire. Even if they are in sync, levels of desire can change due to health concerns, stress, the birth of children, or other issues. It isn't uncommon for married couples to have little or no sex. One 2017 study found that 15.6% of married individuals hadn't had sex the previous year. In addition, 13.5% hadn't had sex for five years.[3]

Nature has played a cruel trick on us. While men find easy release with penetrative intercourse, a minority of women find it satisfying by itself. It is easy, therefore, for sex to focus on the man's needs and proceed at his pace. Men need to ensure this does not become the case, and women need to speak up for their needs. Men who take their cues about women's sexuality from porn or movies may not realize what it takes to pleasure a woman. They may need to tune in to their partner's subtle emotional and sensual needs. Research has found that among married women, sexual satisfaction seems to correlate significantly with overall feelings of connection and warmth in the relationship. Married women whose husbands focused on giving orgasms reported greater sexual satisfaction. Research has found that women in lesbian relationships have more orgasms than those in straight relationships, which seems to be because the partners take the time to pleasure each other.[4] For sex to be satisfying for women—and therefore for their partners—it needs to consider her desires and rhythms.

Sovereignty has two different shades of meaning. It can refer to power over someone else, or it can refer to autonomy, self-rule, and independence. When Gawain cedes the decision about her beauty to Dame Ragnell, he is gifting her sovereignty in the second sense of the word. The story turns on a decision, and it is a decision that at first appears to be Gawain's to make. Should she be beautiful at night for his pleasure in the bedroom? Or beautiful during the day to make him look good among others at court? What would be best for him? Too often, sex can feel like this for women. What's best for *his* ego or *his* pleasure?

Gawain reverses this tendency. He freely gives the decision over to Ragnell. What would *she* like, without needing to concern herself with his needs? This was the space that opened for Emily in her mutual attraction to her young student. In her fantasies of being with Lilian, Emily could feel an expansive sexual freedom to imagine her pleasure in a joyous and unpressured way.

What Lilian gave to Emily in fantasy was a delightful experience of sovereignty over her sexuality. Emily was wise enough to know that a real relationship with another person would inevitably be more complex than a fantasy. The gift was a changed relationship with herself and a connectedness with her body and her desire as her sexuality waned.

ARTEMIS

The image of the virgin has often symbolized the experience of being sovereign over one's pleasure and sexuality, and the Greek goddess Artemis carries this sense of womanly autonomy and independence.

Twin sister to Apollo, she asked her father Zeus to grant her "eternal virginity." As goddess of the hunt, she carried a silver bow and was associated with the moon. She was also the goddess of midwifery and childbirth and the protector of women and girls. Because she was a virgin, Aphrodite, the goddess of lust and love, had no power over her.

By remaining a virgin, Artemis is free, untamed by marriage and the need to yoke herself to the demands of a relationship. She is "one unto herself," whole and independent. Mythologist and author Christine Downing beautifully sums up this aspect of the goddess.

> Artemis is not willing to hide her sexuality as Athena does—nor yield to it. She is not going to let herself be raped as her mother, Leto, was by Zeus; nor will she be co-opted into denying her sexuality so as to make things easier for the men who might feel desire for her. That is their problem, not hers. She is neither seductive toward men nor protective of them. She refuses to allow herself, her sexuality, to be defined by theirs. The passion of Artemis is not repressed like Hera's nor sublimated like Athena's nor lived out in relationships like Aphrodite's. Artemis is the Lady of the Wild Things—including the wildness within herself. Hers is a claimed, a chosen, wildness; a preference, not a given. She is the goddess of the instinctual, not the rational or the civilized. Though Artemis chooses to live in the woods rather than on Olympus, she is not a primal earth goddess like Gaia but a goddess who lives *outside* civilization. What passion means in the realm of Artemis is unflinching knowledge of one's own savagery, instinctuality, bodily desires and responses. To know one's body, one's emotions, one's longings as one's own—that is Artemis.[5]

The myths hint at Artemis taking a female lover. Callisto was the most beautiful of all of Artemis's nymphs and her favorite. When Zeus saw her, he was filled with desire, but he knew that Callisto would refuse advances from a man because the nymphs of Artemis took an oath of virginity. So he approached her disguised as Artemis herself, and in this guise, his kisses and caresses were welcomed, signaling that Callisto and the goddess must have been lovers.

Artemis took her sexual sovereignty deadly seriously. When Actaeon the hunter spied on her as she was bathing, she turned him into a stag, and he was then torn to pieces by his pack of hunting dogs. She also killed Orion after he attempted to rape either her or one of her followers. She expected the maidens who hunted with her or served her to remain virgins while in her service. When Callisto broke her vow of chastity and lay with Zeus—even though he was disguised—Artemis turned her into a bear to punish her for her insolence. When Komaitho took a lover in Artemis' temple, the goddess sent a terrible plague and demanded a yearly human sacrifice before she could be appeased.

Artemis oversaw the initiation of girls into womanhood, and young girls played an important role in her cults. Worshippers of Artemis at Brauron in Attica participated in a ritual known as the Arkteia, in which young girls between the ages of five and ten were consecrated to the goddess. They dressed as bears while worshipping Artemis as the great She Bear and underwent a period of ritual wildness. Scholars believe that "playing the bear" was meant to prepare girls to be future mothers.

"Playing the bear" as a young girl would seem to sacralize and protect the instinctive wildness and naturalness of girlhood, perhaps fencing it off and creating a ritual space for it so that it could have its rightful existence in the future wife and mother's life. It would be an experience that a woman could look back on once she had been "tamed" by marriage, recalling the time she had been consecrated to the goddess who served only herself and no one else. She would therefore have had a reference point of a time when she was not bound by a man's expectations of how she was to look or act.

Mythologist Christine Downing has written about Artemis and her possible role in consecrating girls unto themselves.

We do not know if Artemis, the goddess involved with all the mysteries of female embodiment—menstruation, defloration, marriage, childbirth, death—was also imagined as the goddess who might initiate young girls into the mysteries of their own sexuality. Did the girls sacrifice their virginity to the virgin goddess—and thus keep it? That is, did they learn that their sexuality was their own, that it did not exist primarily for male gratification nor for producing children so that the ongoing life of the polis might be assured?[6]

Perhaps all women need a metaphorical temple to Artemis, even within their marriage. In this place, they can be one unto themselves without having to look after the needs of their husbands or children. For Emily, the sacred space of her attraction to Lilian had been such a temple for a short time. A medieval legend from France underscores the importance of women having their own private area.

MELUSINA

A knight named Raymond was hunting in the forest when he accidentally killed his friend. He was wandering through the woods, thinking about what to do. He sat beside a fountain and was met there by a woman of great beauty and charm named Melusina. She helped him to disguise the accident and consented to be his on the condition that her Saturdays would be spent in complete seclusion upon which he would never intrude. The couple had six sons, all of whom were disfigured in some way. They all grew up to be powerful heroes or warriors.

In all the years that they lived together, Raymond never intruded upon his wife during her Saturday solitude until one day his brother shared that gossipers were spreading nasty rumors. Distraught, Raymond rushed to his wife's apartments. They were empty, but one door was locked. When he looked through the keyhole, he saw her in the bath, and her lower extremities were changed into a fish's tail.

Raymond was beside himself—not with disgust, but with the knowledge that he would now lose his beloved wife. But she did not seem to know that he had seen her, and, for a time, all went on as before. However, upon learning that one of his sons had attacked and killed another, he cried out to Melusina as she came forward to comfort him, "Away, odious serpent! Contaminator of my honorable race!" At this point, Melusina cried in despair that she would leave him and he would never see her again, which is what happened.

There is something strange and sinister about Melusina. She gives birth to children who are impressive and accomplished, but also monstrous. She can receive Raymond in his sin and darkness partly because there is something not entirely wholesome about her. She is a powerful water fairy, aligned with the natural world and the forces of the unconscious. Like Lilith, Melusina isn't fully civilized and is in touch with raw nature. To retain her integrity, she must maintain this connection, which gets renewed every Saturday. Also like Lilith, she has no intention of sacrificing her wild instinctuality for a man. Female sexuality can never quite be tamed. Women have a dilemma. How can we continue to belong to ourselves and at the same time partner with someone? The story offers a possible solution to this thorny problem.

Margaret had always considered herself a seductress, artist, and muse. She spent her twenties and early thirties in tumultuous, intense liaisons with men. She found herself oscillating between fear of being abandoned and fear of being suffocated and would often sabotage her relationships. Finally, at thirty-five, she became involved with Max. Max was a stable and solid partner. He was grounded and knew what he wanted from life.

"We had fun together—our bond was based in the present, material world. We laughed, and we loved eating, drinking, and traveling together. We had a very physical relationship," Margaret recalls. "But I didn't feel that he was interested in my deeper, darker, more mysterious, creative side—a side I had always idealized and looked to men to validate for me. I wanted to reel men in and captivate them. But he wasn't interested in that part of me. So I resisted this relationship for a long time, even ending it for a while, believing that he didn't see me for who I was and that I could never be happy in such a dynamic."

Around this time, she had the following dream.

> I am in a small wooden boat with Max in the middle
> of the ocean. He has oars in his hands, and the seas are
> calm and placid. I look over the edge of the boat into
> the deep blue waters and want so badly to dive in. I
> look back at Max, who has no interest in what's below;
> his eyes are set on the horizon. I decide to dive in. At
> first, I am scared. The water is cold and dark, but the
> deeper I go, the better I can see, and then suddenly, I
> realize I can breathe underwater. A whole world reveals
> itself to me down there, the most beautiful, serene,
> deep world, and though I am alone, I feel the opposite
> of lonely. I swim and swim. Finally, I decide to surface.
> I come back up to the boat and to Max, who is there,
> still rowing the boat—content as ever, as if I never
> left. I feel the urge to tell him about what I saw, but I
> know he won't understand or won't be interested, so
> I don't. I just enjoy being in the boat, on the surface.
> Then again, I feel the urge to dive in, and I do, but this
> time I swim farther than before, and when I come up,
> I am on a deserted island. I am naked and free. I am
> my most wild and uninhibited self. Again, after some
> time, I get tired of being on my own and swim back to
> Max on the little boat. There is something comforting
> to me about his presence there, floating on the surface,
> keeping this safe, dry place for me between heaven and
> the depths below.

Importantly, Margaret took the dream to mean that this wild, instinctual part of herself was for *her*, not for a man. Like Melusina, she could have her deep and watery sojourns that were nourishing and renewing and not for men's benefit. This dream was an initiation into the cult of Artemis.

"I took this dream to mean that I need to remain open to the possibility that I can be with a man who loves the more quotidian and mundane parts of me but who gives me space to live out the exciting and mysterious parts. I've also come to realize (since marrying this man and having a child with him) that it is my longing for my *own* validation of those dark, mysterious, and creative parts that I was projecting onto men. I am often grateful for the strange and unexpected partnership and how perhaps some deeper part of me has circumnavigated my ego's desires to bring me back face-to-face with my real soul's longing for itself."

Saturday is the day that belongs to Saturn, the destroyer, the god of limitation, time, and death, and the dark spirit lying captive in matter. Because of our biology, women have a more specifically embodied experience of limitation, time, and aging than men do. Our bodies count out the months, and we are acutely aware of when our childbearing potential begins at adolescence and when it ends at menopause. Melusina gets one day to herself to commune with her lower, instinctual nature, to revert to her fishy, watery self, to be in her full embodiment that brings with it the deep knowledge of the passage of time and an awareness of mortality.

The story comes to its inevitable end when the husband cannot hide his disdain for her serpent-like aspect. Perhaps a woman's essential nature can never be entirely contained in the vessel of marriage. There is some Lilith part of a woman's untamable, earthy sensuality that needs space to live its own life—at least one day per week. Feminine, Lilith nature can't be fully accommodated in everyday waking life.

The story underscores that there is some part of a woman's soul that cannot be contained in a relationship with another. If we find ourselves disappointed with our partnership, it may be that we need to carve out some private emotional space in which we can return to our sovereign sense of wildness and aliveness and claim our sensuality. We can choose ourselves, as Melusina did. Our dream life is an infinitely vast expanse in which we can discover ourselves. Writing in a journal, dancing by candlelight when we are by ourselves, or setting aside time to walk alone in nature without the distraction of podcasts, music, or phone calls can give us a few moments to make contact with our deep, instinctual nature. These are precious gifts we can give to ourselves.

Because her instinctuality will never be accepted, Melusina must carve out her inviolable space to honor her full self. So, perhaps, must all women. Most of us become sexually active in adolescence or young adulthood. We may spend years having sex with casual and serious partners without a deeply satisfying experience of communion. Like my client Emily, we may be so focused on our partner's needs that we haven't allowed space for the Lilith or the Melusina in us. If our capacity for a rich, unencumbered experience of sexuality is part of what got left in our lumber room, reclaiming this can be full of pleasure and joy and offer us the opportunity for deeper self-knowledge and acceptance. Christine Downing notes that "Artemis does not say 'choose me,' or 'choose women,' but 'choose yourself.'"[7] A full experience of sexuality requires most of all a love of ourselves.

QUESTIONS FOR REFLECTION

1. In "The Wedding of Sir Gawain and Dame Ragnell," King Arthur must discover what women want. Men have often asked this question, but how often do women ask it of themselves? When was the last time that you really asked yourself what you want? How did you create space to allow an answer to emerge? What did you do to honor the answer?

2. Dame Ragnell is hideously ugly. If we are not conventionally beautiful, we may feel invisible. What is your relationship with your physical appearance like? Do you feel beautiful and confident in

your looks? How has your appreciation of your own attractiveness changed over time?

3. Dame Ragnell reveals to Arthur that what women want is sovereignty. Sovereignty means, in part, the ability to make our own decisions. Would you agree with Dame Ragnell that this is what women want? Why or why not? What has your relationship with sovereignty been? In what ways have you sought sovereignty in your life?

4. Dame Ragnell won't agree to marry Gawain in a private ceremony. She wants everyone to witness the wedding and is not ashamed of her grotesque appearance. When we feel inadequate in some way, we may have difficulty standing up for ourselves. We may want to remain small and hidden because we feel ashamed. Where in your life have you insisted on being visible even when it was difficult?

5. If you had to choose between being beautiful by day and hideous by night or vice versa, which would you pick? Why?

6. Melusina asks only to have one day of the week to herself. Where in your life do you carve out time or space where you answer only to yourself?

7. When Melusina is alone, she becomes a mermaid. How do you connect with your instinctual nature?

CHAPTER 7

Rage: Heeding Your Limits

It is important to recognize the difference
between personal anger in intimate
relationships, and transpersonal rage that erupts
from an archetypal level, the level at which the
Goddess enters. When that differentiation takes
place and the rage is appropriately released,
the Goddess can turn her other face. Then the
soul can take up residence in its vastly enlarged
home and go about its own creative life.

—Marion Woodman, *The Pregnant Virgin*

The world has always been afraid of women's anger. Lilith could give full voice to her wrath in her fight with Adam, and she wasn't placated by the three angels who sought to mollify her. In contrast, many of us lose access to this vitalizing emotion. As children, we may have been taught that anger, especially in girls, was unacceptable. When we lost control in anger, we may have been overwhelmed with guilt or worried that others would shun us. When rage enters a woman's life, its effects can be destructive, but it always shows up in service to authenticity. Rage is an immediate, ungovernable response that contains wisdom and power. It is embodied. Anger alerts us that our boundaries have been crossed. It is a warning bell to our nervous system that we have been violated.

Lilith's anger was a key feature of the goddess. An earlier Babylonian depiction describes her rageful aspect.

> Fearsome and savage is her nature. Raging, fearsome, terrifying, violent, rapacious, rampaging, evil, malicious, she overthrows and destroys all that she approaches. Terrible are her deeds. Wherever she comes, wherever she appears, she brings evil and destruction. Men, beasts, trees, rivers, roads, buildings, she brings harm to them all. A flesh-eating, blood sucking monster is she.[1]

Expressed by a woman who is uninitiated, anger can be shrill, ineffective, or indiscriminately wounding. We may end up in tears when we speak our rage, or explode in an unrestrained barrage of insults. Unbridled outbursts can leave us feeling guilty or ashamed in their wake. And yet, the rising column of molten rage that runs through our bodies reminds us of our connection with the vital spark that enlivens and sustains us and the unbridled life force at our core. Anger can help us maintain contact with ourselves and our authentic needs and desires, for it is an aspect of the central fire.

THE FURIES

The Furies, or Erinyes, of Greek mythology were images of female rage, an ambivalent force that could never be entirely propitiated. They were ugly winged women with snakes entwined around their arms. These primitive goddesses punished those who had committed crimes.

Feminine anger is earthy, ancient, ugly, and subterranean. The Erinyes are the children of Night (Nyx), and they dwell in the depths. They can never be entirely civilized. Unlike a man's anger, which can be easily assimilated in public life, female rage is primal and usually not welcome in polite society. According to Aeschylus, the Erinyes are "wingless, black, utterly loathsome; their vile breath vents in repulsive snoring; from their eyes distils a filthy rheum; their garb is wickedness to wear in sight of the gods' statues or in human homes. They are creatures of no race I ever saw."[2]

The most famous story about the Erinyes comes from the cycle of plays known as the *Oresteia* by Aeschylus. Agamemnon is the king of Mycenae and the husband of Clytemnestra. When Agamemnon prepares to fight in the Trojan War, his ship is unable to sail because he has offended the goddess Artemis by hunting and killing one of her sacred stags. She causes the winds to be still in retribution. The seer Calchis declares that only Agamemnon's sacrifice of his daughter Iphigenia can appease the goddess. At first, Agamemnon refuses, but when pressed by his commanders, he relents. Agamemnon has Iphigenia and Clytemnestra brought to Aulis under the false pretext of having the girl married. In some versions of the story, Iphigenia remains unaware of her imminent death, believing until the last minute that she is being led to the altar to be wed.

Clytemnestra is heartbroken and furious about the sacrifice of her daughter. Agamemnon sails to Troy, and while he is gone fighting the Trojan War, Clytemnestra takes a lover named Aegisthus and plots her revenge on Agamemnon. When he returns ten years later, Clytemnestra and Aegisthus kill him. Agamemnon's son Orestes is angered by his father's murder and eventually kills Clytemnestra and Aegisthus to avenge this crime, as directed by Apollo. The deceased Clytemnestra calls upon the Erinyes to avenge her and bring retribution upon her son. The goddesses leave the underworld and begin to torment Orestes. He is aided by the god Apollo, while the ghost of Clytemnestra is spurring on the Furies.

At the direction of Apollo, Orestes flees to Athens and asks Athena to try his case. Athena is afraid of making the Erinyes angry but agrees to oversee the trial. Literature's first courtroom drama begins with Athena presiding as judge. The Erinyes represent the prosecution, while the defendant Orestes is aided by the god Apollo. The Furies argue that Clytemnestra's life is worth as much as Agamemnon's, but Apollo claims that a man's life is worth more than a woman's. The jury is split in its decision, and Athena casts the deciding vote, acquitting Orestes of his crime.

The remainder of the play is a discussion between Athena and the Furies. The Erinyes are horrified and feel their power has been usurped, but Athena mollifies them by promising them a home in Athens where they will be revered. The play ends with the goddesses being accompanied to their temples far below the earth.

BANISHING WOMEN'S ANGER

The *Oresteia* shows the ancient, primal power of women's rage and how it was mistrusted and supplanted by the more patriarchal attitudes represented by Apollo and his sister Athena. Athena, after all, was born from her father's head. Apollo cites this fact as proof: "The mother is not the true parent of the child which is called hers. She is a nurse who tends the growth of young seed planted by its true parent, the male."[3] The contributions of women, then, are minimized. Other ancient stories describe the banishment of women's power and righteous anger, including that of Lilith.

In the *Oresteia*, the tragic cycle began with Agamemnon sinning against the goddess Artemis. This crime sets off a chain of conflicts that pit men and women against each other. Agamemnon betrays his wife and daughter by sacrificing Iphigenia to further his war aims. Clytemnestra murders him to avenge the death of her daughter, and Orestes murders his mother to avenge the death of his father. In the conflict between feminine and masculine values, the masculine prevails. Though the play ends on a celebratory note, the ultimate fate of the Furies is ambivalent. They have been bought off with promises of being revered in Athens, yet they are relegated to a home deep under the earth. The older, earthy gods of raw emotion have given way to the newer gods of thought, such as Apollo and Athena.

We may banish our anger along with Lilith and the Erinyes, but doing so will cut us off from our power and our connection to the inner flame. We may feel our anger is unjustified or struggle to express it because we fear being misunderstood. The rage then stays in our gut, where it festers and ferments, sometimes poisoning us with resentment or even causing physical pain or illness. Rage can erupt in uncontrolled and destructive outbursts. When this happens, those around us may be shocked because they did not know what was cooking in our innards for long months. Such rage may sweep away rigid attitudes and expectations, perhaps clearing the way for new ones to take their place.

Female rage has an archetypal taproot. It arises when the feminine has been dispossessed. It has an unsettling, uncanny feel, as if it rises, with the Erinyes, from Tartarus and is not quite human. It is frightening. It sweeps over us and overtakes us, filling our bodies with strength and fury, turning us fleetingly into a Fury. When we are filled with fury, we are momentarily overtaken by these ancient, archetypal goddesses. We may temporarily lose access to our ability to govern our impulses. Anger is a sentinel that lets us know when our boundaries have been crossed. It can be clarifying and protective, but when it sweeps over us, it can be as if these archaic goddesses have arrived from the underworld and have taken us over. This can leave us feeling out of control.

A Liberian fairy tale gives us an evocative image of how rage can possess us and cause us to act in surprising ways. When we are in such a state, we may be in danger of lashing out and hurting even those we love. However, when the heroine of the tale experiences the transformation wrought by rage, she is able to enforce boundaries and ensure that her needs are not forgotten.

THE LEOPARD WOMAN

A man and a woman were making a difficult journey through a dense forest. The woman had her baby strapped to her back. They had no food and grew desperately hungry. Then, unexpectedly, they came upon a vast, grassy plain upon which many animals were grazing contentedly.

Now the woman could turn herself into anything she liked, and her husband said to her, "Turn yourself into a leopard and kill one of those animals so that I may have something to eat." The woman looked at her husband pointedly. "Do you really mean what you say?" she asked. "Yes!" replied the husband, for he was very hungry.

The woman took her baby off her back and placed the child on the ground. Hair began growing all over her body. She dropped her clothes, and a change came over her face. Her fingers and toes became claws. Within a few moments, a fierce leopard stood before the man, staring at him with hungry eyes. He was scared to death and clambered up a tree for protection. When he climbed up, he could see that his infant child was nearly in the leopard's jaws, but he was too frightened to climb down and rescue him.

When the leopard saw that she had frightened her husband good and proper, she ran off to hunt as he had asked. She captured a young heifer and dragged it back to where her husband and child were. Her husband cried out, begging her to transform herself back into a woman.

Slowly, the hair disappeared, and the claws turned back into fingers and toes. Finally, she was a woman once more. Her husband was so frightened that he would not come down from the tree until after she had put her clothes back on and tied her baby to her back again. Then she said to him, "Never ask a woman to do a man's work again."

This simple tale is full of evocative imagery that illustrates the enormous power inherent in a woman's anger. This power has both a destructive and life-giving aspect, but once unleashed, it can be difficult to control. The tale begins with the couple undertaking a long journey together with their young child, but their reserves are depleted—there is no food. We might liken this to the stage of a marriage in which there are young children and insufficient resources. Both partners work hard, and there is little time or energy for enjoyment or relaxation. In such a state, both parents feel resentful. We can regress to a feeling of childlike entitlement that our partner should care for us. We might be looking for emotional tending, attention, or affection. Certainly, these are all

essential and legitimate needs in any relationship, but when both partners are stretched thin, either partner can unconsciously demand that
his or her needs be put first.

This is what happens to the couple in this story. Both the husband and wife are hungry and under duress. The wife is caring for
the child. It is selfish of the husband to demand that she hunt for him.
The tale seems to pick up on the reality that women are often asked
to carry more than their share in relationships. "Emotional labor" is
a term coined by the sociologist Arlie Russell Hochschild to describe
the invisible work that is done to track and respond to the needs of
others to keep things running smoothly. This work is often done by
women. In families, it is usually the woman who knows that the
twelve-year-old is anxious about her history test tomorrow while
the eight-year-old is upset because she didn't get invited to a birthday party. Dad, meanwhile, may be blissfully clueless about these
fraught, complicated dynamics. Women can take on emotional labor
for their partners as well, putting their own needs aside to tend to
their husbands after a long day at work. If one member of a couple
is always the one soothing the other's anxiety, helping to patch up a
bruised ego, or smoothing over conflicts between the other spouse
and the kids, that person is doing the bulk of the emotional labor. In
heterosexual relationships, it can be the man who takes on this role,
but it is more often the woman.

We might imagine that this fairy tale shows us such a dynamic
in symbolic language. Both partners are stretched thin and are being
asked to carry heavy burdens, but then the husband unfairly imposes
himself on her. He is selfishly asking her to do more than her share.
One aspect of any committed relationship is an economy of mutual
care. There is always some negotiation about who gives the care
and attention and who receives it. His unfair demand unleashes
her rage—she becomes a ferocious leopard. The transformation is
an image of becoming fiercely embodied and fully engaged in an
instinctual way of being. When rage overtakes us, we become consumed by this archetypal, instinctual force. We become something

not quite human. We access some primal part of ourselves, and the usual values according to which we operate are momentarily overturned. In her leopard form, the woman is even a potential danger to her child. And yet the leopard aspect of the woman is powerful and able to provide food for her family.

If we find that we are doing most of the emotional labor in our relationship, we can begin to address this imbalance by becoming more conscious of our tendency to take responsibility for someone else's discomfort. As we become more aware, we will more easily be able to set limits around this impulse. Even if our partner is making unfair demands on us, we have the power to decide whether we will meet them or not. The woman's final statement that ends the tale—"Never ask a woman to do a man's work again"—is a clear no! This can serve as a reminder to us to create firm boundaries around what we are willing to take on.

The poet David Whyte notes that "anger truly felt at its centre is the essential living flame of being fully alive and fully here."[4] Anger puts us in touch with our ancient capacity for self-protection. It is immediate access to the vital spark within. It connects us with the primordial substrate of the sympathetic nervous system. Our heart thumps. Our blood pressure rises. We feel a rush of adrenaline. Anger alerts us to the body's raw, unedited wisdom, a deep knowing about our limits and boundaries that we may have forgotten, but Lilith remembers well. Our anger may mark her occasional, often unwelcome, reappearance.

Tellingly, the woman in the story doesn't refuse the man's demand. Rather than saying no, she does as he asks, becoming fierce and potentially destructive. Women may be prone to swallowing our resentment and taking on too much. If we do more than our share of the physical, emotional, or practical tending and caregiving, built-up rage can be the outcome. This was the case with my client Elle.

ANGER DEFERRED

Elle was fifty-one when she first came to see me and was anticipating an empty nest in a few years. Early in our relationship, I heard Elle's frustration and resentment toward her husband, though when I reflected this to her, she stopped and looked at me, surprised. She had not consciously known that she was so angry. Her husband was loyal, solid, and committed. However, he was somewhat depressive and had never taken responsibility for his own happiness. As a result, he felt resentful and entitled to be in a permanent bad mood. Over the two decades that they had been married, Elle had become accustomed to accommodating his perpetual grumpiness.

"The image I have," she told me, "is that I've been on a long train journey seated next to a stranger who has fallen asleep on my shoulder. As the journey has progressed, he has leaned more and more of his weight on me. In the beginning, I didn't notice it so much, or it felt as though I could handle it. But now I realize I am quite uncomfortable."

Like the woman in the fairy tale, Elle had been asked to do more than her share. She was the primary parent and worked part-time outside the home. Over the years, it had become part of her role to tend to her husband's endless work anxieties and minor physical complaints. And because her husband was chronically slightly depressed and tired, engaging the kids in fun activities or planning enjoyable get-togethers fell to her. Absorbed in a demanding and exhausting job, Elle's husband had little time or energy left over to take an interest in the children, much less Elle's emotional or professional life.

The situation came to a head when Elle was diagnosed with an autoimmune disorder that left her occasionally disabled and required painful disruptive treatments. Elle's husband dutifully took time off to take her to medical appointments and reluctantly stepped up to help their youngest with college essays. When Elle was laid up in bed and couldn't cook, he made meals or got takeout. But she never experienced him as comforting or able to offer her solace as she dealt with the fear and grief that came with the diagnosis. "Practically, he was there," she told me. "Emotionally, he wasn't."

One day, when Elle was in a lot of pain and feeling particularly low and frightened, her husband came in from work. He began a long story about a tense encounter with a colleague without asking her anything about herself. Elle felt he was looking to her to help him handle his irritation, upset, and anxiety, but she was in no place to offer comfort, and she erupted. She turned on him and icily cut him down. After a long exile, Lilith returned. Decades of disavowed needs rose from the pits of Tartarus, demanding their due. She tore into him, and her anger surprised and frightened her.

That night, she had the following dream:

> I'm in the car with my husband. He is driving. We are going to a restaurant out in the suburbs. He is driving fast the way he usually does. At first, I feel nervous, but then I remind myself that he is a good driver and that I can relax. We arrive at the restaurant and eat. It is a large open space. There are not many other couples there. We are talking about a band of marauders that has been terrorizing the community, breaking into people's houses and killing them. In the dream, I understand this band of marauders to be like John Brown's army in Bleeding Kansas. They are filled with righteous fury but are indiscriminate in their use of violence. As we are discussing this, we hear gunfire in the distance. I look at my husband and tell him I think we should leave right away. I feel bad for leaving the bill unpaid, but I tell myself that I will call the restaurant the next day and give them my credit card number. We go outside into the parking lot, and for a moment I feel relieved that we are getting away. Then I look up the hill and see the band of marauders emerging from the tree line, streaming down toward us. They are close now. I know we won't make it to the car. I briefly wonder if we should go back inside, but it is

too late. The conflict is unavoidable. The leader of the
band is a woman, full of fury.

The dream is an eloquent statement about the state of the marriage,
how it got that way, and where it might be going. Elle's association to
the suburbs was that they are an inauthentic place where people go
to escape from the real-world tensions of the city. Therefore, dining
in the suburbs represents a flight from the conflict in her marriage. It
pictures her tendency to go along with things and pretend that all is
well—a strategy she had employed for much of her marriage.

Elle described the scene in the restaurant as serene and elegant, if a
bit stuffy. This provides a sharp contrast to what comes later. The restaurant offers an image of what her marriage had become. On the surface,
things looked calm and pleasant, but it was also bloodless, lacking much
authenticity of feeling. In the dream, there are rumors of forces that will
change everything.

VENGEANCE

Elle loved history and had recently been reading a book about John
Brown and his role in Bleeding Kansas, the period leading up to the
US Civil War. She explained that in May of 1856, the abolitionist
John Brown had marched through the town of Pottawatomie Creek
in the Kansas territory along with seven men in response to the Sack
of Lawrence, an attack on another town committed by a proslavery
group. One night, John Brown dragged five men from their homes
and hacked them to death. He felt he had a divine mission to mete
out God's justice.

Elle's association to John Brown opened a rich discussion in which
the historical complexities resonated with her psychic situation. John
Brown's cause was an eminently righteous one. He was deeply committed to abolition and racial justice. He was in communication with
Harriet Tubman and collaborated with Frederick Douglass. Yet he also
exhibited signs of zealotry and extremism. Psychologically, we might

say that he was inflated. He saw himself as an instrument of God and believed that his anti-slavery work was a sacred obligation. Because he believed God tasked him to strike a blow against slavery, the ends justified the means, and he was given to excesses and fanaticism. After his time in Kansas, he organized the raid on Harper's Ferry, which resulted in his eventual capture and execution. Some remember him as a visionary and martyr, and others as a madman and terrorist.

This kind of righteous fury, then, is deeply ambivalent. Brown felt that violence was necessary, as other means to address racial injustice hadn't worked. Such extreme approaches to a problem can get things unstuck, shake things up, and create new possibilities. However, it is also indiscriminately destructive. Many people died during Brown's Kansas activities and his raid on Harper's Ferry. John Brown's actions and the extensive attention his trial received were important catalysts of the Civil War—the deadliest war the US has ever fought and the war that ended slavery.

Slavery had been a poisonous fault line present at the nation's founding that would eventually demand a reckoning—and a violent one at that. Elle's psyche called up this history as a metaphor for her marriage. At the beginning of her union, she had made an unconscious decision to sacrifice her stance in the interest of harmony. Like the infamous Three-Fifths Compromise in the US Constitution, Elle's concession may have allowed for harmony in the medium term, but it was just a way of delaying an eventual conflict.

John Brown's brutality in Kansas prefigured the enormous violence and loss of life brought about by the Civil War less than a decade later. The repressed liberatory urge, once unleashed, was not moderate or circumspect, but full of righteous fury. The dream put Elle on notice that a similar process was at work within her psyche. The needs she had daily disavowed, the myriad ways she had capitulated on small things that nonetheless mattered a lot, all of these came sweeping out of her. That kind of rage isn't good at making fine-tuned differentiations. As in the dream, the use of "violence" is indiscriminate.

Of course, the suffering inflicted on enslaved people is unfathomable and can't realistically be compared with Elle's struggles in her marriage. One truth about dreams is that they often speak in hyperbole. The tendency of the unconscious to overstate things in no way minimizes the very real violence and injustice that resulted from slavery.

Instead of John Brown, a woman leads the dream's marauding band—a striking and terrifying image of the goddess herself. Like Erinyes summoned from Tartarus by Clytemnestra, she has appeared on the scene to enact vengeance and strike a blow for liberation from outworn attitudes. Yet, like John Brown, she is ambivalent. She brings the energy and moral rectitude that forces a reckoning and ends old, stuck ways of being and relating. And she is frightening.

In the dream, Elle seeks to avoid confronting this furious energy. The dream strategy reflects her waking attitude of being conflict avoidant. During her marriage, she had often shut the conversation down to avoid an argument or rationalized away an irritation or disappointment. Leaving the check unpaid speaks eloquently to all the emotional debt she had accumulated through the years due to this approach. Always ready to put off conflict and pay the cost tomorrow, she had many unpaid bills. The dream shows that she is again trying to avoid conflict, but it's too late. The goddess of fury is upon her. There will be a reckoning. Some old attitude will die, and some version of herself or her marriage will be brutally executed.

A VISIT FROM THE GODDESS

In the quote that begins this chapter, Jungian analyst Marion Woodman makes it clear that an eruption of archetypal rage such as the one that Elle experienced is a visit from the Goddess. When dealt with appropriately, such a visitation can create for us a "vastly enlarged home."

But how do we release this rage appropriately? As we have seen, it is capable of great destruction and life-giving renewal. Sedna, a principal goddess of the Inuit, is another dispossessed and rageful goddess whose story can offer us some wisdom about how to approach this dilemma. Although there are many different versions of her story, important elements are consistent.

SEDNA

Sedna was a beautiful young woman with many suitors, but she rejected them all. One day, a man she had never met before arrived to pay court. He was exceedingly handsome and well-dressed. Sedna quickly agreed to marry him. He took her far away to his home island, where he revealed that he was not a man, but a seabird. She was forced to live with him and eat fish, for that was all he could catch. Sedna missed her family. She missed meat and warm furs.

In the springtime, when the ice began to break up, Sedna's father got in his kayak and went to visit his daughter. When he learned how she had been deceived and saw how she was living, he was enraged. He killed her bird husband, put his daughter in the kayak, and set off for home. But when the bird man's friends returned and found him dead and his wife missing, they flew to the kayak and beat their wings, causing a great storm. The small boat rocked treacherously in the waves. Sedna's father knew that he was about to die unless he could think of something to save himself. He thought the birds might spare him if he threw his daughter overboard. After all, she had brought this situation about by refusing to marry any of the local suitors who had sought her hand. He tossed her overboard, but she clung with desperation onto the side of the kayak. Her father took out his ax and cut off her fingers to the first knuckle. The tips of her fingers became seals. Still, she hung on. Her father chopped off her fingers down to the next knuckle, and these parts of her fingers became sea lions. Yet, she hung on. Finally, her father chopped off the rest of her fingers, and these became whales. Then, Sedna sank to the bottom of the ocean.

Sedna became the goddess of the underworld as well as the life-giving goddess who controlled access to the animals the Inuit depended on for food. When she rages, she causes great storms and withholds the animals from the hunters. Then, a shaman must journey to the depths and appease her by combing her hair.

Sedna is an image of the dispossessed, archetypal feminine. She has been punished and rejected for her lack of humility and obedience. Her resulting rage is wordless and elemental. Just as the Erinyes are relegated to a subterranean home beneath Athens and Lilith removes herself far from Eden, so Sedna sinks into wordless obscurity at the bottom of the ocean. There, she is the giver of life and the provider of all nourishment. It isn't possible to resurrect or redeem her. She is too primitive for that. But she can be honored, and she can be lovingly tended to when she is distraught.

LONG-STANDING RESENTMENTS

Rage can be borne of ancient resentments, and intimate relationships breed daily, myriad irritations. Harmony in close relationships requires compromise, meaning that we may have to accommodate ourselves to things that irritate or disappoint us. Making a marriage work, for example, will demand of us that we let some things slide. Choosing to focus away from minor irritations or disappointments can be in the interest of preserving intimacy and good feelings. However, irritation can also be the first, quiet warning note that something is amiss, that we are being ignored, devalued, or disparaged. Ignoring such a warning is an act of self-betrayal, but our bodies don't let us forget even if we try to. Resentments build up like so much dry kindling, as they did for Elle. The poet Dorsha Hayes has captured the peril of unaddressed resentments in her poem.

FIRE HAZARD

Filled with a clutter of unsorted stuff
a spark can set a man ablaze. What's there
heaped high among stored rubbish at a puff
will burst in flame. No man can be aware
of how inflammable he is, how prone
to what rage beyond control, unless
the piled up litter of his life is known
to him, and he is able to assess
what hazard he is in, what could ignite.
A man, disordered and undisciplined,
lives in the peril of a panic flight
before the onrush of a flaming wind.
Does it now seem I seek to be profound?
I stand on smoking ash and blackened ground.[5]

Unaddressed resentments can build up in our lives—and our marriages—like so much combustible garbage. When this is the case, the vital spark of our anger can set off a conflagration.

This is what happened to Elle. Her argument with her husband that night set off a long-postponed confrontation in which she struggled to express her hurts and resentments through the years and to take responsibility for her needs and desires. The feared fury that the dream heralded was destructive, but mostly of old attitudes and outmoded ways of being. Their destruction was necessary. The conflict had been inescapable.

When long-standing resentments build up between two people, they function like a thick carapace that prevents us from feeling warmth or connection. The air between two people gradually chills until it can become icy. For feelings to thaw, resentments must be aired. We must be able to speak about our hurts and disappointments to our partner and know that they have been received with compassion—and we have to be able to do the same thing for him or her. The moment that we begin to address our resentments, however, is full of peril, just as it was for Elle. When resentments catch fire, they can burn things to the ground if the blaze gets out of control. Such work must be done in a measured way, while we also try to return to vulnerability and connection with our partner. Then the hurt and anger from the past can be aired without inflicting so much damage that it can't be repaired. If long-standing resentments clutter your relationship like the unsorted flammable refuse in Hayes' poem, it can be helpful to have a skilled couples therapist as a guide. He or she can help create space for old hurts to be heard and help douse fires that threaten to get out of control.

When Yellowstone National Park was first established, the US Army worked to suppress any natural fires that occurred due to lightning strikes. However, ecologists have come to understand fire as an important and necessary element of change in a forest. When fires are allowed to burn naturally, they consume dead branches, leaves, and other debris, helping to forestall larger, more destructive conflagrations. Fires return nutrients to the soil and open up space so that light can reach the forest floor, allowing new, young trees to grow. The seeds of the iconic lodgepole pine are sealed tight within their pinecone by a tough resin that can only be melted by extremely high temperatures. These beautiful trees are dependent on fire to release their seeds and allow new life to begin.

Rage is not an emotion that can be easily tamed or civilized. Perhaps it can be released in a controlled, slow burn, or allowed to have its own realm at the bottom of our psychic oceans. We can recognize its importance, its protective and even life-giving capacity. We can appreciate our ability to become enraged, and when anger shows up, we can honor its intent to guard and shelter us, and to rid our souls of dead wood to make room for new life. Instead of dismissing our anger or feeling ashamed of it, we can see it for what it is—a conduit for ancient wisdom that slumbers within. This dormant capacity is an aspect of the untamable fiery goddess alive in each of us, and we can turn toward her with tenderness and gratitude, combing her hair in the depths, grateful for the gifts that she provides.

QUESTIONS FOR REFLECTION

1. In "The Leopard Woman," the couple is making a difficult journey. How have you managed in your relationships when life has been full of challenges? Have you taken on more of your share of the burden, or do you seek to be taken care of?

2. In the story, the woman turns into a dangerous leopard. What happens when you get angry? Where do you feel it in your body? How do you express it, and how does it usually manifest itself in your close relationships?

3. When we get in touch with archetypal rage, we may become afraid that we will lose control or hurt someone. When has your own anger made you afraid? What have you done in these circumstances?

4. The leopard woman may be a danger to her husband and child, but she also captures food for them. Anger can be lifegiving, helping us to set limits and go after what we want. Where has anger been beneficial for you? When has it helped you to achieve a goal?

5. When Sedna becomes angry, she creates storms in the world above. Anger arises first in our bodies, and we may feel its effects on the surface only after some time. How do you know when you are angry? What subtle—or not so subtle—sensations do you notice?

CHAPTER 8

AUTHORITY: CROSSING THE THRESHOLD

. . . Awakening inner authority requires
submitting to genuine authority in others.
Authority issues can only be solved through
developing genuine inner authority. "Authentic
authority" and submission go together; there
is no learning one without the other.

—Michael Meade, *The Water of Life:
Initiation and the Tempering of the Soul*

E leanor Roosevelt's childhood was marked by hardship. Her
father was an alcoholic and she lost both parents and a brother
by the time she was ten years old. As a child, she was timid, insecure,
and awkward. Three years of study in London during her adolescence
helped her to become more confident and exposed her to social issues
and the world of ideas. Her involvement with the settlement house
movement in New York City opened her eyes to progressive causes.
But her marriage to her distant cousin Franklin Delano Roosevelt
brought a sudden end to her expansive interests. Franklin's mother
Sara regulated nearly every aspect of Eleanor's life, and the younger
woman found herself striving to please and losing confidence in her
abilities and ideas.

When children came, Sara worked hard to usurp Eleanor's role as mother, insisting on ordering everything herself and implying at every turn that Eleanor was incompetent. "I was your real mother," she told the children. "Eleanor merely bore you."[1] Sara oversaw the design and construction of two conjoined townhouses—one for Franklin and Eleanor, and the other for herself. There were connecting passageways between the two houses on every level so that Sara could come and go freely in her son and daughter-in-law's home.

Under the influence of her controlling mother-in-law, Eleanor abandoned her interests in progressive issues and parroted the older woman's narrow views. She withdrew from former activities and focused on being a conventional wife and mother. "She offered few opinions, never disagreed, rarely indicated her true feelings about anything. But she was often miserable."[2]

Things changed for Eleanor when Franklin entered politics. She enthusiastically encouraged and advised her husband. When he won a seat in the New York State Senate, the couple moved to Albany, and Eleanor enjoyed physical distance from her mother-in-law, allowing her to become mistress of her own home for the first time. Here, she was able to assert her authority and come into her own. In the years to come, Eleanor Roosevelt would be an essential advisor to her president-husband, an outspoken supporter of civil rights for African Americans, and an advocate for refugees, women, and the impoverished. She is widely considered to be America's greatest and most influential first lady.

Inner authority comes not from power, position, or title but from a deep, wordless knowing of who we are. We come into the world with the capacity for this knowing, but we may become divorced from it as others tell us who we should be or what we should desire. In our culture, ads and other messages bombard us and manipulate us into wanting things. Our fears speak to us and tell us to choose safety and ignore those other voices that whisper about ancient longings. Authority is about reclaiming what we most deeply know about ourselves. It requires us to connect with our fiery wisdom that never lost touch with our most authentic truths.

Like Eleanor Roosevelt, we can leave behind the role of the pleasing maiden and become the powerful matron as we age. To achieve this milestone, we must claim our authority. Doing so will inevitably involve a challenge to those who have been our seniors. The conflict between a woman and her mother-in-law is an archetypal expression of the contest for dominance between generations. Women will need to navigate this struggle whether or not they have an actual mother-in-law. Challenging those who have held authority over us will require strength, boldness, and courage. Developing these potentials will help us go from being a girlish young woman to a strong matriarch.

There is a reason that mother-in-law jokes abound. Terrible mothers-in-law show up frequently in movies and TV shows. Mothers-in-law also feature in many fairy tales and myths, where they often undermine and oppress the daughter-in-law. The Old Testament story of the tender relationship between Ruth and her mother-in-law Naomi is a notable exception. In our lives, issues between mothers- and daughters-in-law can appear in myriad permutations. Many a young wife has felt chastised or rejected by her mother-in-law. Older women can often feel disrespected or pushed aside by a daughter-in-law who doesn't value her wisdom and position. On the other hand, real-world relationships between the two women may be warm, loving, and supportive.

Mother-in-law stories appear worldwide because the generational tension represents a universal pattern. In other words, conflict between a man's mother and his wife is archetypal. The mother-in-law is an aspect of the mother archetype that stands in our way as we navigate claiming our authority. The negotiation between a mother-in-law and daughter-in-law is symbolic of a developmental challenge that all women must confront.

Because this is an archetypal pattern, it can show up in many places in our lives—not just with actual mothers-in-law. Camilla had worked in a small design firm for the better part of her career. The woman founder of the firm had hired Camilla when she was young and had been an important mentor. But as Camilla grew into her own abilities and authority, she found that old relationships that had felt supportive now chafed. "No one did anything wrong," she told me. "But I found I had my own knowing and way of doing things and opinions, and I was clashing a bit too much with some of the women with authority." She eventually left the firm to work as a freelancer. Though she maintained good relationships with her former bosses and colleagues, the time had come for her to claim her inner authority and stand on her own.

A myth from ancient Greece tells the story of Psyche, who had to go through many trials before asserting her own deep, inner authority. Unfortunately, she also happened to have perhaps the worst mother-in-law ever—the goddess Aphrodite.

EROS AND PSYCHE

There once lived a king and queen with three beautiful daughters. The eldest two were lovely beyond words, but the youngest, Psyche, was so beautiful that even the goddesses were envious. The people of that land began paying Psyche the honors usually reserved only for Aphrodite herself. Aphrodite was filled with rage when she saw this. She sent her son Eros to Psyche so that he would cause her to fall in love with a vile and lowly creature. But when Eros saw the beautiful Psyche, he fell in love with her and chose to disobey his mother.

Meanwhile, Psyche's father had gone to consult the oracle of Delphi to understand why there were no suitors for Psyche. Men were happy to admire her, but none had come to offer themselves as her husband. The oracle gave a most terrible prophecy: Psyche's father was instructed to dress his daughter in black and leave her alone on a mountain to await her suitor, a winged serpent who would come and take her.

Therefore, Psyche was left alone and terrified on the mountain; her family mourned her as if she were dead. While she sat trembling, a soft breeze came and transported her to a beautiful valley beside a magnificent palace. A voice told her that the palace was hers and instructed her to make herself at home. During the day, she was waited upon by invisible hands. She bathed and ate, and was always accompanied by the soft sounds of the harp. Though she saw no one else, she knew her husband would come at night. In the darkness, he came to her. He spoke lovingly, and she knew great happiness.

Psyche spent her days wandering about the beautiful palace and being waited upon by her unseen servants, and she spent the nights in the arms of her loving husband. For many months, she felt great joy. But after some time had passed, she began to feel bored and lonely during the day, and she grew dissatisfied that she did not know what her husband looked like, for he came to her only in the darkness of night. Moreover, she missed her family and knew they must worry about her or think she was dead. At length, she asked her husband whether her sisters could visit her to pass the time and reassure her parents that all was well. At first, her husband said no, but Psyche grew so sad that he finally relented. But he warned her that she must not allow herself to be influenced by her sisters, or it would mean the end of their relationship.

The next day, Psyche's two sisters were transported by the gentle west breeze to the palace. They were overcome by the beauty and riches of their youngest sister. They enjoyed the soft music and the delicious wines, and envy began to take root in their hearts. All day, they plied Psyche with questions about who her husband was. Only a king or even a god could have such fantastical wealth. Who was he? What did he look like? Psyche had no answer. Overcome by envy of Psyche's favored position, the sisters developed a plan. They planted doubt and fear in Psyche's heart. They told Psyche that her husband must indeed be the winged serpent the oracle foretold. Perhaps he was loathsome and ugly or even dangerous. "How can you sleep with such a horrible creature?" they asked her.

From this day forward, Psyche's feelings about her husband were poisoned by corrosive doubts. Why doesn't he allow himself to be seen? What reason could there be other than that he is a hideous monster? Such thoughts haunted her for many days until she finally decided she would expose him that night. After her husband fell asleep, she quietly lit a candle. Psyche gasped. The pool of light that fell about her sleeping husband revealed not a monster but the most beautiful man she had ever seen. But as she sat gazing upon his beauty, a drop of wax fell from the candle onto his back. He awoke with a start. Grasping all at once what had happened, he rushed from the room.

Psyche realized that her husband was none other than Eros, the god of love and the son of Aphrodite. In sorrow and despair, she began searching far and wide for her beloved, but in vain. Even Hera and Demeter refused to help her, as they feared offending Aphrodite, who was still jealous of Psyche's beauty and angry that her son had disobeyed her. At last, Psyche had no choice but to go to the temple of Aphrodite and confront her mother-in-law.

The enraged goddess took hold of Psyche by her hair and rent her clothing. "Ah! . . . So you condescend to pay your respects to your mother-in-law, is that it?" she said. She berated Psyche for her foolishness. Then she sent her two servants, Sorrow and Sadness, to torment the young woman by giving her formidable tasks. For her first task, Aphrodite mixed a great quantity of wheat, millet, poppy seeds, peas, lentils, and beans. She then instructed Psyche to separate the heap into distinct piles within a single day. Psyche was overcome when she saw the scope of the task before her and began crying. An ant heard her and took pity on her. He called all the other ants, and they quickly sorted the pile of seeds together.

The goddess was not assuaged and set Psyche another task. A flock of murderous sheep with sharp horns grew golden fleece. Aphrodite tasked Psyche with gathering the golden wool from these deadly creatures. Once again, Psyche despaired. This time, a reed growing along the river banks sang a sweet melody to her, advising her to wait until the sheep fell asleep during the heat of the day and then gather the wool caught in the briars. Psyche did as she was instructed and brought heaps of soft golden fleece to pile in Aphrodite's lap, but the goddess was not satisfied.

She gave Psyche a jar and told her that she must return with it filled with water from the headwaters of the river Styx. Psyche climbed treacherous heights to reach where the waters burst from a steep and slippery slope. Dragons prowled both banks. Psyche was sure that this would be the end of her. But then Zeus's eagle saw her from afar. The bird owed Eros a favor, so he swooped down, took the jar from Psyche, deftly filled it before the dragons could swat at him, and returned it to Psyche.

When Psyche returned the jar to Aphrodite filled with Stygian water, the goddess was more determined than ever to set the young girl a task to finish her off. Aphrodite instructed Psyche to travel to the Underworld and fill a box with some of Queen Persephone's beauty, then bring it back to Aphrodite. Under no circumstances was the younger woman to open the box, however.

Now, Psyche was truly despairing, for she recognized that she could only travel to Tartarus as one of the dead. Would she have to kill herself to undertake this task? She climbed a high tower, prepared to throw herself from it, but the tower spoke to her. It told her how she might enter the Underworld. It further instructed her to bring coins to pay Charon, the ferryman who transported souls across the river Styx. The tower also told her to get two pieces of honey-soaked bread to give to Cerberus, the three-headed dog who guards the entry to Tartarus.

The tower further warned her that a corpse would float by and beg to be hauled into the boat as she was being ferried across the Styx. Under no circumstances was Psyche to succumb to pity for this person. She must stop up her ears and ignore his pleas. The tower warned her that, once ashore, three women would be weaving cloth and would ask for her help, but she must refuse them. Finally, the tower instructed her to use the sops to appease Cerberus. By following the tower's instructions, Psyche was able to complete her task, and she found herself carrying the beauty box back with her toward the upper world. But at the last moment, her curiosity got the better of her. "I would be a fool to be carrying this box of divine beauty and not to take a very little bit of it for my own use," she told herself. So she opened the box and in that instant, was overcome with a deep sleep. She fell down and lay as still as a corpse.

Since leaving Psyche, Eros had been held as if a prisoner by his angry mother. But he could bear to be parted from his love no longer.

He flew now to Psyche and brushed the cloud of sleep away from her. He closed the box and handed it to her, telling her to complete the task his mother set her. Then he flew to Olympus and begged Zeus to bless his marriage to Psyche, which Zeus was happy to do. To assuage the wrath of Aphrodite, Zeus invited Psyche to Olympus and had her drink the nectar of the Gods so that she would become immortal. In this way, Aphrodite would not have to feel that her son had married beneath him.

The wedding of Psyche and Eros was celebrated with great merriment. Even Aphrodite danced a lively dance. In due time, Psyche gave birth to a daughter, and her name was Pleasure.

From the tale's beginning, the central conflict is between Psyche and Aphrodite. The younger woman presents a challenge to the supremacy of the older woman—Psyche's beauty is revered even above that of the goddess of love herself. A powerful woman who experiences herself as attractive, confident, and capable can feel threatened by the arrival of someone younger, full of promise and beauty. This psychological situation may play out in the personal or professional sphere—it has an archetypal foundation. There is a time in life for claiming our power and authority. However, at another time, we must cede these to the next generation. The story of Psyche and Eros illustrates the universal bones of this situation and reveals the considerable task that the younger woman may have as she navigates this generational transfer of power.

Psyche draws Aphrodite's envy through no fault of her own. In the first part of the story, she is passive, floating about in the breeze. She doesn't seek the acclaim that comes to her or respond to her situation with agency. She finds herself the blameless victim of Aphrodite's jealous attacks. Later, she becomes the secret bride of Eros. She doesn't even show much curiosity about where she is, how she got there, or who the strange man is who visits her each night.

Psyche's passivity results in a kind of provisional resolution by the middle of the story. She is mostly happy in her beautiful palace with her mysterious husband. However, she begins to grow lonely and bored. Loneliness and boredom are feelings that can come over us when we start to recognize that we are stuck. We feel restless or ill at ease. We may not be able to articulate what is wrong, but we sense that something is off. These feelings often prompt us to take action, sometimes impulsively. Even if the step is not well thought out, it can sometimes set something in motion and end the stalemate.

So it is in Psyche's case. Her feelings of restlessness bring about a desire to see her sisters. Psychologically, we could say that some part of her recognizes that change and disruption are needed. This part is aligned with the sisters. The sisters are motivated by jealousy and plot to end Psyche's happiness. But we can also see them as psychic factors that are intent on breaking up stale or overly rigid ways of being. The sisters are not going to allow Psyche to remain passive and unconscious.

When Psyche lights the candle, she brings consciousness to the situation. There is a moment when we get sick of being in denial and choose not to keep ourselves in the dark any longer. In the story, this moment begets clarity and knowledge—Psyche now knows she is married to none other than Eros himself. And yet it is also a tragedy. She has betrayed her love, and, in so doing, she has lost him.

Becoming conscious of her situation precipitates the sorrowful search for her lost love and necessitates a confrontation with her mother-in-law. At first, Psyche must acknowledge the older woman's power and authority and submit meekly to her punishments. As we step toward claiming our authority, an attitude of hubris will not do. We do not come by authority by denigrating someone else's. Psyche must give the older woman her due. She earnestly completes each task that the goddess sets her.

But just as Psyche must show respect to her mother-in-law, so it is also vital that, at the right moment, she challenges the supremacy of the older woman. Psyche's boldness in opening the box is necessary for her transformation and the story's ultimate resolution.

At this moment, she dares to ask something for herself. Here she *consciously* asserts her status as equal to that of her mother-in-law. She connects with her vital spark and finds her ability to be a little selfish and demand something. In the beginning of the tale, she aroused Aphrodite's anger because others held her up as equal to or surpassing the goddess, but Psyche herself could not claim this. The opening of the box is an act of rebellious self-assertion that brings about a happy ending and releases Psyche from her supplicant status. She becomes a full equal to her divine mother-in-law. The story is an important prescription for how to grow into one's authority. It tells us that you must first humbly acknowledge the wisdom and dominance of the elders and be willing to pay your dues. But when the time is right, you must be ready to step into your own.

WHO HAS THE POWER?

When Josie first came to see me, she had just given birth to her second child. She was petite with wild blonde curls and a self-deprecating sense of humor. Josie had married the love of her life—a tall, elegant surgeon who made her laugh and shared her love of cooking. Her husband's family was from Nigeria and had immigrated to the US when her husband was a small child. Shortly before coming to see me, she and her husband had moved to the area to be close to his parents, so Josie found herself in a strange city surrounded by her husband's extended family.

Josie's husband was the eldest son. As is often the case in such a configuration, he was the "prince" of the family, much beloved by his mother, who felt no one was good enough for him. Josie had a lively career as a fabric designer, but this did not garner any respect from her husband's family, who valued academic achievement and intellectual pursuits above all else. Josie was aware that her mother-in-law did not like her from the beginning. This situation had become the subject of much hilarity between her and her husband as they used humor to deal with the uncomfortable relationship tensions. But now that she was living among his family, the constant stream of critique—both explicit and implicit—left her feeling distressed and isolated.

Josie's mother-in-law found fault with her cooking, housekeeping, and parenting. In addition, the older woman had gone back to school to pursue a PhD and made subtle disparaging comments about Josie's work. Worst of all, she often criticized Josie in front of Josie's children. Josie was formidable in her own right, and she had her husband's absolute—if passive—support, but in the face of such a stream of negativity, she found her self-esteem crumbling.

In one tearful session, she shared her fears that her husband would find her inadequate and leave her and that her children would come to share her mother-in-law's disdain for her. To that point, Josie had deflected her mother-in-law's attacks with humor. In effect, she had never dealt with them head-on or taken them seriously. After I empathized with the pain she was feeling, I told her flatly that she, in fact, had all the power in the situation. This simple sentence stopped her in her tracks. She was silent for a moment and then asked me what I meant.

"You have this woman's son who is loyal to you first. You also have her grandchildren."

My reframing of the situation shifted Josie's attitude. She went from batting away her mother-in-law's critiques to engaging with her in a confrontation that honored both the older woman's wisdom, power, and age and her own talents, position, and authority. Just as Psyche approached her mother-in-law with respect before asserting herself, Josie started to have serious conversations with her mother-in-law, in which she acknowledged the considerable achievements of the older woman. But she did so while claiming her position of power and setting limits. For example, she calmly made it clear that she would not tolerate being criticized or insulted in front of her children.

Josie had to complete her version of Psyche's tasks. Although she had her husband's support, she had to negotiate the relationship with her mother-in-law mostly on her own, just like Psyche. She and I worked together to discern what belonged only to Josie and what belonged to the situation that had become constellated between herself and the older woman. Together, week after week, we carefully put each seed in its correct place. Things did not always go smoothly. Josie's mother-in-law did not relish having her position of supreme authority usurped, and there was more than one ugly confrontation. But Josie never again retreated into a self-deprecatory stance, nor did she stoop to treating her mother-in-law with anything but respect even as she set firm limits. It took a few years, but eventually, a truce was struck. It was clear that Josie's mother-in-law respected her, even if she never overtly stated this. Eventually, Josie's mother-in-law sought her son's advice on medical matters, but she looked to Josie for help and guidance on many other issues—and Josie was genuinely pleased to provide it.

As with Josie, sometimes we have an outer mother-in-law against whom we are tested and need to find our sense of self-assertion. But sometimes, what holds us back from stepping up and assuming more authority in work, personal relationships, or life involves an *inner* mother-in-law that makes it difficult for us to grow into our mature stance.

CAPITULATION

When I was twenty-two, teaching at the girls' boarding school—the same one where I figured out I could break back into my room by tricking the lock with an ID card—I still had not developed a firm stance in the world. I was young and unsure of myself. As a "house mother" to a small dorm, I held authority given to me by my position at the school, but I didn't have a consolidated sense of personal power. Part of my role as dorm parent was to police rules and regulations. Smoking was strictly forbidden, but unsurprisingly, as the year concluded, I frequently smelled cigarette smoke coming from the upper floors of the dorm where there was a small attic. On these occasions, I marched loudly upstairs so the girls would hear me coming and put the cigarettes away before I came upon them. Getting caught smoking came with a severe punishment and a permanent mark on one's record, so I never wanted to see them. Instead, I would reprimand them and pretend I was frustrated at not having caught them red-handed. After several weeks of this charade, I had a pretty good idea of who was smoking and where and when they were doing it.

One day, I was called to the office of the head of school. Dr. Houston was a stern, unapproachable older woman. She sat behind an imposing desk in her oak-paneled office with another senior administrator, and I took a seat across from her in a high-backed leather armchair. The two older women told me they had proof that Alice, a girl in my dorm, was supplying the others with cigarettes. According to Dr. Houston, some other students had come forward with incontrovertible evidence. Dr. Houston and the other senior administrator were serious and intent. They planned to proceed with disciplinary action against Alice.

I hesitated. "Who is accusing her?" I asked. "We can't tell you that," answered Dr. Houston. Something didn't feel right about the story. Alice was from Louisiana, making her an outsider at this New England prep school. She had struggled all year with feelings of homesickness. I knew the other girls didn't like her. I felt pretty sure that, although she was one of the girls whom I had almost caught smoking, she was hardly the ringleader as was being claimed. In my gut, I knew that something was wrong, but I wasn't strong enough to assert this inner knowing. I folded and acceded to their plan to punish Alice. She was understandably distraught and defiantly pro-claimed her innocence. A month or two later, it was revealed that things were as I had suspected. Alice had been set up by some of the girls in the dorm and was not the main culprit in the dorm smoking scandal, even though she took the fall for it.

My instincts had been right. I knew the people and the situation on the ground more intimately than Dr. Houston in her stately office with its high ceilings and velvet drapes. And yet I hadn't stood up for Alice—or myself. I wasn't ready yet to take on the next generation. I was still deferential and assumed that someone as qualified and revered as Dr. Houston would know better than I.

Being able to listen to our intuition can be an important aspect of finding our authority. I had my own sense of what was going on but was unable to hold onto it or assert it. Intuition offers us clarity rather than certainty. It is quietly sure of itself. It speaks without urgency or anxiety, even when it is warning us. Speaking up for what I knew to be right would have required me to be in contact with my intuition and to find the authority to assert the knowledge that it offered, but I was years away from reaching that.

BEYOND THE INGENUE

Through her encounter with her mother-in-law, Psyche grows beyond being the beautiful young woman—what Jungian analyst Linda Leonard refers to as "the eternal girl"[3]—and becomes powerful in her own right. When the actress Reese Witherspoon was in her thirties, she found she was no longer being offered choice roles, even though she had won accolades for her previous work. Her financial advisor told her to start saving money because she would likely work even less in her forties. As for many actresses before her, Witherspoon was having difficulty navigating the transition from ingenue to mature woman.

In response to this crisis, Witherspoon founded her own production company at the age of thirty-six. Pacific Standard was established with a goal to create films with strong female leads. The company produced the Oscar-nominated 2014 film *Wild*, which featured Witherspoon in the lead role as a woman at midlife seeking to reconnect with herself after a period of depression and substance abuse left her life in shambles. Witherspoon forged her own path from the young blonde "it" girl to a mature, seasoned actress playing psychologically complex roles. In recent years, her career has continued to blossom, both on and off camera.

Assuming authority means being willing to leave behind old ways of being in the world and step into new skills. It requires getting in touch with the creative energy of the goddess and being unafraid of her dark side. While the ingenue is sweet and unassuming, the mature woman has access to authority that can flow only from the dark depths of the personality. A mother-in-law fairy tale from India shows us how a beleaguered daughter-in-law could assume her authority after making contact with the fiery, feminine divine.

THE CLEVER DAUGHTER-IN-LAW

There once was a mother-in-law who was a terrible tyrant. She made her daughter-in-law do all the housework, look after all the animals, and carry water from the well. Then the mother-in-law and her son would eat a big meal themselves and give the young woman stale leftovers. If the woman dared to complain, the mother-in-law would pick up a broom and beat her. If she wept, the old woman would rain down curses and insults, calling her a slut and worse. The husband was meek and never said anything to protect his wife.

In the backyard of the house grew a snake gourd plant. The young woman's mouth watered whenever she looked at the growing snake gourds. Semi-starved, she fantasized about eating a big bowl of delicious snake gourd talada.

One day, she returned from the market with important news for her mother-in-law. The older woman's sister was taken ill and called for her family to come immediately. The mother-in-law left in a hurry, but the mother-in-law asked her daughter-in-law to finish cooking the talada.

The daughter-in-law was excited. She made more talada. She made several other dishes and served her husband a big, delicious meal. Then, she took a big bowl of the talada to the temple of the goddess Kali—the only place where she could find peace. She closed the door behind her and sat down to eat the talada. She ate and ate such a quantity that the goddess was shocked and put her hand over her mouth in disbelief. The young woman was so busy eating that she didn't notice this. She scraped the bowl clean, let out a big belch of satisfaction, and went down to the river to wash the bowl.

When she returned home that evening, her mother-in-law was very angry. Sparks were flying from her eyes. She had a stick in her hand,

and blows fell on the young woman's back and waist till she fell to the ground crying pitifully. "You daughter of a whore, how long have you waited to cheat me like this? You've gobbled up a pot full of talada like a buffalo, you dirty slut!" screamed the woman, and she rained some more blows. When the husband came home, he, too, joined in the punishment.

Meanwhile, the whole town was buzzing with the news that the statue of Kali in the temple now had its hand on its mouth. People from other towns also came to see this miracle, and everyone had their own interpretation. Everyone was scared that this was a bad sign. Something terrible was going to happen to the village, they thought with a shudder. Worship and rituals were performed all over the village.

"Someone has polluted the goddess. That's why she has shut her mouth with her hand. She is angry. There won't be any rain. No children will be born in this village anymore," they said, terror-stricken. They arranged festivals and sacrificed goats. But nothing seemed to please the goddess. So the village elders sent the town crier through the area to announce a big reward to anyone who would make the goddess remove her hand from her mouth. No one came forward.

The daughter-in-law watched all this and came to her mother-in-law one day and said, "Mother-in-law, tell the elders we'll get the goddess to remove her hand from her mouth. I know how to do it."

The mother-in-law was furious at first. "Look at her! She wants me to lose face in the village. She wants to act big, as if she is a holy woman. What no one could do, she says she'll do. Fat chance!" she sneered. But the daughter-in-law persisted and convinced her that she knew something no one else knew.

On the appointed day, she took a broomstick and a garbage basket full of rubbish and went to the temple. She shut everyone out and closed the door behind her. She put down the basket in front of the Black Goddess and, brandishing her broomstick, challenged Kali: "You jealous female! What's it to you if I ate my snake gourd talada? Why do your eyes burn? If you'd only asked me, I'd have given you some. May your face burn, your cheeks swell and explode, and your eyes sink and go blind! Will you take your hand off your mouth now or shall I beat you with my broomstick?! Now!"

There was no answer. The daughter-in-law was furious and looked like Kali the Black Goddess herself. She went up to the image and gave Kali's face several whacks with her broomstick. Kali whimpered and cried out. She removed her hand from her mouth, and the image now looked as it had always looked. "That's better!" muttered the daughter-in-law. She picked up her basket and broom and came home with the news that she had managed to get Kali to remove her hand from her mouth.

The whole village was agog with the news. Everyone ran to the temple to see for themselves and couldn't believe their eyes. They praised the daughter-in-law as the greatest of chaste wives whose virtue had given her miraculous powers. They gave her a big reward and many gifts.

Now the mother-in-law was terrified by this incident. She felt that her daughter-in-law had strange powers and would take revenge against her for all the terrible things she had done all these years. The young woman must know some magic, and who knows what she could do?

On a dark night, mother and son whispered to each other. She said to him, "Son, this one frightened even Kali the Mother Goddess, and made her take her hand off her mouth. She won't let us go unharmed. We have beaten her, starved her, and given her every kind of trouble. She'll take revenge. She'll finish us off. What shall we do?"

"I can't think of anything. You tell me," said the cowardly son.

She said, "She's now asleep. We'll gather her up in her mat, take her to the fields, and burn her in the pit there. I'll get you a beautiful new bride."

"All right, let's do it right now," he said, and they gagged her quickly and rolled her in her bedclothes and mat. The daughter-in-law woke up, but she lay still and pretended to be sleeping. They carried her to the pit in the field outside the village and hid her behind the bush while they went looking for twigs and firewood. As soon as they left, she rolled around and loosened the mat around her. She slid out of it, pulled at the string around her hands and tore it, took the gag from her mouth, and found a log nearby, which she wrapped in her bedclothes and mat. Then she walked a little distance, climbed a banyan tree, and hid in its branches.

The mother and son came hurrying back, spread twigs and branches all around the bundle in the mat, put logs over it, and lighted it. They covered it with dry straw. It glowed with leaping flames as they watched it burn and burn. When the knots in the fuel crackled and burst, they said, "The bones, the bones are splitting." When the log inside caught fire, its knot cracked in the flames and went off like a gunshot. They were satisfied that the skull had now exploded as it does in a cremation. It was dawn, and they went home.

The daughter-in-law crouched in the branches. That night, four robbers sat under the tree, dividing up some loot among themselves. They had just broken into a rich man's mansion and plundered jewelry, gold, and cash. As they sat down, they saw a fire burning at some distance. So one of them climbed the tree to see if anyone was near the fire. He came right up to the branch where the daughter-in-law was perched. When he saw someone sitting there, he said softly, "Who's there?" She boldly put out her hand, gently shut his mouth, and whispered, "Ssh, not so loud. I'm a celestial. I'm looking for a good handsome man. I'll marry you and make you rich beyond your dreams. Just be quiet!"

The robber couldn't believe what was happening to him. He held her hand and said, "Are you for real?" She said, "Hmm." Then she slowly pulled out her little satchel of betel leaf and nut, gave him some, and put some into her mouth. He came closer to kiss her. She turned away, saying, "Look, we're not married yet. But you can put your betel leaf into my mouth with your tongue. I'll be as good as your wedded wife when I've eaten from your mouth. All right?"

He was beside himself with joy. He put out his tongue with the chewed betel leaf and brought it close to her mouth. She at once closed her teeth on his tongue powerfully and bit it off. Screaming with unbearable pain, he lost his grip and fell down. The robbers below ran helter-skelter in panic. The man who had fallen had lost his tongue and could only babble and blabber and spit blood, making noises like "*Da da dadadada . . .*" as he, too, ran after his companions. His noises scared them even more, and they fled faster, with him squealing behind them.

When dawn came, the daughter-in-law cautiously climbed down the tree and saw to her amazement lots of gold, jewelry, and money. She quickly bundled them all up and went straight home. When she tapped on the door, calling out, "Mother-in-law, Mother-in-law, please open the door!" the mother-in-law opened the door hesitantly, her face blanched with fear. There, in front of her, was her smiling daughter-in-law. The mother-in-law fainted. The daughter-in-law carried her into the hall, sprinkled cool water on her face, and revived her. Her son just stood there, not knowing what to think.

When she came to and opened her eyes, the mother-in-law asked her, "How did you . . . ? How is it you are . . . ?"

The daughter-in-law briskly replied, "After you cremated me, messengers from Yama, the god of death, took me to Him. His eyes were shooting flames like our Kali, our village goddess. As soon as He saw me, He said, 'Send this one back. Her mother-in-law is a sinner. Bring *her* here and put the Iron Crow to work on her, to tear her to pieces with its beak. Dip her in cauldrons of boiling oil.' He ranted on like that about you. I fell at His feet and begged Him, 'Don't do this to my mother-in-law. She is really a very fine woman. Give me whatever punishment you wish. Please spare my mother-in-law.' He was pleased, even smiled, and said, 'You can go now. We'll do as you say. But if your mother-in-law ever troubles you, we'll drag her here. My messengers will always be watching.' Then He gave me all this gold, jewelry, and money and sent me home. People say bad things about the god of death. But He was so good to me."

The mother-in-law embraced her daughter-in-law with fear and trembling in her heart.

"You're really the angel of this house. You've saved me from the jaws of death's messengers. So, from now on, I'll do as you say. Just forgive everything I've done to you. Will you, my darling daughter-in-law?" she said, touching the daughter-in-law's chin tenderly.

The daughter-in-law was now the boss in the house. Her mother-in-law and her husband followed her wishes and everyone was happy.

Many Indian fairy tales involve mistreatment by a mother-in-law. This theme may reflect the practice common in India for a bride to leave her family to live with her husband's mother and father. It also reflects the archetypal pattern we have explored in this chapter—the transfer of authority from one generation to the next.

The daughter-in-law begins the story unquestioningly subservient to her mother-in-law, just as Psyche was initially. Her transition to head of the household starts when she furtively satisfies a deep desire. Just as Psyche opens the beauty box, the heroine of this story sneaks away to Kali's temple to eat her fill of the talada. In both tales, a fervent wish impels the heroine to transgress, to cross a forbidden line. Claiming authority will often involve challenging a collective norm or taboo.

Both stories involve an arrogation of divine power. Psyche, at first, unwittingly challenges the goddess Aphrodite by being more beautiful than she is. Later, she consciously chooses to take a little of Persephone's beauty for herself. In the Indian tale, the daughter-in-law's fortunes change for the better when she directly confronts the goddess Kali and threatens and beats her. Later, she tricks the thief by telling him she is a celestial. Finally, she represents herself to her husband and mother-in-law at the end of the tale as carrying the authority of the god of death. In mythological stories, one of the quickest ways to earn a terrible punishment is to challenge a god's or goddess's supremacy. However, Lilith isn't bothered when we confront her. She has been exiled for too long and is overjoyed to return to us. She cheers us on when we ask that we be treated as her equal. Reconnecting with her won't be hubris; it will be life-giving.

Daring to claim a bit of divine authority seems to be required for a woman to grow up and become powerful. Authority always rests upon a transpersonal basis—most kings claimed their power came from the gods. Finding personal authority will require us to connect with the divine principle, or that which is larger than self. Having a living connection to the goddess helps us to know our place in the cosmos. We are neither too arrogant, nor too humble, but we can claim our rightful place because a relationship with the divine sustains us.

Kali and Lilith could be sisters. Kali is the divine mother, and the ultimate manifestation of Shakti, or primordial cosmic energy. She is also the goddess of time, change, power, and destruction, and is most often pictured in her terrifying aspect. Her skin is deep blue, and her tongue lolls out of her mouth. She wears a necklace of severed human heads, and around her waist she wears a girdle of severed human arms. That the daughter-in-law in the story can easily command the goddess indicates that renewed contact with this fierce energy is welcomed and appropriate. She has been nice and subservient for too long.

The clever daughter-in-law has come to Kali's temple to nourish herself and fulfill a deep need for sustenance. When we pursue our needs with clarity of intention, we encounter our destiny. The daughter-in-law shocks the goddess by how much she eats. When we pay attention to our needs and desires, our large appetite for life can be an asset, putting us in contact with divine energies. In such a case, the goddess will help us. Our audacity is rewarded. In the Indian tale, the heroine must confront the goddess before taking on her mother-in-law. Once she stands toe-to-toe with the goddess, she is invincible.

For a woman to assert her authority, she must know her inner Kali or Lilith. Attempts to assert oneself without this deep inner contact will fail. The clever daughter-in-law goes into Kali's temple to have her secret rendezvous with nourishment. Owning her needs is a sacred act. Tending those needs puts her in right relationship with the goddess and cements their connection. When we honor our needs, we commune with the goddess. The fairy tale tells us that encountering this energy is facilitated by expressing our deepest yearnings and desires. It is the daughter-in-law's destiny to become a matriarch. There is always something divine about encountering our destiny.

The daughter-in-law is kind to her mother-in-law in the end. She doesn't seek revenge and is a good manager. The daughter-in-law was able to overthrow the oppressive authority of her mother-in-law and assume her rightful place without becoming tyrannical herself.

THE STRENGTH OF CONVICTION

Holding authentic authority means having confidence in our perceptions and analysis, even when no one else sees what we see, or what we see threatens the status quo. Ivana had grown up in the former USSR and had vivid recollections of what the abuse of power and silencing looked like. Though she initially came to see me because of her troubles with her teenage son, another issue eventually took center stage in our sessions. She began to suspect that the clinic where she worked as a nurse was engaged in unethical and fraudulent practices. In our weekly meetings, she shared her suspicions with me. These eventually became a conviction that something was amiss. She brought her observations to her superiors and was shocked when they accused her of misunderstanding and intimated that it would be better for her to drop her concerns. At first, she questioned herself. Had she misunderstood? Her superiors' effort to undermine her faith in her own perceptions is another example of the phenomenon of gaslighting that we explored in chapter 3. But because she had grown up in the former Soviet Union, she was aware of how such tactics were used to silence and discourage those who dared to question. Whenever she calmly considered the facts of the situation as she had been observing them, she found again the conviction that she could trust her own perceptions, and the courage that flowed from that. Ivana struggled with what to do, and we considered the options. She could continue working and remain silent, quit and move on without looking back, or report the practice to the regulating body.

Ivana quickly rejected the first option. She was a conscientious person, and simply continuing to work to pick up the paycheck while turning a blind eye to the unethical practice going on was not something she could stomach. She considered simply quitting. Her skills were in demand, and it would be easy for her to get another job. However, it didn't feel right to her to move on without saying anything. Becoming a whistleblower felt like the right ethical choice, yet there were many dangers and disadvantages. It could embroil her in legal and administrative procedures and harm her career, as others in the field could be reluctant to hire her. Reporting the clinic would also mean betraying her supervisors, whom she had previously held in high regard and to whom she still felt some loyalty.

Ivana loved being a nurse. Jeopardizing her career was no small matter to her. Many days, she was filled with self-doubt. Had she misinterpreted the evidence? But she kept coming back to her own knowing. Ultimately, she decided to trust herself. She knew it was right to step into her authority. Despite the risks, Ivana reported the clinic's ethical breach. Subsequent proceedings revealed that she had been correct in her assessment of the situation. It was a challenging time, and there were many losses and difficulties. However, once she took this step, she felt how right it was. She felt a deep sense of relief. "I'm sleeping better," she told me. She confidently claimed her knowledge, power, and personal authority. She was asked to testify and made frequent media appearances when the scandal was uncovered. Her surefootedness and confidence in these high-pressure situations surprised Ivana. She felt fully alive and in possession of her strengths even though some were trying to discredit her publicly. Her heightened visibility and confidence eventually led her to a leadership role in healthcare, where she thrived.

Ivana had been understandably afraid of taking such a bold step. Embracing her authority did bring chaos and destruction. Ivana lost friends. She saw some people she had liked and admired lose their jobs. Her relationship with her husband suffered as she became increasingly preoccupied. There were times when she was plagued by doubts. And yet, she had clarity that she had done the correct thing. Standing up for what was right, even in the face of risk, felt like a triumphant claiming of power, agency, and authority. It was an exultant recognition that she could trust her inner knowing and that when she did so, her life grew larger.

Crossing the threshold to authority comes at a cost. We must give up illusions and face ugly truths about ourselves and the world. We must sacrifice the comforting belief that others know better than we and will tell us what to believe and make everything right. We must take responsibility for our own considerable power, which we may secretly fear. The vital spark invites us to step out of the shadow of obedience and into the center of our lives. It welcomes us to become our own master, to connect with our deep knowing and consciously claim our potency and aliveness.

QUESTIONS FOR REFLECTION

1. In the beginning of "Psyche and Eros," Psyche is very passive. It is only once she has the confrontation with her mother-in-law that she begins to find her agency. Where in your life have you been passive? Where in your life right now are you reactive rather than agentic?

2. Psyche is happy to enjoy her nights with her mysterious husband. How have you allowed yourself to be unconscious about important things? Perhaps you let your partner handle the finances, or you allow yourself not to think about important issues that you will nevertheless have to face someday. What do you think the costs are of remaining unconscious of these things?

3. Aphrodite doesn't like Psyche very much and sets her many impossible tasks. Where is there an Aphrodite in your life? Perhaps it is another person who carries authority—a boss, a family member, or even a literal mother-in-law. Perhaps it is an institution to which

you are answerable that makes many demands on you. What is the attitude you carry toward this person or thing?

4. Psyche must be sure to avoid succumbing to pity for the corpse if she is to complete her final task. Carrying authority often means making difficult decisions and valuing structure and fairness over concern for the plight of the individual. Where does pity get in the way of you making hard choices?

5. Psyche opens the beauty box, and the clever daughter-in-law secretly eats the *talada*. The stories show us that claiming something for ourselves is part of assuming authority. Where in your life have you been bold in reaching for something that you want? How did doing so help you become more authoritative?

6. The daughter-in-law in the Indian tale is badly mistreated by her husband and his mother, but she doesn't try to leave her situation or seek revenge. Instead, she uses her wits to become a worthy opponent and, in that way, prevails. Though leaving a bad situation is sometimes the best thing to do, we may have more power to make changes than we thought we did. Think of a time when you were being treated badly. In what way were you able to become a worthy opponent and advocate for yourself or assert yourself to make changes?

CHAPTER 9

RUTHLESSNESS: OWNING
AGGRESSION

> Only we ourselves can fight for our
> own lives, taking full responsibility for
> what we encounter along the way.
>
> —Aldo Carotenuto, *Eros and Pathos*

Shirley Chisholm was the first Black woman to be elected to the United States Congress. Her first committee assignment was to the House Agriculture Subcommittee on Forestry and Rural Villages. Chisholm challenged congressional traditions by refusing to accept this assignment—she wanted something more relevant to the urban Bedford-Stuyvesant community she represented. Speaker John McCormack encouraged her to "be a good soldier," but Chisholm didn't back down. She was eventually removed from Agriculture and assigned to Veteran's Affairs.[1] Shirly Chisholm didn't worry about stepping on toes. When she saw something that needed to be done, she did it even if it upset others. In the politicking leading up to the 1972 Democratic convention, Black leaders favored different strategies and couldn't agree on a unified approach. Amid the confusion, Chisholm stepped up and announced her bid as a candidate for the US presidency. One of her aids later noted that "they were standing around, peeing on their shoes . . . and so Shirley finally said to hell with it and got a campaign going."[2] Chisholm was known for being intelligent and a remarkable public speaker, but her easy access to sure-footed aggression was one of her most well-known qualities. Her campaign slogan was "unbought and unbossed."

While compassion and pity are admirable qualities, relying too much on them can cut us off from our authentic needs and desires and extinguish our glowing coals. Sometimes, what life requires is ruthlessness. Accessing ruthlessness and aggression when necessary will allow us to find an authoritative stance. In English many centuries ago, *reuthe* meant "pity" or "compassion." To be ruthless, then, is to be without pity. It means we can turn coldly away from the needs of others. Finding our ruthlessness won't be easy for many of us. To do so, we must get to know Lilith in her darkest and most frightening aspect. Encountering this side of our fiery spirit means facing unyielding, unpitying nature—that which unmercifully demands of us that we accept responsibility for ourselves and, in so doing, helps us to grow. If we can honor the dark goddess and apprentice ourselves to her, we can lay claim to some of her power.

Aggression and ruthlessness are qualities that many of us find especially difficult to own and develop. They are particularly forbidden, fraught, and potentially dangerous. It may feel shadowy and uncomfortable even to admit that we have the capacity for ruthlessness. Owning our aggression may be particularly challenging if we have had a difficult relationship with a parent who was ruthless with us. We may have survived childhood by telling ourselves that we would never be like our mother. Our sense of "not like mother" may have become a core belief about ourselves that we need to hold onto. In such cases, opening to the possibility that we, too, have the capacity for aggression may feel threatening to our very sense of self. It is important to remember that aggression related to in a conscious manner is not about wanton cruelty or selfish power-seeking. Married with awareness, aggression and ruthlessness become tools that may be used with care in service to growth.

We cannot thrive if we are not willing, at times, to assert our needs, sometimes even at the expense of another. Those who are incapable of learning this lesson exhaust and deplete themselves in their endless efforts to care for others. Though they seem selfless, they inevitably become resentful. Their denied needs and the resulting bitterness tend to seep out in subtle ways, often poisoning relationships with others. To avoid this, we must become friendly with the dark side of the goddess—she who is unyielding and able to harness her capacity for aggression in service to her goals.

AGGRESSION

One of the meanings of aggression is "readiness to attack or confront." Access to our aggressive capacity doesn't mean that we get into random fights or vent our frustrations at will. Instead, it means we have integrated a sense of our power and ability to stand our ground. As the dictionary definition implies, we are ready to fight when it matters. Others sense this about us implicitly, and this awareness subtly alters how they respond to us.

Access to our aggressive capacity tends to go underground for girls in adolescence when we become oriented to the needs and expectations of others. Since we don't develop a conscious relationship with this capacity, it can feel out of control and threatening when it asserts itself. If our aggression has been disavowed and unused for a decade or two, we may find it unwieldy, awkward, uncomfortable, and frightening. When we pick it back up, it may feel like a tool that is too big for us. Unintegrated aggression often gets expressed in a manner that is heavy-handed, cruel, or ineffectual.

Henpecking is an example of aggression that is not well directed. It may develop in a marriage when we have not integrated our aggression and learned to wield it well. When a woman henpecks her husband or partner, she engages in constant criticism, often laced with disdain. Though men can also treat their partners with contempt, it seems that women are the ones who most often engage in the particular behavior we think of as henpecking. When we henpeck, our vital assertive energy is not well channeled. We may have very legitimate reasons to feel irritable, put upon, or disappointed with our partner, but daily complaints and scolding are not effective at bringing about the changes we want, and they undermine intimacy and connection. If you find that you are frequently subjecting your partner to withering criticisms or mean-spirited teasing, you may want to give yourself credit for your healthy impulse to assert yourself while also considering the potential destructive nature of how it is showing up in your life. Integrating our capacity for aggression takes work. It requires us to accept that we are capable of inflicting harm and to take responsibility for this. It invites us to become fully conscious of our power. And it requires us to gain intimate knowledge of Lilith and her mythological sisters.

As we strive to become familiar with our dark, feminine power, we can't be naive about its destructive potential. If we treat it too casually, we can be harmed—or harm someone else. A Grimms' tale warns us of the dangers that can befall us if we underestimate this power.

FRAU TRUDE

Once upon a time, there was a small girl who was very strong-willed. Whatever her parents told her to do, she disobeyed them.

One day she said to them: "I have heard so much about Frau Trude. Someday I want to go to her place. People see amazing things there, and such strange things happen there, that I have become very curious."

Her parents strictly forbade her, saying: "Frau Trude is a wicked woman who commits evil acts. If you go there, we fear terrible things will happen to you."

But the girl paid no attention to her parents and went to Frau Trude's place anyway.

When she arrived there, Frau Trude asked: "Why are you so pale?"

"Oh," she answered, trembling all over, "I saw something that frightened me."

"What did you see?"

"I saw a green man on your steps."

"That was a huntsman."

"Then I saw a black man."

"That was a charcoal burner."

"Then I saw a blood-red man."

"That was a butcher."

"Oh, Frau Trude, it frightened me when I looked through your window and could not see you, but instead saw the devil with a head of fire."

"Aha!" she said. "So you saw the witch properly outfitted. I have been waiting for you and wanting you for a long time. Light the way for me now!"

With that, she turned the girl into a block of wood and threw it into the fire. When it was thoroughly aglow, she sat down next to it and warmed herself by it, saying: "It gives such a bright light!"

This brief story surprises us. It does not have the happy ending we expect from a fairy tale. It must have served as a warning tale to disobedient children. But it also contains profound psychological truths. Frau Trude is an image of the dark feminine goddess—of the destructive aspect of nature. We experience this destructive power when we age, become ill, or die. We witness it in floods, earthquakes, and natural disasters of all kinds (though many of these have a human-made component as well). Jung pointed out that the unconscious is also a manifestation of nature. We can see the destructive element of nature at work in the psyche when the unconscious overwhelms consciousness, such as in psychosis or other extreme mental states.

I have a small pond in my backyard that is home to many creatures, including fish, frogs, and dragonflies. Several times each summer, the frogs lay masses of eggs near the bank. Then I get to observe the hundreds of tiny black dots become tadpoles that eventually wriggle free of the gelatinous egg mass. As the weeks pass, these little tadpoles get larger. Occasionally, I witness a ferocious dragonfly nymph eating them. I love frogs—their eyes are like jewels, and they sing on summer afternoons. I am always excited to see a fresh batch of frog eggs because I know it will mean more frogs. Seeing the lobster-like dragonfly nymphs catch and eat the tiny tadpoles pains me, but this is nature's plan. Too many frog eggs are produced—more than the pond could support if they all grew to adulthood. The tadpole carnage and destruction I witness are part of the inexorable cycle of life and death in which we are all embedded. To nature, an individual life is just another piece of Frau Trude's kindling.

The girl is fascinated by the stories she has heard of Frau Trude. Examples of nature's destructiveness such as tornadoes or volcanoes mesmerize us because they are darkly numinous. Nature's ability to destroy is dispassionate and impersonal. Illness and death visit us indiscriminately. In the story, the parents are aware of the destructive potential of this energy and command their daughter to stay away.

The girl, however, is insufficiently reverent toward this dark goddess. She has the wrong attitude toward the unconscious. She takes her safety for granted and hubristically assumes that nature's destructive aspect cannot touch her or that it should be there for her amusement and thrill.

As an aspect of nature, the dark feminine is unyielding and unsentimental. Nature doesn't coddle or show mercy but requires us to give life our best effort, just as she does with every one of those tadpoles. She is uncompromising and expects nothing less from us than our all. It demands of us that we accept responsibility for ourselves and grow into the fullest version of ourselves.

An engagement with the dark goddess will be an initiatory encounter that requires us to claim our capacity for darkness and aggression. A similar theme is explored in a Russian fairy tale in which the heroine takes quite a different attitude than the little girl in Frau Trude.

VASILISSA THE BEAUTIFUL

In a certain Tsardom far away, there lived a merchant. He and his wife had one daughter, Vasilissa the Beautiful, and they loved her dearly. When the little girl was eight years old, the mother fell ill, and it became clear that she was going to die. She then called her daughter to her and spoke solemnly.

"My dear daughter, these are my last words. Listen carefully to what I have to say and carry out my wishes. I am dying, and I give you this little doll along with my blessing. Protect it, never show it to anyone, and carry it with you always, for there is no doll like it anywhere in the world. Whenever you are troubled by sorrow or evil, take the doll into a corner, give it something to eat and drink, and then tell it your troubles. It will tell you how to act in your time of need." And then she kissed little Vasilissa on the forehead and took her last breath.

Little Vasilissa grieved greatly for her mother, and in the long nights that followed, she could not sleep but lay in bed and wept. Then, one night, she remembered the little doll. She took it out of her pocket and gave it something to eat and drink. "Oh, little doll!" cried Vasilissa. "Listen to my grief. My dear mother is dead, and I am lonely for her!"

The doll's eyes began to glow like fireflies, and suddenly it came to life. It ate a little, drank a little, and then began speaking.

"Don't weep, little Vasilissa. Grief is worse at night. Lie down, shut your eyes, comfort yourself, and go to sleep. The morning is wiser than the evening." So Vasilissa the Beautiful lay down, comforted herself, and went to sleep, and the next day her grieving was not so deep, and her tears were less bitter.

After some time had passed, the merchant thought of marrying again. There was a widow in a nearby village with two daughters. The merchant thought she would be a good companion and house-keeper and a kind stepmother to little Vasilissa. So he married her and brought her home, but Vasilissa soon learned that the woman was not as her father had hoped.

She was cold and cruel and had only married the merchant for his wealth. She had nothing but envy and spite for Vasilissa, for she was becoming a great beauty as she grew, while the stepmother's daughters were thin and homely. The stepmother and stepsisters gave Vasilissa endless chores, hoping she would be worked to the bone and grow worn and tired. Meanwhile, they lay about the house, pampering themselves. But it didn't work. The stepdaughters remained gaunt and unattractive while Vasilissa grew more beautiful every day.

Now the reason for this was Vasilissa's doll, without which she could never have managed to bear the cruelty of her stepmother and stepsisters. Each night, after everyone else was asleep, Vasilissa would go into a closet and take the doll out of her pocket. She would give it something to eat and drink, then tell the doll her troubles. The doll's eyes would glow, it would eat and drink a little, and tell Vasilissa what to do. Then, while Vasilissa slept, the doll would clean the kitchen, bring the water from the well, weed the garden, and get the stove heated just right so that all Vasilissa needed to do the next day was rest in the shade.

Now it happened that the merchant had to travel to a distant Tsardom. When he was gone, the stepmother contrived a plan to get rid of her stepdaughter once and for all. In the evening, she gave each daughter a task. The eldest had to make a piece of lace, the next to knit a pair of hose, and Vasilissa had to spin flax. She ordered them not to stop before they had finished. Then she lit a single candle, put out all the fires elsewhere in the house, and went to bed. After the girls had been working several hours, the eldest daughter pretended to straighten the wick, but in doing so, she put out the candle as her mother had instructed so that now there was no more light.

"There is not another fire in the house, and our tasks are not done. Vasilissa, you must go to fetch fire at our closest neighbor's house."

Now the closest house was the hut of the terrible witch Baba Yaga, who lived in the middle of the gloomy forest. The stepsisters locked Vasilissa out of the house and told her not to come back in unless she brought fire with her.

Vasilissa sat down on the doorstep and wept. Then she took her doll out of her pocket and gave it something to eat and drink.

"Oh, little doll! I must go to the house of the terrible witch, Baba Yaga, and ask for fire, and I am afraid she will eat me! What shall I do?"

After the doll had eaten and drunk, it spoke. "Do not fear, Vasilissa! Go where you have been sent. No harm will come to you." So Vasilissa put the doll back in her pocket and started walking into the forest's depths.

She walked all through the night, and the going was hard. After many hours of walking, she heard hooves. A man dressed all in white galloped by on a white horse. As soon as he passed, cool dawn appeared in the sky. She continued walking. Many hours later, a man dressed all in red on a bright red horse passed her, and the sun reached its zenith in the sky.

She walked and walked, and as evening fell, she came upon a neat green lawn. In the midst of it stood a little hut raised high off the ground on chicken legs. A fence of human bones surrounded the green lawn. On the top of each fence post was a human skull. The gate's hinges were made from foot bones, and the lock was made of jaw bones. Vasilissa stopped and stood still in fear. At that moment, a man dressed all in black and riding upon a black horse galloped past. Night fell, and the eyes of the skulls on Baba Yaga's fence began to glow red.

Just then, there was a terrible rushing sound. Baba Yaga came flying through the forest, riding in a great mortar and pushing herself along with a pestle while sweeping away the tracks behind her with a broom. When she arrived at the gate, she spoke. "Little hut, little hut! Turn the way your mother placed you!" Then the hut spun around on its chicken legs and faced the witch. Baba Yaga was about to open the gate and let herself in when she stopped and sniffed. "I smell the blood of a Russian!" she said.

Vasilissa was terrified, but she remembered the encouraging words of her little doll. She drew near to Baba Yaga, bowed very low, and said, "It is only I, Grandmother, Vasilissa. My stepsisters sent me to borrow some fire, for all our lights have gone out."

"Well, I know your stepsisters. If you are going to borrow light from me, you must stay and work for me. If not, I'll eat you for my supper!"

Baba Yaga turned and commanded the gate, upon which it sprang open. The witch went whistling in, and Vasilissa followed her timidly. The gate snapped shut and locked behind her.

Once inside, Baba Yaga spread herself out on the stove and commanded Vasilissa to bring her all the food in the oven. Vasilissa brought forth enough food to fill three strong men. She also brought up beer, wine, and honey from the cellar. Baba Yaga ate and drank it all, leaving Vasilissa only a crust of bread and some cabbage soup.

After she had eaten, Baba Yaga grew drowsy, but she spoke sternly to Vasilissa before falling asleep. "Tomorrow, after I drive away, clean and sweep the yard. Then take a measure of wheat from the storehouse and pick out all the specks of dirt and wild peas. Then, be sure to have a hearty meal prepared for me when I return. If you do not do this, I will eat you for my supper!"

Presently, the old woman turned toward the wall and soon snored loudly so that Vasilissa knew she was sound asleep. Then, Vasilissa went into a corner, took out her doll, gave her a bit to eat and drink, and told the doll that Baba Yaga had set her impossible tasks.

"Do not be afraid, Vasilissa. Say your prayers and go to sleep, for the morning is wiser than the evening."

So Vasilissa lay down on the floor and fell asleep.

When Vasilissa rose the next morning, it was still dark. She looked out the window to see the white rider on his milk-white horse gallop past and jump the fence just as dawn was breaking. Baba Yaga had already left. The girl wondered at the witch's cottage, so filled with all manner of wonderful things. Then she remembered the tasks she was to do. Imagine her relief to find that the yard had already been swept and tidied and to see her little doll picking out the last of the specks of dirt and peas from the wheat. All Vasilissa had to do was cook Baba Yaga's supper, and she set out to do this with great diligence.

As evening drew near, Vasilissa saw the black rider on his black horse gallop past and jump the fence. Just after, there was a terrible whistling noise, and Baba Yaga swept into view. The witch inspected the yard, the hut, and the wheat, saying that if she found any fault, she would eat Vasilissa for supper. But so perfectly had the doll performed the tasks that Baba Yaga could not find a weed in the yard or a single pea or speck of dirt in the wheat. She was furious but tried not to show it. Instead, she clapped her hands three times and called for her faithful servants. Immediately, three pairs of hands appeared, took the wheat, and began to grind it.

Then Baba Yaga sat down, and Vasilissa served her an enormous meal, enough for four strong men. Baba Yaga ate it all, including the bones. After dinner, she commanded Vasilissa to complete all of the tasks she had done that day on the next, but, in addition, she was to take a measure of poppy seeds and clean them one by one. Then she turned toward the wall and once again began to snore.

Vasilissa took the little doll from her pocket and went into a corner. As on the previous evening, the doll comforted her. "Go to sleep now, Vasilissa, for the morning is wiser than the evening." So Vasilissa said her prayers, lay down and went to sleep.

The next morning, she found that the doll had completed all of the tasks Baba Yaga had set and that she only had to cook the old witch's dinner. At dusk, she once again heard the roaring of Baba Yaga's approach just as the man in black on his coal-black horse galloped past. The sun set and the eyes of the skulls began to glow, and in came Baba Yaga, sniffing around and carefully inspecting everything. But as on the previous day, she could not find any fault with Vasilissa's work. Once again, she clapped her hands and called for her servants, and three pairs of hands appeared to carry away the poppy seeds to press them for oil.

Then Vasilissa served the meal she had prepared, enough for five strong men, and she also laid beer and honey on the table. Baba Yaga ate every morsel while Vasilissa stood nearby.

When she had finished eating, Baba Yaga snapped at her. "Why do you just stand there as if you can't speak?"

"I didn't wish to speak without your permission, Grandmother, but if you will permit me, I will ask you some questions."

"Well, just remember that not every question leads to good. If you know too much, you will grow old too quickly."

"As I walked through the woods, I saw a man on horseback dressed all in white on a milk-white horse. Who is he?"

"That was my white, bright day. He is a servant of mine, but he cannot hurt you. Ask me more."

"Later in the day, I was overtaken by a second rider dressed all in red on a bright red horse. Who is he?"

"That was my round, red sun. He is also my servant, but he cannot hurt you. Ask me more," she said, grinding her teeth.

"I saw a third rider, dressed in black on a coal-black horse. Who is he?"

"That is my servant, dark, black night. He cannot hurt you. Ask me more!" she demanded, growing furious. But Vasilissa was silent.

"Ask me more! Ask me of the three pairs of hands that serve me!" But Vasilissa saw the eagerness in Baba Yaga's manner.

"Three questions are enough for me. I would not grow old too soon by knowing too much."

"It is good for you that you asked only about what you saw outside the hut. If you had asked about the three pairs of hands, they would have seized you and carried you away to become my food just as they did the wheat and the poppy seeds. Now I have a question to ask you. How is it that you have been able to complete all of the tasks I set you?"

Vasilissa was so frightened to see the way that the witch ground her teeth that she almost told her about the little doll, but she thought quickly and only replied, "The blessing of my dead mother helps me."

Baba Yaga sprang up and started shouting. "Leave my house immediately! I want no one who bears a blessing to enter my house! Leave at once!"

Vasilissa ran out of the hut and into the yard. Behind her, she heard Baba Yaga yelling at the gate to open. Then Baba Yaga grabbed one of the skulls from the fence post and threw it after Vasilissa. "There is the fire for your stepmother and stepsisters! Take it to them, and may they have joy in it!"

Vasilissa put the skull on a stick and ran as fast as she could through the forest. It was night, but she found her way by the light of the skull's glowing eyes, which only went out at daybreak. She walked all through the day, and in the evening, she found herself once more at her stepmother's house. She thought to herself that, by this time, they must surely have found some other source of light, and she threw the skull into the hedge, but it spoke to her.

"Do not throw me away, beautiful Vasilissa. Bring me to your stepmother."

So Vasilissa brought the skull inside to her stepmother. When she did, the eyes of the skull began to glow fiercely, and its gaze followed the stepmother and stepdaughters wherever they went until they were burned to death.

At the beginning of the story, we learn that Vasilissa has a good mother. The little doll is an eloquent image of an internal ability to self-soothe and find inner resources. Such a capacity is the gift we receive when we are adequately mothered. If our mother or caregivers reliably comforted us when we were distressed, we internalize this ability and can do it for ourselves. Such an internal good mother is a kind of magic in our lives, an inexhaustible font of wisdom and comfort. Vasilissa's magical doll is a perfect image for this inner capacity to self-soothe. We always carry it with us, but we may not even be aware of it until we need it. Our capacity to lovingly tend to ourselves when we are distraught manifests mainly in how we speak to ourselves in our inner voice. There is a difficulty with having a good mother, however. When we are well-loved and cared for, it may be more difficult for us to find our aggression. "Good enough" mothering may teach us to trust ourselves, regulate our emotions, and expect the world to treat us fairly, but it may leave us without important access to the ruthlessness that we may need if things take a dark turn.

THE INNER VOICE

Most of us don't pay much attention to inner self-talk, but this voice enormously impacts our moods, self-assessment, and overall resilience. If we constantly berate ourselves or indulge our doubts and fears, this voice will have a corrosive effect on our souls. If we speak to ourselves with gentleness and compassion, we will be soothed and strengthened, ready to face potential challenges.

What any of us need when we are upset—from our mothers, partners, or ourselves—is first, a listening ear. Our feelings need to be heard and met. It feels terrible when we are distraught and the person we confide in tells us we are overreacting or minimizes our concern. The doll provides this receptive listening for Vasilissa, who gets to pour out her troubles.

Once we have been heard, we often feel a little calmer. Then, it can be helpful to have someone engage with us in perspective-taking or problem-solving. The little doll does for Vasilissa what a good mother does for a child and what resilient people do for themselves. Psychologists call it *decatastrophizing*. When faced with a problem, we all tend to become overwhelmed. We then lose perspective, and the difficulty often appears worse than it is. We may assume that the outcome will inevitably be the worst one possible. Such an attitude can induce feelings of panic and even paralysis. Not only do we feel worse when we engage in this kind of thinking, but we also become too frightened and helpless to act effectively. Being tired or hungry can make it more likely that we will respond to a challenge by catastrophizing.

The doll reminds Vasilissa that "the morning is wiser than the evening." This admonition is a beautiful, poetic way of stating an essential truth—that problems often look more manageable after we have had the chance to sleep on them. It doesn't make much sense to ruminate about our troubles late into the evening when we are depleted. We can give ourselves the gift of rest, knowing that we will likely be able to face a challenge with renewed energy when we awake. When we defer addressing a difficulty until the morning, we can give our problem to the unconscious while we sleep. Like the doll who works to do Vasilissa's chores at night, the unconscious works on our issues while we rest.

Having an internalized good mother allows us to relate to the unconscious as a source of comfort and wisdom we can turn to in times of distress. Positive parental complexes have a powerful impact on a person's life because we internalize the ability to soothe ourselves and manage distressing emotions. However, positive experiences with our parents may leave us unprepared for the world in other ways. If our parents tended to us lovingly when we were children, we might not realize how harsh the world can be. We don't expect others to be unkind or manipulative. And we've rarely had to mobilize our aggression to get what we want or protect ourselves. If we have had the blessing of a good mother, we will have to learn to serve the dark goddess before we can be initiated into the use of our aggression. Vasilissa must go to Baba Yaga to find fire because she is not yet in touch with this aspect of her own vital spark.

LEARNING RUTHLESSNESS

Baba Yaga is complex and ambivalent. She is not only horrid, dangerous, and frightening, she is also fair and wise. She gives Vasilissa the fire she promised and recognizes that Vasilissa will need the skull to deal with her stepmother and stepsisters. In other Russian tales, Baba Yaga's role as a wisdom figure is featured. For example, in "Marya Morevna," the hero Ivan seeks Baba Yaga's help—Koschei the Deathless has captured Ivan's warrior princess wife Marya Morevna. Ivan must go to Baba Yaga and seek a magic horse, otherwise he will not be able to defeat Koschei. After making Ivan prove himself, Baba Yaga provides him with his magic steed.

Like Kali, Baba Yaga is a sister of Lilith—fierce, unlovely, and uncompromising. She has jurisdiction over the sun, dawn, and night. She is the keeper of ancient secrets and great wisdom. She is more than just a witch. She is an archaic nature goddess, a primordial Slavic deity who has persisted through the ages. When Vasilissa bravely faces Baba

Yaga and agrees to work for her, Vasilissa becomes a kind of acolyte to this dark goddess. Lilith and Baba Yaga both know how to be ruthless. This capacity for ruthlessness is the skill that Vasilissa needs. She has been well mothered, but she doesn't have access to her fire.

When Baba Yaga gives Vasilissa the skull with the instruction to give it to her stepmother, she shares the gift of fiery aggression, a boon the young woman could not have gained from her mother. Once home, Vasilissa has an impulse to revert to her "nice girl" self and throw the skull away, but the skull speaks, reminding her that Baba Yaga told her to deliver it to the stepmother. Just as the little doll is an image of the nurturing, soothing capacity that Vasilissa gained from her good mother, so the skull can be seen as the voice of the dark mother Baba Yaga that she now carries with her.

Our ability to be aggressive—to stand up for ourselves, set limits, and, when necessary, turn our fiery anger on someone who would hurt us—is a quality that comes from the goddess. It is darkly divine, not quite of this world. It is dangerous and should not be used wantonly or indiscriminately. There are several different endings to the tale, but in most, Vasilissa buries the skull after her stepmother and stepsisters are burned to death. Vasilissa seems to recognize that this divine capacity is something that isn't safe to wield. The act of burying the skull is an image of what culture expects from women. We have been taught to bury our aggression. That the story ends in this manner reveals how profoundly ambivalent it is for women to access this kind of inner potential.

A 2006 film explores a similar story of a young, innocent woman who must apprentice herself to the dark goddess. She must discover what really matters to her and learn to be ruthless in service to her most deeply held values.

THE DEVIL WEARS PRADA

The Devil Wears Prada features a beautiful ingenue, Andy Sachs (Anne Hathaway), who works at a fashion magazine as an assistant to her larger-than-life boss, Miranda Priestly (Meryl Streep). Andy's story mirrors that of Vasilissa. Andy is an earnest recent college graduate who has just arrived in New York City. Though her resume is impressive, she struggles to find a good job in journalism. Finally, running out of options, she applies to become an assistant to the editor of *Runway*, a prestigious fashion magazine. Andy's earnest social justice sensibility and lack of fashion sense are at odds with the obsessive focus on appearance and the cutthroat atmosphere at *Runway*, but she gets the job.

Miranda Priestly, Andy's boss, is renowned for her ice-cold demeanor and demanding temperament. Miranda is a force to be reckoned with. She can wither with a look. Miranda is more than an image of ruthless competition and self-absorbed importance. She is a manifestation of the dark goddess. Like Baba Yaga, she is an image of pure nature—unforgiving, unsentimental, sometimes ruthless, and sometimes life-giving. Though Andy has never heard of her, everyone repeatedly reminds her that "a million girls would kill for this job," and that a good recommendation from Miranda will open any door.

Like Vasilissa, Andy is given a series of seemingly impossible tasks. She must order and fetch Miranda's lunch from a steakhouse and deliver it at precisely the right moment. Miranda even asks that Andy procure the unpublished manuscript of the next *Harry Potter* book for her two daughters—a feat as challenging as any assigned to Vasilissa.

Miranda, like Baba Yaga, seems to be (or imagines herself) in the realm of the superhuman. One scene shows her haranguing Andy to find her a flight out of Florida. It becomes clear that Miranda is in the middle of a hurricane and no planes are flying, but she dismissively refers to the storm as "an absurd weather problem."[3] We see trees lashing violently in high winds through Miranda's hotel window as she demands that Andy find her a way to get home. While Baba Yaga controls the day, noon, and night, Miranda believes the weather ought to obey her commands.

Andy's initiation into the world of high fashion is full of comedic moments. Her slight disdain and sense of moral superiority is not lost on Miranda. While Miranda is inspecting outfits for an upcoming photo shoot, she deliberates out loud about which belt to choose, and Andy giggles audibly. In the shocked silence that follows, she nervously explains that she is "still learning about this stuff." Miranda turns on her, glowering.

> This . . . stuff? Okay. I understand. You think this has nothing to do with you. You go to your closet and select, say, that lumpy blue sweater because you're trying to tell the world that you take yourself too seriously to care about what's on your body. What you don't know is that your sweater is not blue. It's not even sky blue. It's cerulean. . . .
>
> That color is worth millions of dollars and many jobs. And here you are, thinking you've made a choice that exempts you from the fashion industry. In truth, you are wearing a sweater that was selected for you by the people in this room. From a pile of stuff.[4]

Andy must learn to respect Miranda's power and relate to it with reverence before she can experience the helpful side of this ruthless energy.

STEPPING UP

A turning point comes after Andy is unsuccessful at getting Miranda back from Florida during the hurricane in time to see her daughters' piano recital. Miranda gives her a cutting dressing-down for her failure. Andy runs tearfully to her colleague Nigel, who is a senior editor at the magazine and a close colleague of Miranda's. He expresses stoic disinterest in Andy's distress. He accuses her of whining and encourages her to quit if she doesn't like it.

> We could replace you in five minutes with someone who really wants this job . . . You want me to say poor you, Miranda is picking on you? She's just doing her job. Wake up! . . . You have

no idea how many legends have walked these halls and what's worse, you don't care. Because this is a "stepping stone" for you. This place, that people would die to work, you deign to work. And you want to know why she doesn't give you a kiss on the forehead and put a gold star on your homework?[5]

Nigel's reproach wakes something up in Andy. He is telling her that nature—that life—doesn't reward us for tepid, self-congratulatory efforts. It demands everything, a total commitment to our unfolding. Andy has been behaving like a girl, wanting to get a gold star for being a good student. Until this moment in the film, she hasn't taken full responsibility for herself. Unconsciously, she has not been fully in her life. At this moment, things change.

She sees that she has been holding herself aloof from Miranda and the magazine's mission, secretly disdainful of fashion. Now she commits. She asks Nigel to help her change how she dresses, and we see her transform from a frumpy, midwestern college student into an elegant fashionista. Andy now holds nothing back. She lets her defensive disdain and judgment disappear and begins seeing the world through Miranda's eyes. Her initiation has begun.

Andy's foil throughout the film is Miranda's senior assistant, Emily Charlton (played by Emily Blunt). Emily is wound tight and obsessed with fashion. We learn early on that, as Miranda's senior assistant, Emily will accompany her to Fashion Week in Paris and that this trip is of supreme importance to her. She spends all of her time prepping for it, dieting for it, and anticipating it. After Andy commits to Miranda, the older woman offers her the glowing skull and urges her not to shrink from taking it.

MIRANDA: Paris is the most important week of my year. I need the best possible team with me. That no longer includes Emily.

ANDY: Wait. You want *me* to—oh, no. No, no. Emily would die. Her whole life is about Paris. [*Miranda stares. Doesn't care.*]

ANDY: She hasn't eaten in weeks. I can't do that, Miranda. I can't.

MIRANDA: If you don't go, I'll assume you're not serious about your
　　future at *Runway* or any other publication. [*Andy looks at her.*]
MIRANDA: The decision is yours.[6]

Andy chooses to go to Paris, taking the knife Miranda has handed
her and planting it squarely between Emily's shoulders. Miranda has
challenged her to recognize her excellence, drop her midwestern niceness, and prioritize her needs and desires even when it means being
ruthless. This is the lesson Andy needed to learn.

Later in the film, Andy proves she can draw on her newly claimed
aggressive capacity. In Paris, she realizes that the world of high fashion
is not where she belongs. Her values are not aligned with Miranda's.
Paradoxically, she is now required to stab Miranda in the back.
Confidently, she leaves Miranda at a critical moment. She tosses the
cell phone that has tied her to her boss into a fountain and leaves that
life behind her. She can harness her aggression in service to her unique
destiny and no longer needs to be Miranda's assistant.

At the film's close, we see Andy at an interview for a plum journalism job. The editor asks her about her time at *Runway*, and Andy
admits she "screwed it up."

EDITOR: That's not what I hear. I called over there for a reference, left
　　word with some snooty girl, next thing you know I got a fax from
　　Miranda Priestly herself saying that of all the assistants she's had,
　　you were by far her biggest disappointment. And that if I don't
　　hire you, I'm an idiot.[7]

Andy passed the test. She won Miranda's approval not because she
was eager to please or conscientious but because she could marshal
aggression in service to herself and her development. Andy succeeded
precisely because she disappointed Miranda. Throughout her appren-
ticeship, she learned to know her needs and desires, and to find the
ruthlessness required to prioritize her soul's unfolding.

WHAT WE DEMAND FOR OURSELVES

Grace is the woman who unwittingly employed trickster energy to get into the college of her choice. When she first came to see me, I was struck by the softness of her voice and the tentativeness she expressed as she spoke. Petite and slight, she sat on my couch tucked to one side as if she wanted to take up the least amount of space possible. Raised in a family with little room for her needs, Grace had difficulty ever doing anything that might hurt or disappoint other people.

By nature, Grace was fiery and strong. She had been blessed with many Lilith qualities but had mostly lost access to these in her childhood, which had been marked by her father's alcoholism and her mother's depression. Part of our work centered around her career. She found herself in an unsatisfying job and longed to quit and stay home with her two small children. Grace felt she couldn't do so, however, in part because she felt indebted to her boss, Cate. Cate was an older, childless woman who had taken Grace under her wing, hired her away from another agency, and mentored her to become her replacement. Cate's fondness for her touched Grace, but she sometimes found the expectations that came with this attention suffocating. As it became clear to Grace that she did not want to continue working, Cate's mentoring began to feel more uncomfortable and pressuring. Grace knew that Cate would be devastated if she quit. Following her own heart required that she be ready to wound someone else.

While considering giving notice, Grace had a dream in which an older woman named Jane told her that she needed to get over her "rotten complex." Jane was a woman that Grace knew from church. Grace shared with me that she found Jane to be abrasive and self-absorbed. She didn't concern herself too much with what other people thought of her. Jane, then, carried some of the fiery, aggressive qualities that Grace needed to find. The "rotten complex" referred to Grace's tendency to experience crippling doubt and guilt whenever she did anything that felt a little selfish. Meeting her own needs had always made her feel rotten.

"We demand from others only what we fail to give ourselves," according to Jungian analyst Edward Edinger.[8] When her Lilith qualities were still stifled, Grace looked to her boss to give her permission to follow her heart, but approval was never going to be forthcoming from that quarter. She had to sanction her own plans, knowing that Cate would feel hurt and betrayed.

Grace eventually found the courage and clarity needed to give notice. Cate was predictably angry and upset and treated Grace coldly for her remaining weeks on the job. For Grace, however, finding the necessary ruthlessness to do what she wanted to do rather than what everyone else wanted her to do was life-changing. As is always the case, taking a step toward wholeness and authenticity led to a general sense of more aliveness and greater well-being. Kindling her forgotten coals, Grace connected with her vitalizing spark. A few months after she left her job, she had the following dream:

> I had found the source of all water in the Arctic. I
> had been kayaking with someone else, and we
> kept traveling farther and farther north. It took a
> surprisingly short time to get there. It was magnificent
> and sacred and also mundane/everyday in the sense
> that it was near a busy road and also had trash in it,
> like a dirty river. I prayed that humanity found a better
> way to treat our water.

Grace was moved by this dream. She understood that, though there was still some work to be done, she had become firmly connected with her own inner, renewing source.

The ability to be ruthlessly aggressive is one of the darkest aspects of human nature. It can be used to threaten, harm, or humiliate others in the interest of gaining power over them, and when we are in touch with our aggression, the temptation to use it to punish is ever present. There are good reasons to be wary of this capacity. However, we will not be able to live out our pattern if we cannot marshal aggression on our own behalf.

When I was in my thirties, I was seeing a psychologist who wasn't a good fit. I knew I needed to end our treatment, but I was worried about hurting her feelings. Around that time, I had the following dream.

> I am in a car in the passenger seat. Tony Soprano is driving.

Tony Soprano is a career criminal and arguably a sociopath, albeit a sympathetic one. But he never shirks from doing the difficult thing. If he has to murder someone to keep his family or his business safe, he will do it. Though it was hard for me to accept my inner Tony Soprano, the dream encouraged me to make friends with him so that I could find the ruthlessness I needed in order to end a relationship that wasn't serving me.

Baba Yaga isn't going to give us a gold star for being compliant. She wants us to show up in our full aliveness. This may mean that we fight to win, setting aside compassion for our competitor. It may mean that we don't shirk from taking a stand we know will inflict discomfort or even pain on others we care about when the situation calls for it. To find our fiery aggression and use it in service to our own growth and unfolding can be a challenging task for women. If we are to bring forth what wants to come into the world through us, we will need to learn ferocity, aggression, and ruthlessness. When these are wielded with wisdom, they give us power to fulfill our destiny.

QUESTIONS FOR REFLECTION ————————

1. The girl in "Frau Trude" doesn't listen to her parents' warnings and becomes firewood for the witch. Where in your life have you been overconfident? Maybe you didn't pay attention to clear warning signs that a situation wasn't right for you. What happened? What did you learn?

2. When Vasilissa is troubled, she has an inner resource that helps her keep things in perspective and face hardships. When you are facing a challenge, what is your inner dialogue like? How do you talk to yourself? What do you tend to do when you are down or facing adversity?

3. Vasilissa has some wicked stepsisters who are selfish and unkind. Where in your life are you like Vasilissa, at the mercy of someone else's meanness? And where are you like the stepsisters, pushy and arrogant?

4. Vasilissa must travel into the depths of the forest to meet Baba Yaga. Vasilissa is frightened, but she knows that she has her little doll in her pocket. Have you ever had a time in your life that felt like a journey into the dark forest? Perhaps you were grieving or depressed. What inner resources did you rely upon during this time?

5. Baba Yaga is an image of a powerful, archaic, transpersonal energy. Living with her, Vasilissa gets in touch with the raw, instinctual wisdom that Baba Yaga carries. When have you made contact with your inner Baba Yaga? What was it like?

6. Vasilissa uses the skull to light her way home, but then almost throws it out once she arrives. When we are adults, we may gain clarity about maladaptive patterns in our family of origin. However, we often find ourselves falling back into the same patterns when we return home for a visit. What are the patterns that you tend to fall into when you visit family members?

7. Vasilissa is able to bring the skull inside—she can now access her aggression. Where in your life are you able to be appropriately aggressive? Where is this difficult for you?

CHAPTER 10

RETURN: LOVING YOUR FATE

The urge to become what one is is invincibly
strong, and you can always count on it, but
that does not mean that things will necessarily
turn out positively. If you are not interested
in your own fate, the unconscious is.

—C. G. Jung, *C.G. Jung Speaking*

We can welcome our fiery qualities back from their exile and make a comfortable place for them within our lives. We can see that these aspects of ourselves are not dangerous or demonic but unwavering allies in our quest for wholeness. Jung said of the unconscious that "it reflects the face we turn towards it. Hostility lends it a threatening aspect, friendliness softens its features."[1] For many of us, our outlaw energies have long been neglected, devalued, and misunderstood, so we have come to fear these. But they are a rich store of glowing coals.

When we welcome them back, they help us to come home to ourselves. Then we value our feminine qualities of relatedness, compassion, and emotionality, yet we can access fiery canniness, trickiness, aggression, and authority in service to our authentic goals and desires. We know our hearts. We can attune and attend to the needs of others but can also make a conscious choice not to do so. Because of this, our love and care are given freely and joyfully, not because we are following some old script or are compelled by undifferentiated obligation.

THE NICE RABBIT

When Lucie first came to see me, she was desperately unhappy. "I feel angry all the time," she confessed tearfully. "I even feel angry that I have to brush my teeth." Lucie had spent her whole life following the rules and doing what others told her to do. Being a "good girl" had come with its perks—she was highly accomplished in many areas. It had also cost her dearly. She was trapped in a miserable marriage and had several friendships that she found draining but couldn't escape. She was a tremendously talented writer and had some success with publication. However, she found it challenging to advocate for herself or tend to her creative offspring with appropriate promotional efforts. Lucie's suppressed anger was just barely in check. Though she tried hard to face life with her sweet persona, her rage oozed, infecting her relationships with other people who could sense her irritability and vulnerability. Because people could feel unconsciously that her considerable anger was turned only on herself, it led them to take advantage of her, which made things even more difficult and miserable for her.

Lucie's family had stressed duty and propriety. Her mother had been brilliant but under-actualized and unhappy. Lucie's younger sister had significant behavioral issues that occupied her mother's attention. Lucie was cast in the role of caregiver, helping to soothe her mother's perpetual anxieties and lift her mood when it darkened. When she found her way to my office at midlife, she had spent decades meeting others' expectations and playing by the rules. She had lost touch with her vital spark early on. Those fiery aspects of herself now protested their exile by creating symptoms for Lucie—depression, irritability, and dark moods.

Early in our work together, Lucie had a dream that eloquently told the story of her wounded instincts.

> There is a brown rabbit huddled in a cage. The cage isn't even all the way enclosed. He could get out if he wanted to, but he doesn't seem to know that. There is a piece of paper pinned to its fur that says, "This is a nice rabbit."

My mother is there. She reaches in, and the piece of
paper comes off, revealing a deep gash underneath it.
The rabbit lunges at me in fear. I get a bloody nose.

Lucie had lived as the "nice rabbit" for many years, her wounds
barely concealed by the declarative efforts she made to present as
"nice." She was so oriented to connecting with and tending to others that she had become disconnected from herself and had difficulty
acknowledging her very significant wounds. There was such a strong
inner injunction against ever being unpleasant, selfish, or entitled that
she could never see that this cage in which she was trapped could be
easily escaped.

In waking life, Lucie often found herself in situations where she
felt put upon or taken advantage of, but, like the nice rabbit, she didn't
know how to get away. Lucie was friends with a woman named
Margaret, who demanded her time. Margaret repeatedly made poor
decisions that resulted in drama and chaos. Margaret would call
Lucie frequently and insist on spending time together. She would
then fill all of the time complaining about these terrible situations in
her life, which were of her own making, and expect Lucie to commis-
erate with her. Margaret was never interested in what was going on in
Lucie's life and was not sensitive to Lucie's needs. If Lucie wasn't adequately forthcoming with attention and sympathy, Margaret would
become disparaging.

The relationship with Margaret brought Lucie nothing but irritation, but when I suggested that she might consider setting some
boundaries with Margaret, Lucie balked. She was so divorced from
her Lilith qualities—from her sense of entitlement to her stance,
from her healthy anger and justified outrage—that setting limits
with Margaret seemed unthinkable. Instead, she internalized her
rage and unhappiness, frequently binging on ice cream after spending time with Margaret.

Similar situations appeared elsewhere in Lucie's life—in her relationships with her mother and sister, at work, and in her marriage.

She spent considerable energy suppressing the wonderful, fiery qualities that could have brought aliveness. Much of the work we did together was aimed at encouraging her to befriend these unlikeable qualities within herself so that she could set aside being the "nice rabbit" and claim her ferocity.

Throughout the years that we worked together, Lucie often spoke of a fellow writer named Kira, who appeared to embody many qualities Lucie had renounced. Kira was prolific and adept at self-promotion. Lucie never had enough time to devote to her writing and didn't produce as much as she wanted. Though Lucie barely knew Kira personally, she found her aloof and haughty when they did have brief interactions. Kira became an image of everything Lucie hated—self-absorption, arrogance, entitlement, and selfishness. These hated qualities were precisely the ones that she most lacked. Week after week, she brought her poisonous envy and resentment about Kira into our sessions. Kira frequently appeared in Lucie's dreams, where she behaved with callous disregard for dream Lucie's feelings.

Somehow, the outlaw energies that Kira embodied felt unattainable to Lucie, who experienced herself as cruelly shut off from these live-giving potentials. When we had been working together for a few years, she brought in this dream:

> I am searching in shallow water for lost things—
> flippers, water shoes. There are two small, uninhabited
> islands a little ways off shore. I think it is the Pacific
> Northwest. The islands look lush and beautiful. I feel
> sad that I have never been down to the water. I think
> I have never been down to the water and visited those
> islands, but then I must have been there since the
> swimming things were mine. I thought they would be
> hard to find, but then they were right there.

In the dream, Lucie wistfully gazes at the water and the islands, assuming they are out of her reach. The dream lets her know that, in fact, she has been there before. When she had this dream, Lucie could not feel that this tranquil scene was one she had regular access to, just as she could not see that Kira's enviable qualities were hers to claim as her own. Throughout our work together, Lucie's envy and even hatred of Kira melted gradually into a kind of intense curiosity and painful longing. I encouraged her to lean into these feelings, and Lucie bravely did so, both imaginatively and in the real world.

Opportunities for connection with Kira presented themselves, and Lucie took them. She got to know Kira better—Kira the real person—and discovered that she liked her very much. This outer connection corresponded with a rapprochement with her inner Kira. She found the courage to leave her marriage. She became bolder and less self-effacing as regards her writing and committed to larger and more ambitious projects.

Her feelings for Kira softened and deepened into genuine admiration and affection, along with a continued longing for more closeness. After many years, she had the following dream:

> Kira has written me a letter. I know it's special and
> about how much she cares for me, though I haven't
> read it. She leaves it for me in a pile of other things—
> art, clothes—all special as well. But then I can't find
> the letter. I don't give up, I go back to the place
> multiple times to look. I don't feel defeated; I am
> determined—in a way that feels "soft," gentle, not
> stressful or pressured—to keep going back to look.

"We always rediscover our unconscious psychic contents in other people," wrote Jung.[2] In Kira, Lucie had found those outlaw energies of self-protection and self-assertion that had been so forcefully disallowed earlier in her life. Lucie had found a way to open to this formerly forbidden aspect of herself and discovered that these features are not, in fact, destructive. Though still elusive, her inner Kira is a loving friend.

When we can turn toward the disowned parts of ourselves, our lives change. A Greek fairy tale poignantly illustrates this and can help us understand Lucie's story more deeply.

THE ILL-FATED PRINCESS

There once was a queen with three daughters for whom she could not find husbands. One day a beggar woman came to the palace. She saw the distress of the queen and offered advice. "I can help, but you must do as I say. Tonight when your daughters go to bed, notice how they sleep and come and tell me about it in the morning." The queen did as she was told and noted that her eldest daughter slept with her hands on her head, her middle daughter slept with her hands on her bosom, while her youngest daughter slept with her hands in her lap. The queen reported all of this to the beggar woman.

"Listen well! Your youngest daughter, who sleeps with her hands in her lap, is the ill-fated one. Her evil Fate is affecting those of her sisters as well."

The queen was disturbed by this news and did not know what to do. But her youngest daughter came to her. "I heard everything, mother, and I know that my evil Fate keeps my sisters from getting married. I know what I must do. Have the gold of my dowry sewn into the hem of my dress and let me go."

Her mother tried to dissuade her, but the girl's mind was made up. She packed a few things, dressed in simple clothes, and said farewell to her mother and sisters. As she left, she saw two bridegrooms approach the palace on horseback.

The girl walked and walked, and by nightfall, she had arrived at a cloth dealer's house in a village. She asked if she could spend the night there and was given a place to stay in the basement. That night, her Fate came and began to tear all the cloth stored in the basement. The Fate overturned the bolts of fabric and ripped everything to shreds. The princess begged her Fate to stop, but she threatened to tear the princess into shreds as well.

In the morning, the fabric dealer was distraught. "What will become of me! You have ruined me!" But the princess took some gold coins from the hem of her skirt and gave them to the dealer. Then she took her leave and wished him well and kept walking. At night, she came to the home of a glass merchant and asked to spend the night. The same thing happened as on the first night. Her Fate came and broke all of the glass in the shop, screeching and howling as she did so. When the glass merchant awoke and saw what had happened, he was beside himself, but the princess gave him some gold coins from the hem of her dress and went on her way.

Now she walked until she came to the royal palace of that country. She sought out the queen and asked for work. The queen was a wise woman and could see that the princess was of noble birth even though she was dressed simply. The queen had the princess sit beside her and embroider pearls, but when the girl set to work, the pictures fell from the walls, and the pearls scattered everywhere. While the princess stayed with the queen, the dishes flew off the shelves at night, and the servants complained, but the queen told them to be patient. "She is a princess but is under an evil Fate. Have pity on her!"

One day, the queen said to the princess, "You cannot go on in this way, with your evil Fate always pursuing you. You must find a way to change your Fate." But the princess did not know how to do this, so the queen explained. On a high mountain far away lived all the Fates. The princess needed to travel to the mountain and seek out her Fate. "Give her a piece of the bread that I will give to you," explained the queen, "and say to her, 'Fate who decreed my fate, change my fate.' Do not leave until she has taken the bread."

The princess did as the kind queen had instructed. She took the bread and walked and walked until she had climbed the far mountain and arrived at a gate. When she knocked, a beautiful woman in fine clothes appeared. The woman looked at the princess for a moment, said, "You are not mine," and then left. A few minutes later, another Fate appeared, just as beautiful as the last. "I don't know you," she told the princess. Things continued in this manner for some time until a hideous woman with wild, matted hair and twisted features approached the gate. The girl quaked, but she was determined. "Are you my Fate?" she asked, anticipating the answer. The ugly woman laughed cruelly, and the girl knew she had found the right Fate.

The princess handed her the bread and said, "Fate who decreed my fate, change my fate!" But the haggard woman threw the bread back and spit at her, shouting at her to leave. But the princess did not give up. Each time her Fate threw the bread back to her, she picked it up, handed it again to her evil Fate, and asked her to change her fate. At last, the Fate snatched the bread. "Listen to me!" she said and drew a ball of silk thread from her pocket. "Take this ball of thread and keep it for yourself until someone comes looking for it. Then, demand its weight in gold."

The girl took the ball of thread and returned to the queen. Now, there were no more broken dishes or spoilt embroidery.

It came to pass that the king of the neighboring land was ready to marry, but the bride's dress was missing some silk thread. The king's men were searching near and far for the right thread, and learned about the princess in the next kingdom who had a ball of silk thread. They sent a messenger to ask her to come to the palace and bring the silk to see if it matched. When the princess arrived and held up her thread, everyone could see that it matched the bride's dress perfectly. The princess said she would happily sell the ball for its weight in gold. They placed the thread on one side of the scale and a quantity of gold on the other, but the scale would not balance. They went on heaping gold on the scale, but it never moved. Then, the king's son, the prince, stepped on the scale—and it balanced perfectly! "If we are to have the silk, then you must have me!" he said. And so the princess and prince were married and lived out the rest of their days in happiness and contentment.

Psychologically, the girl's evil Fate is her capacity for destruction, rage, ugliness, and other shadowy qualities with which she does not have an adequately conscious relationship. "When an inner situation is not made conscious, it happens outside as fate," according to Jung.[3] Because the princess is not in relationship to her inner outlaw energies, they show up in an uncontrollable and destructive fashion. In a similar way, Lucie's banished aggression and anger seemed to happen to her from the outside.

The girl plays the role of family scapegoat. She is the reason her sisters cannot get on with their lives and she must be sacrificed. Whenever there is a degree of dysfunction in a family, it is often the case that one family member bears the weight of being conscious of this fact. Lucie's mother could wrap her deep dissatisfaction with her life in myriad small complaints about the health of her dog. Lucie's sister could play the diva at family gatherings, soaking up attention while avoiding addressing the real issues. Only Lucie seemed to have to suffer consciously the family trauma. Like the girl in the story, the scapegoat is often the person tasked with transforming and redeeming the family pain through conscious suffering.

The girl must leave home for the story to have a happy ending. Confronting our Lilith qualities will require separating psychologically from our family of origin. Our parents were likely complicit in encouraging us to divorce ourselves from our assertive instincts. Even where this is not the case, integrating shadowy qualities always requires that we become a version of ourselves that is not yet known to us. We cannot stay the child of our parents and become the person we were meant to be. As mythologist Michael Meade writes, "It is difficult for parents to see through the veil of their own expectations to the inner nature of the child born to them. And each child carries something that waits to be born in the world beyond the parent's door."[4] The girl in the tale must leave home to meet her fate. Likewise, Lucie had to do much hard work to separate from the identity that her mother had thrust upon her. Leaving home—discriminating our values from those of our family—is the first step toward psychological maturity.

The fairy tale heroine suffers greatly until she meets the queen, who can see her true nature and encourages her to have the fateful encounter on the mountain. Though we can see the queen as an inner figure—a source of wisdom and encouragement within—we also sometimes meet such people in the outer world. Such people see our essential character and call us forth toward claiming it. The fairy tale maiden finds the courage to confront her dark aspect and even to make friends with it. Doing so is no easy task. When we have spent a lifetime avoiding knowing about our capacity for ugliness, turning to face this can be frightening, humiliating, and even destabilizing.

In my work with Lucie, I sometimes reflected to her that she wasn't, in fact, a very nice person. Her true nature was fiery, passionate, acerbic, and incisive. These were wonderful qualities, but they were not ones she allowed herself to own. It wasn't comfortable for her to hear me say that I didn't think she was naturally sweet and compliant. Over time, Lucie began to feel that she had permission to express these other aspects of herself.

Changing one's fate isn't a simple, straightforward process. There is no recipe for transformation. Often, people in analysis come to an awareness of their "evil fate"—the inner attitudes and constellations of past hurts and defensive injunctions that constrain and restrain them. Then they ask with some despair, What do I do about this? The answer is imaged in this story. To bring about lasting psychological change, we must be prepared to confront that part of ourselves that holds us back, and then we must be willing to remain in relationship with it. The princess patiently and persistently tosses the bread back to her fate without rancor. There is no wish to dominate or surrender, just an earnest desire to be recognized and received. When we long to transform some painful aspect of our lives, we will need to stick with it—to keep noticing our patterns every day, to be curious about what motivates us, and to look for new ways of approaching old, sticky issues. We will have to turn toward these dark, messy parts of ourselves with a friendly face, wanting to get to know them. We will meet them in our dreams, and this will give us an opportunity to learn from them. We'll need to have faith that things are changing, even when it's hard to see that they are.

The poet Rainer Maria Rilke gave advice to another young poet that captures the nature of the transformation process imaged by the tossing of the bread:

> Be patient toward all that is unsolved in your heart and . . . try to love the *questions themselves* like locked rooms and like books that are written in a very foreign tongue. Do not now seek the answers, which cannot be given you because you would not be able to live them. And the point is, to live everything. *Live* the questions now. Perhaps you will then gradually, without noticing it, live along some distant day into the answer.[5]

When we are groping to find a way forward and are not sure what to do, we just have to keep tossing the bread to our fate, keep living and loving our questions.

The ancient Greek philosophers spoke of a love of one's fate, or amor fati. To love our fate will require us to find room for all the messy, disagreeable parts of ourselves. When we have spent a lifetime denying a part of our soul, it becomes wild and feral. It can't be easily tamed. Integration doesn't happen because we make a superficial effort. Our attempt to connect with our wildness and ferocity must be sincere. We must be willing to offer something that matters. When the first sister in "Fitcher's Bird" gives the sorcerer bread, she gives away her life force to a sabotaging energy that can overwhelm and gain control of her. When the princess gives the bread to her Fate, she is nurturing a connection with a vital and long-forgotten part of herself and welcoming it home.

Lucie's fiery qualities felt so forbidden that, at first, she could only experience them as belonging to Kira, for whom she initially felt envy and hatred. Lucie worked hard to befriend her grotesque, hateful qualities. Allowing herself to get closer to Kira was part of this work. In time, she could love these qualities both in Kira and eventually in herself. This change shifted the center of gravity in her personality. She no longer felt the need to be compulsively nice. She set boundaries with people and situations that she found draining and claimed more time for her writing. She cultivated those relationships that fed her and became better at allowing herself to feel pleasure. She really had changed her fate.

When we have ready access both to our connecting, tending qualities and to our assertive, fiery qualities, the way we are in the world will change. We won't feel so downtrodden. We'll feel more comfortable with ourselves. We'll experience less self-doubt and more joy. When faced with hardship, we'll have rich inner resources to draw upon. Whatever fate befalls us, we will be able to meet it with agency and resilience.

QUESTIONS FOR REFLECTION

1. Nothing ever seems to go right for the heroine of "The Ill-Fated Princess." Where in your life have you felt that nothing ever goes your way, as if you were ill-fated? How do you understand that situation? What did you do to try and change your fate?

2. When the princess realizes she is the reason her sisters aren't marrying, she decides she must go. She leaves home to meet her Fate. Where in your life have you made a bold decision to leave familiar things behind? How have these experiences worked out for you?

3. The princess works for a queen who understands her predicament and can help her with it. She did not find this same understanding and aid from her mother. Sometimes, we need to find someone outside of our family who can help us understand our fate and learn what to do about it. Doing this hard work of changing our fate always requires that we separate psychologically from our parents. Where in your life have you found help in understanding yourself that you could not get in your family of origin?

RETURN: LOVING YOUR FATE

4. The princess must find her Fate and convince her to take a gift. Confronting our fate means being able to acknowledge both the strengths and limitations inherent in ourselves and in our life situation. When in your life have you been asked to confront your fate? What was the result of the confrontation?

5. The princess's Fate gives her a ball of thread, but it isn't clear at first how this will be helpful. Sometimes, life gives us unlikely gifts and we are not sure how they will serve us. What are the talents or fortunate happenings that you have had that, at first, you were not clear on how they would be helpful to you? How have they developed over time in your life?

Coming Home to Yourself

The fire burns right through you. That
which guides forces you onto the way.

—C. G. Jung, *The Red Book*

Fire is an ancient symbol of transformation. It purifies by burning away what no longer serves. It melts what has become rigid and alters the very nature of the thing it touches. If parts of ourselves have felt numbed or emptied of meaning, rekindling our vital spark can bring renewed warmth, aliveness, and the burning authenticity that comes from being in touch with the central fire.

It is difficult to retain our connection to the central fire. Its intensity can be too much, so we distract and distance ourselves. It feels easier to focus on what the outer world asks of us and so we forget to tend our inner flame. Recovering the glowing coals we left behind in the lumber room is a lifetime project. When the better part of us has become a stranger, calling her home will be bittersweet. We'll have to acknowledge the wasted years. We'll have to give up the comforting fantasies. But we will be restored to ourselves. We will be renewed. A poem from Derek Walcott describes this tender homecoming.

LOVE AFTER LOVE
The time will come
when, with elation
you will greet yourself arriving
at your own door, in your own mirror
and each will smile at the other's welcome,

and say, sit here. Eat.
You will love again the stranger who was your self.
Give wine. Give bread. Give back your heart
to itself, to the stranger who has loved you

all your life, whom you ignored
for another, who knows you by heart.
Take down the love letters from the bookshelf,

the photographs, the desperate notes,
peel your own image from the mirror.
Sit. Feast on your life.[1]

It is our destiny to be consumed by the flames of life; we each have a choice whether we embrace this destiny or shrink from it. Reclaiming our capacity for creative aggression, fiery sexuality, emboldened disagreeableness, sharp-witted trickery, burning desire, clearsighted shrewdness, empowering anger, and bold authority will allow us to set our lives ablaze. When these traits are incorporated into consciousness, they no longer pop up in ineffective and passive aggressive ways, but are at our disposal to be used in service to our growth. They become part of our repertoire, along with those qualities that help us care for others—nurturing, empathy, kindness, gentleness, and generosity. When we have access to both sets of traits, we can move through the world with greater consciousness, power, and agency.

Integrating these traits will be difficult. Doing so will require us to grow beyond limited but safe conceptions of who we are. It will challenge us to explore forbidden rooms, give voice to prohibited thoughts, and wield new weapons. The call to learn cunning, the summons to sensuality, and the demand to claim desire will burst the seams of the too-narrow garments we had sewn for ourselves. We'll have to get used to being bigger.

Jung spoke of the advantages of living fully, of those who "filled up the beaker of life . . . and emptied it to the lees." Jung predicted that, in such cases, "they would have kept nothing back, everything that wanted to catch fire would have been consumed, and the quiet of old age would be very welcome to them."[2] By finding the glowing coals hiding beneath the gray ash, we can live life with more fire, setting alight all the combustible material our nature provided us with. We can drink life to the lees and leave no fuel unspent. And we can come home to our essential nature. We can return.

ACKNOWLEDGMENTS

This book is a bit of a stew. In it, I've combined different ingredients from various sources. I may have chopped and sliced and seasoned, but many of the ideas in this book are ones I learned from my teachers, including Jungian authors and instructors in my Jungian training program, as well as C. G. Jung himself. Still other ideas were born of discussions with colleagues and friends or in the process of analytic work with my patients. So many contributed in some way to the development of these ideas that I couldn't possibly name them all, but there are a few to whom I am particularly indebted.

The voices of Joseph Lee and Deb Stewart are woven into every page. They are my thought partners and dear friends. I'm grateful to Anne Walsh for guidance and insight, especially during the past few years. I am indebted to Julie Bondanza for all her years of teaching and supervision. The section on the Erinyes would not have been written without her, and she was generous enough to take the time to discuss this material with me once again. Allison Colby helped me hone my ideas both as a friend and later as an early reader of my manuscript. Hanne Steen was supportive of my first book and made important contributions to this one. Parand Meysami and Manijeh Rabiei-Roodsari offered insightful fairy tale advice. Though the tale didn't make it into the final version of this book, I'm very thankful for the deepened understanding.

I'm grateful to my clients, from whom I have learned so much. I'm especially appreciative of those who generously allowed me to use their material. I'm thankful for the women who joined me for retreats in which we worked on several of the fairy tales in this book. The insights and experiences we shared have helped shape my ideas, and I am grateful.

Bea Gonzalez and Lewis LaFontaine have both been important resources. Bea's social media accounts @SophiaCycles offer a generous sharing of Jungian quotes, and she's always been willing to help me find something when I've asked. Lewis's website carljungdepthpsychologysite.blog has come to my rescue countless times when searching for citations, and he has also generously helped me source quotes. Roxy Runyan has been flexible, encouraging, and stalwart as a publicist. Faith Tillery designs exquisite author websites and is always cheerful and helpful even when I'm terribly disorganized. I am full of gratitude for the invaluable assistance of my literature, film, and video game consultant, my daughter.

There are no words of thanks adequate to the task of acknowledging Adriana Stimola. She has seen the value in my work and always has time for an encouraging word. I'm still not sure what I did in a past life to merit having Haven Iverson as an editor. She is unfailingly warm, supportive, and encouraging, but at the same time has an unflinching editorial eye. She embodies the powerful combination of qualities I have attempted to describe in this book. I'm also thankful for the entire team at Sounds True. It has been the perfect home for my books.

Lastly, great thanks to Dom for his forbearance and support. I'm so grateful you've been up for coming on this journey with me.

NOTES

Introduction: Banishment

1. Siegmund Hurwitz, *Lilith, the First Eve: Historical and Psychological Aspects of the Dark Feminine*, Kindle ed. (Einsiedeln, Switzerland: Daimon Verlag, 2012), 119.

2. Marie-Louise von Franz, foreword to *Lilith, the First Eve*, by Hurwitz, 13.

3. Murray Stein, *Jung's Map of the Soul: An Introduction* (Chicago, IL: Open Court, 1998), 11.

4. Jennifer Connellan et al., "Sex Differences in Human Neonatal Social Perception," *Infant Behavior and Development* 23, no. 1 (January 2000): 113–18, doi.org/10.1016/s0163-6383(00)00032-1.

5. Carol Gilligan, *In a Different Voice: Psychological Theory and Women's Development* (Cambridge, MA: Harvard University Press, 2016).

6. Paul Holdengraber, "Adam Phillips, The Art of Nonfiction No. 7," *Paris Review*, no. 208 (Spring 2014), theparisreview.org/interviews/6286 /the-art-of-nonfiction-no-7-adam-phillips.

7. Marie-Louise von Franz, *The Interpretation of Fairy Tales* (Boston, MA: Shambhala, 1996), 2.

8. Heinz Westman, *The Springs of Creativity* (London: Routledge & Kegan Paul, 1961), 12.

9. C. G. Jung, *The Collected Works of C. G. Jung*, vol. 8, *The Structure and Dynamics of the Psyche*, ed. and trans. Gerhard Adler and R. F. C. Hull, 2nd ed. (Princeton, NJ: Princeton University Press, 1970), para. 772.

10. "Obituary: Grandma Moses Is Dead at 101; Primitive Artist 'Just Wore Out,'" *New York Times*, December 14, 1961, timesmachine.nytimes.com /timesmachine/1961/12/14/118526623.html?pageNumber=1.

11. Arnold B. Cheyney, *People of Purpose: 80 People Who Have Made a Difference* (Parsippany, NJ: Good Year Books, 1998), 110.

12. C. G. Jung, *The Collected Works of C. G. Jung*, vol. 14, *Mysterium Coniunctionis*, trans. Gerhard Adler and R. F. C. Hull (Princeton, NJ: Princeton University Press, 1970), para. 623.

Chapter 1—Division: Losing Your Fire

1. C. G. Jung, *The Collected Works of C. G. Jung*, vol. 8, *The Structure and Dynamics of the Psyche*, ed. and trans. Gerhard Adler and R. F. C. Hull, 2nd ed. (Princeton, NJ: Princeton University Press, 1970), para. 757.

2. Mary Bray Pipher, *Reviving Ophelia: Saving the Selves of Adolescent Girls* (New York, NY: Riverhead Books, 2005), 19.

3. Liz Dennerlein, "Study: Females Lose Self-Confidence Throughout College," *USA Today*, September 26, 2013, usatoday.com/story/news /nation/2013/09/26/study-females-lose-confidence-college/2871111/.

4. Katty Kay and Claire Shipman, "The Confidence Gap," *The Atlantic*, May 2014, theatlantic.com/magazine/archive/2014/05 /the-confidence-gap/359815/.

5. Clarissa Pinkola Estés, *Women Who Run With the Wolves: Myths and Stories of the Wild Woman Archetype* (New York, NY: Ballantine Books, 2003).

6. Marie-Louise von Franz, *The Collected Works of Marie-Louise von Franz: Archetypal Symbols in Fairytales*, vol. 3, *The Maiden's Quest* (Asheville, NC: Chiron Publications, 2021).

7. *Ex Machina*, directed by Alex Garland (Santa Monica, CA: Universal City Studios Productions, 2014), 1 hour 48 minutes.

8. Edward F. Edinger, *Ego and Archetype* (New York: Pelican Books, 1973), 160–61.

Chapter 2—Disagreeableness: Flinging the Frog

1. Yanna J. Weisberg, Colin G. DeYoung, and Jacob B. Hirsh, "Gender Differences in Personality Across the Ten Aspects of the Big Five," *Frontiers in Psychology* 2 (August 2011): 178, doi.org/10.3389/fpsyg.2011.00178.

2. Christian Jarrett, "Do Men and Women Really Have Different Personalities?" BBC Future, October 12, 2016, bbc.com/future /article/20161011-do-men-and-women-really-have-different-personalities.

3. C. G. Jung, *The Collected Works of C. G. Jung*, vol. 7, *Two Essays on Analytical Psychology*, trans. R. F. C. Hull, 2nd ed. (Princeton, NJ: Princeton University Press, 1972), para. 254.

4. James Hollis, *Mythologems: Incarnations of the Invisible World* (Toronto, Canada: Inner City Books, 2004), 62.

5. Safron Rossi, *The Kore Goddess: A Mythology and Psychology* (Arroyo Grande, CA: Winter Press, 2021).

6. Natalia Klimczak, "2,500-Year-Old Mummified Crocodile Yields Surprises," Ancient Origins, last updated November 18, 2016, ancient-origins.net /news-history-archaeology/2500-year-old-mummified-crocodile-yields -surprises-007031.

7. Lora E. Park, Ariana F. Young, and Paul W. Eastwick, "(Psychological) Distance Makes the Heart Grow Fonder: Effects of Psychological Distance and Relative Intelligence on Men's Attraction to Women," *Personality and Social Psychology Bulletin* 41, no. 11 (2015): 1459–73, doi .org/10.1177/0146167215599749.

8. *Howl's Moving Castle*, directed by Hayao Miyazaki (Tokyo, Japan: Studio Ghibli, 2004), 1 hour, 59 minutes.

9. *Howl's Moving Castle*.

10. *Howl's Moving Castle*.

11. Dorothy Parker, *Enough Rope: A Book of Light Verse* (Bristol, UK: Ragged Hand, 2022), 72.

CHAPTER 3—SHREWDNESS: GETTING OVER INNOCENCE

1. Mark Winborn, *Interpretation in Jungian Analysis: Art and Technique* (New York, NY: Routledge, 2019).

2. Clarissa Pinkola Estés, *Women Who Run With the Wolves: Myths and Stories of the Wild Woman Archetype* (New York, NY: Ballantine Books, 2003), 47.

3. *I, Tonya*, directed by Craig Gillespie (Los Angeles, CA: Lucky Chap Entertainment, 2017), 1 hour, 59 minutes.

4. *I, Tonya*.

5. Heidi Anne Heiner, *Sleeping Beauties: Sleeping Beauty and Snow White Tales from Around the World* (Nashville, TN: SurLaLune Press with CreateSpace, 2010).

6. C. G. Jung, *C. G. Jung Letters*, vol. 1, 1906–1950, ed. Gerhard Adler and Aniela Jaffe (New York: Routledge, 1973), 237.

7. *The Wizard of Oz*, directed by Victor Fleming (Beverly Hills, CA: Metro-Goldwyn-Mayer, 1939), 1 hour, 42 minutes.

8. *The Wizard of Oz*.

9. *The Wizard of Oz*.

10. *The Wizard of Oz*.

11. *The Wizard of Oz*.

12. *The Wizard of Oz*.

13. David Kealy, George A. Hadjipavlou, and John S. Ogrodniczuk, "On Overvaluing Parental Overvaluation as the Origins of Narcissism," *Proceedings of the National Academy of Sciences* 112, no. 23 (2015): E2986, doi.org/10.1073/pnas.1507035112.

14. Dieter Baumann, "Quo Vadis, Helvetica?" in *The Rock Rabbit and the Rainbow*, ed. Robert Hinshaw (Einsiedeln, Switzerland: Daimon Verlag, 1998), 110.

Chapter 4—Trickster: Opening to the Unexpected

1. *Quo Vadis, Aida?*, directed by Jasmila Žbanić (Sarajevo, Bosnia and Herzegovina: Deblokada Film, 2020), 1 hour, 41 minutes.

2. I Love Lucy, "Return Home From Europe," directed by James V. Kern, written by Jess Oppenheimer, Madelyn Davis, and Bob Carroll, featuring Lucille Ball, Desi Arnaz, and Vivian Vance, aired May 14, 1956.

3. Richard Burton, *The Richard Burton Diaries*, ed. Chris Williams (New Haven, CT: Yale University Press, 2012), 352.

4. Lucille Ball, *Love, Lucy* (New York: Berkley, 2022), vii.

5. Lewis Hyde, *Trickster Makes This World: Mischief, Myth, and Art* (New York: Farrar, Straus and Giroux, 2010), 9.

6. Hyde, *Trickster*, 13.

Chapter 5—Desire: Embracing Life's Fire

1. David Shipman, *Judy Garland: The Secret Life of an American Legend* (New York: Hyperion, 1994).

2. C. G. Jung, *Visions: Notes of the Seminar Given in 1930–1934*, vol 2., ed. Claire Douglas (Princeton, NJ: Princeton University Press, 1997), 758.

3. C. G. Jung, *Nietzsche's Zarathustra: Notes of the Seminar Given in 1934–1939*, vol 2., ed. James L. Jarrett (Princeton, NJ: Princeton University Press, 1988), 801.

4. Matthew 13:45–46.

5. Charles Dickens, *Oliver Twist*, Townsend Library ed. (West Berlin, NJ: Townsend Press, 2007), 12.

6. Leslie Jamison, "Why Everyone Feels Like They're Faking It," *New Yorker*, February 6, 2023, newyorker.com/magazine/2023/02/13 /the-dubious-rise-of-impostor-syndrome.

7. Brené Brown, "Listening to Shame | Brené Brown," TED, March 16, 2012, YouTube video, 20:38, youtube.com/watch?v=psN1DORYYVo&ab_channel=TED.

Chapter 6—Sexuality: Loving Yourself

1. M. Esther Harding, *Woman's Mysteries Ancient and Modern* (Boston, MA: Shambhala Publications, 1971), 125.

2. Christine Downing, *Myths and Mysteries of Same-Sex Love* (Lincoln, NE: Authors Choice Press, 2006), 205.

3. Jean H. Him, Wilson S. Tam, and Peter Muennig, "Sociodemographic Correlates of Sexlessness Among American Adults and Associations with Self-Reported Happiness Levels: Evidence from the U.S. General Social Survey," *Archives of Sexual Behavior* 46, no. 8 (November 2017): 2403–15, doi.org/10.1007/s10508-017-0968-7.

4. Joanne Bagshaw, "Why Do Lesbians Have More Orgasms than Straight Women?" Psychology Today, February 16, 2016, psychologytoday.com/us/blog/the-third-wave/201602 /why-do-lesbians-have-more-orgasms-straight-women.

5. Downing, *Myths and Mysteries*, 210.

6. Downing, 197.

7. Downing, 211.

Chapter 7—Rage: Heeding Your Limits

1. Siegmund Hurwitz, *Lilith, the First Eve: Historical and Psychological Aspects of the Dark Feminine* (Einsiedeln, Switzerland: Daimon Verlag, 2012), 36.

2. Aeschylus, *The Oresteian Trilogy*, trans. Philip Vellacott (New York: Penguin Books, 1956), 149.

3. Aeschylus, *Oresteian Trilogy*, 169.

4. David Whyte, *Consolations: The Solace, Nourishment, and Underlying Meaning of Everyday Words* (Langley, WA: Many Rivers Press, 2021), 19.

5. Dorsha Hayes, *The Bell Branch Rings* (New York: W. L. Bauhan, 1972), p. 26.

CHAPTER 8—AUTHORITY:
CROSSING THE THRESHOLD

1. Blanche Wiesen Cook, *Eleanor Roosevelt: Volume One: 1884–1933* (New York, NY: Penguin, 1993), 179.

2. Cook, *Eleanor Roosevelt*, 179.

3. Linda Schierse Leonard, *The Wounded Woman: Healing the Father-Daughter Relationship* (Athens, OH: Swallow Press, 1982).

CHAPTER 9—RUTHLESSNESS:
OWNING AGGRESSION

1. Susan Brownmiller, "This Is Fighting Shirley Chisholm," *New York Times*, April 13, 1969.

2. Evelyn M. Simien, *Historic Firsts: How Symbolic Empowerment Changes U.S. Politics* (New York, NY: Oxford University Press, 2016), 32.

3. *The Devil Wears Prada*, directed by David Frankel (Los Angeles, CA: Fox 2000 Pictures, 2006), 1 hour, 49 minutes.

4. *The Devil Wears Prada*.

5. *The Devil Wears Prada*.

6. *The Devil Wears Prada*.

7. *The Devil Wears Prada*.

8. Edward F. Edinger, *Ego and Archetype* (New York: Pelican Books, 1973), 161.

CHAPTER 10—RETURN: LOVING YOUR FATE

1. C. G. Jung, *The Collected Works of C. G. Jung*, vol. 12, *Psychology and Alchemy*, ed. and trans. Gerhard Adler and R. F. C. Hull, 2nd ed. (Princeton, NJ: Princeton University Press, 1968), para. 29.

2. C. G. Jung, *The Collected Works of C. G. Jung*, vol. 10, *Civilization in Transition*, ed. and trans. Gerhard Adler and R. F. C. Hull, 2nd ed. (Princeton, NJ: Princeton University Press, 1970), para. 374.

3. C. G. Jung, *The Collected Works of C. G. Jung*, vol. 9, part 2, *Aion*, ed. and trans. Gerhard Adler and R. F. C. Hull, 2nd ed. (Princeton, NJ: Princeton University Press, 1979), para. 126.

4. Michael Meade, *The Water of Life: Initiation and the Tempering of the Soul* (Seattle, WA: Greenfire Press, 2006), 35.

5. Rainer Maria Rilke, *Letters to a Young Poet*, trans. M. D. Herter Norton (New York: W.W. Norton & Co., 1993), 18–19.

EPILOGUE—COMING HOME TO YOURSELF

1. Derek Walcott, *Sea Grapes* (New York: Farrar, Straus, and Giroux, 1976), 66.

2. C. G. Jung, *The Collected Works of C. G. Jung*, vol. 8, *The Structure and Dynamics of the Psyche*, ed. and trans. Gerhard Adler and R. F. C. Hull, 2nd ed. (Princeton, NJ: Princeton University Press, 1970), para. 789.

ABOUT THE AUTHOR

Lisa Marchiano, LCSW, is a Jungian analyst, author, and podcaster. She is the cohost of the popular depth psychology podcast *This Jungian Life*. She is on the faculty of the C. G. Jung Institute of Philadelphia, and she lectures and teaches widely. Lisa is the author of *Motherhood: Facing and Finding Yourself* published by Sounds True in 2021. She lives and practices in Philadelphia.

ABOUT SOUNDS TRUE

Sounds True was founded in 1985 by Tami Simon with a clear mission: to disseminate spiritual wisdom. Since starting out as a project with one woman and her tape recorder, we have grown into a multimedia publishing company with a catalog of more than 3,000 titles by some of the leading teachers and visionaries of our time, and an ever-expanding family of beloved customers from across the world.

In more than three decades of evolution, Sounds True has maintained our focus on our overriding purpose and mission: to wake up the world. We offer books, audio programs, online learning experiences, and in-person events to support your personal growth and awakening, and to unlock our greatest human capacities to love and serve.

At SoundsTrue.com you'll find a wealth of resources to enrich your journey, including our weekly *Insights at the Edge* podcast, free downloads, and information about our nonprofit Sounds True Foundation, where we strive to remove financial barriers to the materials we publish through scholarships and donations worldwide.

To learn more, please visit SoundsTrue.com/freegifts or call us toll-free at 800.333.9185.

Together, we can wake up the world.

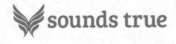 sounds true